The Restless Dead

CRITICAL
MEXICAN STUDIES

CRITICAL MEXICAN STUDIES
Series editor: Ignacio M. Sánchez Prado

Critical Mexican Studies is the first English-language, humanities-based, theoretically focused, academic series devoted to the study of Mexico. The series is a space for innovative works in the humanities that focus on theoretical analysis, transdisciplinary interventions, and original conceptual framing.

The Restless Dead
Necrowriting & Disappropriation

Cristina Rivera Garza
Translated by Robin Myers

Vanderbilt University Press
Nashville, Tennessee

Library of Congress Cataloging-in-Publication Data

Names: Rivera Garza, Cristina, 1964– author. | Myers, Robin, 1987–
    translator.
Title: The restless dead : necrowriting and disappropriation / Cristina
    Rivera Garza ; translated by Robin Myers.
Other titles: Muertos indóciles. English
Description: Nashville : Vanderbilt University Press, [2020] | Series:
    Critical Mexican studies; book 1 | Includes bibliographical references.
Identifiers: LCCN 2020018702 (print) | LCCN 2020018703 (ebook) | ISBN
    9780826501219 (paperback) | ISBN 9780826501226 (hardcover) | ISBN
    9780826501233 (epub) | ISBN 9780826501240 (pdf)
Subjects: LCSH: Authorship—Social aspects. | Technology—Social
    aspects. | Violence.
Classification: LCC PN149 .R58513 2020 (print) | LCC PN149 (ebook) | DDC
    808.02—DC23

LC record available at https://lccn.loc.gov/2020018702
LC ebook record available at https://lccn.loc.gov/2020018703

How much can a dead body experience?
Teresa Margolles

What is offered to us is that community is coming about, or rather, that something
is happening to us in common. Neither an origin nor an end: something *in*
common. Only speech, a writing—shared, sharing us.
Jean-Luc Nancy, *The Inoperative Community*

To see the dead as the individuals they once were tends to obscure their nature.
Try to consider the living as we might assume the dead to do: collectively. The
collective would accrue not only across space but also throughout time. It would
include all those who had ever lived. And so we would also be thinking of the dead.
The living reduce the dead to those who have lived, yet the dead already include
the living in their own great collective.
John Berger, *On the Economy of the Dead*

Contents

Acknowledgments

From 2006 to 2013, I wrote a weekly column of about 5,500 characters for the cultural section of *Milenio*, a newspaper of national circulation in Mexico. The Oblique Hand quickly became a laboratory of ideas where I explored wide-ranging topics and forms: from book reviews to translations, from travel chronicles to film analyses, from notes on contemporary art to discussions of current politics. Felipe Calderón became president, winning a hotly contested election by the slightest of margins. Immediately thereafter, he escalated the so-called War on Drugs: a long-lasting conflict with roots dating back to the late 1960s, when the Mexican state militarized counter-narcotic activities and thus paved the way for the organization of counterinsurgent groups targeting both guerrilla movements and drug traffickers from the 1970s onwards. The violence that spread across the country was hardly new to the early twenty-first century, but its spectacular cruelty defied any semblance of normalcy. Without a program in mind, I began reflecting on the war that engulfed our days and claimed so many lives. The first edition of *The Restless Dead: Necrowriting and Disappropriation*, published in Mexico in 2013, comprised a selection of the articles I devoted to exploring the fraught relationship between violence and writing. These were not academic pieces, but dispatches generated in a swiftly crumbling world, one I found increasingly difficult to explain with accepted truths or rusty tools. I wrote freely, in a style amenable to broader audiences regardless of the complexity, or obscurity, of the subject in question. In my mind, *The Restless Dead* remains a book of writing activism.

In 2008, during one of the gravest financial crises in recent years, I accepted a position as a professor in the MFA program in creative writing at the University of California, San Diego. I continued publishing The Oblique Hand on a weekly basis, but this time I was reporting from the Tijuana-San Diego border, one of the most dynamic geopolitical crossings in the world. I became a migrant in my two countries, perpetually moving back and forth. And back. Although they're growing in number, creative writing programs remain scarce in Latin America, where most writers harbor deep-seated suspicion toward, if not outright dismissal of, the connection between writing and academia. Immersed in the US creative writing world for the first time, and writing mostly for Spanish-speaking audiences in Mexico, I used my column to explore the pros and cons of historically divergent approaches to teaching and practicing writing. In recent decades, grants funded by the Mexican state have played a greater role in supporting younger writers. Until very recently, though, gender and racial discrimination have been the uncontested norm in writing programs taught outside academic environments, and with very little accountability, in Mexico.

While I was able to develop a writing life in Spanish while teaching in English in Southern California, the marginalization of Spanish—and, more generally, of writers of color in US writing programs—proved overwhelming, and especially troubling on the UC campus in greatest geographical proximity to the US-Mexico border. Spanish majors at US campuses deemed Hispanic-Serving Institutions, such as UC Riverside and Santa Barbara, numbered 250 students. At UC San Diego, however, only about twenty-five students declared Spanish as their major in 2016. Meanwhile, students from the Spanish-speaking world entering the MFA program as bilingual writers soon learned that the institution offered English-only courses and only admitted theses written in English. Through this perverse act of erasure, the university paid lip service to the cultural and aesthetic relevance of Spanish while actively ensuring that both the language and its practitioners remained invisible or inconsequential in classrooms and hallways—and, even more importantly, in the writing valued by the system. As is true in universities countrywide, tenure appointments and salary raises continue to dismiss the relevance of work written in languages other than English, often arguing that committee members lack the credentials and linguistic skills to objectively evaluate the standing of publishing ventures abroad. Both the university and society as a whole lose out when people of color are thus impeded from contributing their input, talent, energy, and skills (linguistic and otherwise). As the poet Claudia Rankine has conveyed so electrifyingly in her book *Citizen*,[1] structural racism manifests itself both in outright acts of violence and in everyday microaggressions. Both hurt. Both demand a response. I explored my growing commitment to bilingual writing and to writing in Spanish in the US, both in the pieces I wrote for The Oblique Hand through 2013 (the year my column came to an end) and in my institutional engagements. As for the latter, I accepted a position at the University of Houston to start the first PhD track in Creative Writing in Spanish in 2017, the year Donald Trump became president. In many ways, the articles and personal essays I wrote for magazines and newspapers during those years, some of which have found their way into *The Restless Dead*, constitute an intellectual chronicle of my own journey as a bilingual migrant writer of color in the United States.

As these articles moved from The Oblique Hand and other periodical publications into this book, none of the original texts remained intact. While I tried to maintain the grittiness and immediacy often associated with journalism, I rewrote some in part, others entirely. I recreated arguments in new logical sequences. All of these texts are, in essence, disrupted texts. A sabbatical year at the University of Poitiers in France granted me the time and tranquility to reorganize these materials and shape the book's central contentions. An artist residency at the Centro de las Artes in San Agustín Etla, in the state of Oaxaca, Mexico, allowed me to continue working on the project, introducing various changes and reviewing the entire manuscript in early 2013. This collection of essays wouldn't have incorporated the Mixe concept of communality if I hadn't spent those precious months living in Oaxaca, and if I hadn't traveled its mountains and valleys, its rivers and coasts, in the company of Saúl Hernández Vargas and Matías Rivera De Hoyos, my son. Finally, I wouldn't have dared to let this book exist in its current form, couldn't possibly have interrupted its incessant book-becoming (which is, as we know, an infinite process), if I hadn't been able to test its arguments on the incredibly talented members of the Taller de Re-Escrituras (re-writing workshop) that I taught for two weeks in Oaxaca: Yásnaya Aguilar, Bruno Varela, Patricia Tovar, Efraín Velasco, Noehmí, Amador, Daniel Nush, Gabriel Elías, Andrea Carballo, Miguel, Viviana Choy, Rafael Alonso, Alejandro Aparicio, Josué.

The English version of these texts came about through many months of intense and intensely gratifying work with poet Robin Myers. Since the original version of *The Restless Dead* addressed audiences in the Spanish-speaking world, we prepared the book to cross the border back into the United States by rearranging the order of the chapters and adding several newer essays. The last chapter in this new configuration calls for stubbornness. I may not believe that we have much cause for hope, but we do have reasons—many of them—to keep insisting.

Introduction

Many writers have gracefully, even easily, used the figure of death to analyze the relationships between writing and the context of its production. The experimental US-American writer Camille Roy does it:[1] "In some sense, the writer is always already dead, as far as the reader is concerned."[2] Hélène Cixous does it: "Each of us, individually and freely, must do the work that consists of rethinking what is your death and my death, which are inseparable. Writing originates in this relationship."[3] Margaret Atwood does it in her book of essays on writing, aptly titled *Negotiating with the Dead: A Writer on Writing*.[4] The Lebanese writer Elias Khoury does it, author of *Gate of the Sun*, a book that tackles collective memory and historical tragedy head-on.[5] Clearly, Juan Rulfo does it. All his murmurs, ascending or descending the hillside with the frozen lights of Comala—the great necropolis, populated by the ex-dead—peeking out behind it.[6]

These examples suffice (although we could name countless others) not only to show the close relationship between written language and death, but also to demonstrate that this relationship has been long recognized—and even actively sought out—by diverse writers of both poetry and prose. What remains both an illuminating and a terrifying metaphor for some, however, has for others become an everyday reality. In Mexico, depending on the source, between sixty thousand and eighty thousand people died in situations of extreme violence during a six-year presidential administration that few would hesitate to call the *guerra calderonista*: the Calderón war.[7] Indeed, in 2006, right after a bitter and potentially fraudulent election, President

Felipe Calderón ordered a military crackdown on the brutal narcotrafficking gangs that had presumably maintained pacts of stability with prior regimes. Newspapers, urban chronicles, and everyday rumors all described the growing cruelty and extravagance of the war crimes, the rampant impunity of the criminal justice system, and the general incapacity of the state to protect and defend its people's safety and well-being. Over time, almost everyone lost someone during the war. The nucleus of evil—which pulsed, according to Roberto Bolaño in the section "The Part about the Crimes" of 2666, in the vicinity of Santa Teresa (that is, in the border city of Ciudad Juárez)[8]—crept outward and spread elsewhere. Surrounded by narco-graves, besieged by horror and fear, new and more vicious necropolises cropped up in the northern hemisphere of the American continent: in Monterrey, once known as the Sultan of the North, and especially in another northern state, Tamaulipas, where mass graves containing the remains of seventy-two Central American migrants, brutally murdered by organized criminal gangs, were found in 2010.[9] Culiacán. Morelia. Veracruz. The names of more Mexican cities and states soon joined the longer list of contemporary necropolises. Palestine. Central Africa. Chernobyl.

What does it mean to write, today, in such a context? What are the challenges for writing, when professional precariousness and gruesome deaths are the stuff of everyday life? Which aesthetic and ethical dialogues does the act of writing hurl us into when we are quite literally surrounded by corpses? The following pages ask these and other questions. At the same time, they explore the fact that the literary communities of our post-human worlds are still undergoing what may be the major revolution of our age: the rise and increasing use of digital technologies. To be sure, death often encroaches on the very same territories where internet connections are making their forward march—a sort of contemporary battalion. Blood and screens, conflated. If writing is supposed to critique the status quo, then how is it possible—through writing and with writing—to dissociate the grammar of predatory power from aggravated neoliberalism and its deadly war machines?

In contemporary states, as Achille Mbembe argues in "Necropolitics," an article that appeared in *Public Culture* in 2003, "the ultimate expression of sovereignty resides, to a large degree, in the power and the capacity to dictate who may live and who may die. . . . To exercise sovereignty is to exercise control over mortality and to define life as the deployment and manifestation of power."[10] While the concept of biopower, coined by Michel Foucault, once helped explain "that domain of life over which power has taken control," Mbembe responds with the concept of necropower (that is, "that dominion of death over which power has taken control") in order to understand the complex web that violence and politics have woven together across much of the globe. Mexico is certainly among the places caught in this web. Mexico, which has begun the twentieth-first century as it spent the twentieth: enduring the reformulated terms of capitalist exploitation under the watchful eye of its imperial neighbor, and reconfiguring the terms of its resistance. So it was, too, in the era of the 1910 Mexican Revolution. More than most other countries during this transition, Mexico encounters what Adriana Cavarero has dubbed contemporary horrorism: forms of extreme and spectacular violence that threaten not only human life, but also, and perhaps especially, the human condition itself.[11]

Unlike those of the modern age, today's war machines don't establish states of emergency or produce military conflicts with the goal of territorial confiscation. In a context marked by global mobility and in greater harmony with nomadic conceptions of space as a de-territorialized or segmented entity, necropolitical war machines recognize that "military operations and the exercise of the right to kill are no longer the sole monopoly of states and the 'regular army' is no longer the unique modality of carrying out these functions."[12] The radical transformation of war protocols and changing notions of territory, now seen as networks of mobile bodies in flock-like waves, have turned these conflicts into veritable wars against women. According to feminist sociologist Rita Segato, when populations are not neatly aligned within state lines, belonging and loyalty come to be marked on bodies in spectacular ways. Women's bodies thus become mere canvases on which the masculinity of the war machine inscribes, with tremendous cruelty, its own mandate.[13] As evidenced by narcotrafficking in Mexico, whether autonomous from or directly integrated into the state, these war machines borrow elements of "regular armies," but they also incorporate their own members. Essentially, the war machine takes on multiple functions, from political organization to commercial operations. In fact, under circumstances like these, the state itself may become, or already is, a war machine.

Writing against the status quo throughout the second half of the twentieth century roughly responded to Adorno's legendary warning against the commodification of language and the pervasiveness of instrumental reason under capitalism. To escape this instrumentalization of language, writers of various aesthetic persuasions pursued a series of strategies, including but not limited to rejecting the transparency of language (and the very idea of such transparency) as a mere vehicle of meaning, employing distorted syntax, constantly critiquing referentiality, undermining the position of the lyric "I", and continually upsetting the reader's expectations. A range of modernist and avant-garde movements from both the United States and Latin America embraced these and other strategies to activate the potentiality of language and to unmake existing literary canons.

However, necropolitical strategies of power have rendered many such alternatives obsolete, if they haven't reintegrated them altogether into the capitalist war machine of our times. If, as Agamben has convincingly argued, one of the goals of contemporary states is to de-subjectivize—that is, to remove the subject from language, transforming her from a "speaking being" into a "living being," then many of these once-subversive strategies are in need of urgent revision.[14] A contemporary writer facing in Mexico (or elsewhere) the sequences of horrorism described by Adriana Caravero—the person rendered speechless, paralyzed by the onslaughts of violence—has no option but to critically confront the tools of her trade. What can we do in the face of horror? Can we, in fact, do anything at all? When speechlessness and social paralysis prevail, when resistance and struggle are suffocated as soon as they emerge, the critical relevance of certain community-based writing practices only increases: processes that question the legitimacy or political usefulness of a notion of authorship without community connections; processes that emphasize the material conditions of production that allow writing to exist (or not to exist) in the first place; processes that underline the roles of both authors and readers, and their communities, in the production and sharing of writing materials. These writing practices, which have radically shifted away from the singularity of the author and onto the dynamic meaning-producing roles of readers and communities, calls into question the appropriation of someone else's materials (and, in writing, we are always dealing with someone else's materials). Instead, such practices usher in the disappropriation of these materials. Disappropriation has involved, and still involves, the critical renunciation of what capital-L Literature does and has always done: appropriating others' voices and experiences for its own benefit and its own hierarchies of influence. Disappropriation has involved, and still involves, exposing the mechanisms that permit an unequal exchange of labor: the labor that uses the language of collective experience for the author's individual gain. The comprehensive goal of disappropriation was, and is, to return all writing to its plural origin. In this way, it seeks to construct future horizons in which writing joins the assembly so it can participate and contribute to the common good. A simultaneously backward and forward movement, disappropriation uncovers the past and blazes trails into the future at the same time. Disappropriation, in short, describes the kind of writing that,

in an era marked by the spectacular violence of the open war on populations dubbed the War on Drugs, would open itself up to include the voices
of others in evident and creative ways. In doing so, it would take care to
avoid the obvious risks: subsuming the voices of those others into the author's own sphere or reifying them in unequal exchanges characterized by
profit or prestige for a select few. Critical and celebratory, always carried
out in cooperation with others, disappropriation (in writing) issues a warning about what is in danger here and now: the construction of communal/
popular horizons that secure the collective re-appropriation of the material
wealth available, as Raquel Gutiérrez has argued.[15]

This practice, conducted amid a staggering death toll and in formats
ranging from pen and paper to the digital screen, is what I call *necrowriting*
in this book. They are writing practices that both bear witness to and resist the violence and death resulting from the neoliberal state that has embraced maximum profit as a guiding principle. As for the poetics that sustain necrowriting by constantly challenging the concept and practice of
property (and propriety), I call this *disappropriation*. These terms are less
an academic diagnosis of today's production than a reading effect: the out-
come of reading with lenses informed by aesthetics, ethics, and politics—all
three elements at the same time, intertwined and enmeshed.

This poetics of disappropriation forms *communalities* of writing. In un-
veiling work created by many people in community (as the Mixe anthro-
pological root-word implies), communalities of writing address survival
strategies based on mutual care and the protection of the common good,
challenging the ease and apparent immanence that marks the languages of
globalized capitalism. Unlike the paternalistic "giving voice to the voiceless"
promoted by certain imperial subjectivities, and unlike the naïve putting-
of-oneself into another's shoes, these writing practices incorporate those
shoes and those others into the materiality of a text. Writing always involves a co-authorship; the result is always a text-in-common. And when
I say "in common," I mean not only the physical latticework comprised by
author, reader, and text, but also (to paraphrase a concept of communality I'll revisit later) the experience of mutual belonging, in language and in
collective work with others.

According to the Argentine theorist Josefina Ludmer, Latin America's
most recent textual production is characterized by its disrespect for the
strict division between the literary and the non-literary—an autonomous
notion of literature that capital-L Literature strove to keep alive. Confusing, more than merging, the borders between auto-fiction and fiction,
post-autonomous writings settle for producing (or aspire to produce?) the

present. These are her literal words (in my translation): "These writings don't accept literal readings; this means that we can't be sure, or it doesn't matter, whether they are or aren't literature. Nor do we know, or nor does it matter, whether they are reality or fiction. They are installed locally and in everyday reality to 'create present,' and this precisely is their significance."[16] Electronic writings on social platforms like blogs or Twitter are evidence of such intertwinings thus far. Much of today's documentary writing, both poetry and prose, reflects this urge to shake off the "dominion of what-is-your-own" that subverts conventional uses of archival material. In this way, it also provides an alternative to conventional interpretations of what historical novels are or could be. It subverts, in short, what it means to write history at all. Planetary writings, questioning the universality of a global subject through an interconnection among body, community, and nature, are absolutely part of this critical stance. Here we could also include the many hybridized, fragmentary books that insist on the impossibility of their own classification, even though they are now highly recognizable and recognized among readers.

While conceptualist appropriationism contributed, perhaps paradoxically, to the erasure of co-authorships and the re-instauration of the professional writer as the ultimate owner of discourse, disappropriative strategies approach both what-is-one's-own and what-is-the-other's as, fundamentally, *other*. That is, an entity with material existence—or, so to speak, voice. These voices and their specific material existences necessarily refuse to return to the circuit of authorship and capital, maintaining the inscriptions of the other and others in the textual process. Keeping others' inscriptions, working within this connection or this embrace, is no small matter. As a poetics, disappropriation has stopped believing that the sole outside-of-language (as Barthes would say) or the sole alteration of language (as Benjamin would suggest) is achieved through the literary "code." Therefore, it critically explores the production, distribution, and archival strategies applied to different textual connections with the public language of culture. These are writings that explore both the inside and the outside of writing; that is, their social occurrence in community, right between the discourses and speech-acts enacted by the others we become when we exist relationally with others.

Disappropriated writings, then. Ownerless, in the strict sense of the term. Without property or beyond property. And thus inappropriate. Or, perhaps more precisely put, inconvenient. According to the Real Academia de la Lengua Española (RAE), the Spanish-language dictionary, they would be writings unaffiliated with any particular person or circumstance. Or, better put, affiliated with many. And they are writings that, in not knowing how to behave appropriately, show the most critical face—which is often the other-est face—of what occurs.

A CONVERSATION

Whenever we talk about narration, narrative structures [as Kathy Acker said], we're talking about political power. There are no ivory towers. The desire to play, to make literary structures which play into and in unknown or unknowable realms, those of chance and death and the lack of language, is the desire to live in a world that is open and dangerous, that is limitless. To play, then, both in structure and in content, is to live in wonder.[17]

The desire to live in wonder—this desire to resist, both ethically and aesthetically, beyond the world's ivory towers, organically engaged with the communities that have questioned the inevitability of the capitalist grip—defines one of the most exciting literary conversations of our time. Much ink was spilled in the United States in the heated debate between conceptualist writers and a group of poets known as the Mongrel Coalition against Gringpo—and Carmen Giménez Smith's essay "Make America Mongrel Again" put forth a number of Latinx artists and writers whose work has ceaselessly challenged the racial and gender tenets of the status quo.[18] Echoes of this discussion reverberate in recent works by Raquel Salas Rivera and Vanessa Angélica Villarreal, whose bilingual energy and scope places them in far closer proximity to ongoing deliberations throughout Latin America. Questionable appropriative practices and an utter lack of sensitivity (or even attention) with respect to the privileges granted to white authors, whether male or female, by racist and classist structures, unleashed an urgent debate on the multiple and complex relationships between race and class, on the one hand, and writing on the other.

While this controversy attracted considerable attention in the US, a different—and larger—conversation was also taking place around issues of similar import in other areas of the world and in distinct literary traditions. But a conversation can only take place when those implicated are aware that an exchange of ideas, a dialogue of sorts, is occurring. While it would be difficult to gather conceptualists from the US, authors affiliated with the Nocilla project in Spain, writers delving into post-exoticism in France, and so-called leftist literature in Argentina in the same room, they might share a basic set of concerns that, while shaped by specific literary and social histories, all speak to a desire to engage with writing in ways that are both contemporary and irreverent. With different degrees of enthusiasm and emphasis, these writers have thought long and hard about the close relationship between writing and social change, between literary production and digital technology; the link between the literary realm and the public language of culture through strategies of documentary writing (among others); the subsequent subversion of the narrator's role, or of any other element of conventional fiction, as a sole mechanism of meaning production; the use of translation as an original language; the use of juxtaposition and ellipses as sequential principles; and the dissemination of hybrid genres. Employing allegory and pastiche, subverting classics by recycling them, and trying, in their most visibly poetic moments, to articulate ("redeem," Walter Benjamin would say) public discourse via techniques associated with citationist aesthetics, conceptual writings stressed that literature (now used more as an adjective than a noun) would not emerge unscathed from its pacts with platforms 2.0.

While much of the critical energy in US-American literary discussions was used to unpack the ways that white supremacy structured the literary industry, debunking or rightfully contextualizing works by Vanessa Place and Kenneth Goldsmith, a related conversation unfolded in the Spanish-speaking world.[19]

Writing in another language and on another continent, but facing the same challenges posed by digital technology, the so-called Spanish mutants of the Nocilla generation presented a tract on relationships between contemporary popular culture and a writing style that doesn't hesitate to feed on other texts. These other texts may include both the works of great authors canonized by officialist literary history and shards of urban language found by chance. Eloy Fernández Porta's books—from *AfterPop* to *£®o$*, and even his latest, *Emociónate así*—reflect an interdisciplinary, appropriately mutant body of work, ranging from the graphic to the musical and even video.[20] Agustín Fernández Mallo wrote an essay promoting a post-lyrical, urbanoid poetry, although his most interesting contribution has undoubtedly been *El hacedor (de Borges), Remake*. Following the appropriative principles underlying a great deal of contemporary digital production, Fernández Mallo rewrote a famous text by the Argentine author Jorge Luis Borges.[21] The fact that the poet's widow filed criminal charges against him—and won, forcing Fernández Mallo's book to be pulled from the shelves—only illustrates the threat that strategies of textual appropriation increasingly pose to certain bearers of prestige, authorial authority, and profits.[22] Vicente Luis Mora, another Spaniard, added to the debate with an iconoclastic essay on a recent history of the page and the creation of what he calls the *lectoespectador*, the reader-viewer, a reader for whom reading is seeing. Seeing means looking at screens, too.[23]

In France, Antoine Volodine wrote *Le Post-exotism en dix leçons, leçon onze*, a theoretical manifesto or performance in defense of prison writing—which, in being diametrically opposed to capital, directly attacks conventional notions of authorship and distribution.[24] For Volodine, post-exotic books naturally and perhaps solely speak to people sharing a prison cell. And we all share a prison cell, whether we know it or not. Such books are shared, then, with those who also want to escape. And with them alone. Because they confront power, these writings make peculiar pacts with language that let them fly under the radars of authority. They resemble other kinds of writing in many ways, but in reality, Volodine says, they are always talking about something else. This "something else" belongs to an incarcerated community whose members will ultimately die; their memory, in the narrator's hands, is the only thing that will survive. And this is why post-exotic works exist: to endure, in Volodine's words once again, "through recitation, clandestine copies, or muttering through the doors." Indeed, the aim of the post-exotic writer isn't mass distribution (remember, the enemy often lives among the readers themselves), but rather to meddle in and become part of memory. First memory, then dreams. The afterlife in dreams.

The Argentine writer Damián Tabarovsky uses the term *literatura de izquierda*, left-literature, to describe his critical diagnosis against today's commercial and academic literatures. The title has an unmistakably political charge.[25] Based on a detailed reading of Jean-Luc Nancy and Maurice Blanchot, Tabarovsky offers an updated vision of contemporary Latin American fiction and poetry, focusing on works that keep finding new ways to explode the chambers of authorship, commerce, and prestige. Although his assessment generally favors strategies popularized by various turn-of-the-century modernisms, he also turns to texts distinguished by their careful work with language, especially those written originally in translation. Tabarovsky's essay advocates for a literature "without an audience," a literature that speaks to language itself. Like so many books labeled (often with alarming ease) "cult" works, his position gives off a faint whiff of snobbery.

Iconoclastic, forged beyond the bounds of the academic canon as such, these essays are among the voices in a conversation that no contemporary writer can afford to ignore. Regardless of whatever consensus they can (or can't) produce, such books contain much of the transnational vocabulary that may help us interpret, as well as encourage or question, literary works that want to enunciate themselves in and with their time. In the end, just as the experimentalist writer Gertrude Stein—a student of William James, exiled alongside her companion Alice B. Toklas in Paris—discussed in her essay "How Writing is Written," every writer's challenge is to be contemporary with her contemporaries.[26] In many ways, this set of works examines the subversive potentiality of writing, invoking it and arousing it in the process. While politics vary greatly from author to author, it is certain that politics—and, better put, the political as a field, that inescapable link between aesthetics and ethics—feature prominently in each of them. Controversies now limited to English-speaking authors would only increase if all these works were to be translated into all the languages involved here. Let us hope that such translations are now under way.

THE STATE OF THINGS AND THE STATE OF LANGUAGE: A CRITIQUE

I use the word *necrowritings*—always in plural—for the textual works that emerge, alert, among war machines and digital machines: forms of textual output that seek to shake off the dominion of what-is-one's own. Necrowritings are born into a world of horrific carnage and governed by states that have traded their ethics of accountability to their people for a logic of extreme profit. Nonetheless (and perhaps fundamentally), they incorporate grammatical and syntactical practices, as well as narrative strategies and technological exercises, that question the state of things and the state of the language available to us. I call these writing-related decisions—which are closely associated with contemporary necropolitics, albeit through their opposition to them—*poetics of disappropriation*. I also use this term to distinguish such forms of writing from others that, while they may define themselves as critiques, have continued to rearticulate themselves in the spheres of authorship and capital, exacerbating more than interrogating the spread of writing within the dominion of what-is-one's-own. Political in the broadest sense of the word, violent and violated by the assaults of a twilight world, these inappropriate necrowritings go hand in hand with death, stepping on death's heels, pressing in on death's solar plexus, wherever they may go. This is, in accordance with the term's official definition, the end of life, the moment when something reaches its conclusion. Death. But it also involves (and here I continue to follow the officially accepted definitions; I've translated this one from the RAE) "very intensely feeling some form of affection, desire, or passion." You can die of laughter or thirst or love. Maybe one can even die of the desire to live, as Kathy Acker put it, in wonder. Perhaps one dies of living wonder-fully. Of writing inappropriately.

TEXTUAL CADAVERS

. . . .

. . . .

. . . .

Isn't anyone here? asks the woman
from Paraguay.
Reply: There are no cadavers.

Néstor Perlongher, *Cadáveres* (my translation)

It has become standard practice to address the most important or at least
the most voluminous part of a written work as the "body text." Associated
with a variety of appendices, like the header or the footnotes, and structured through paragraphs or broader sections, like chapters, this body came
to be understood as a type of organism with its own internal functions and
connections, whether explicit or implicit, to other members of its species.
In the end, an organism is defined by its capacity to exchange matter and
energy with its environment. Endorsed by a stable bond with a specific
authorship, the organism we talked about when we talked about the body
text was certainly alive. In this way, many writers, both men and women,
equated the creative process with a gestation period and a book publication with birth. The body text, an organism in and of itself, was also and
above all a living entity. No one gave birth to cadavers. Or no one accepted
that they did.

The conditions set by contemporary necropolitical war machines have
severed, by force, the longstanding equation of the body text with life. An
organism isn't always a living thing. What's more: as a living thing, an
organism is defined, as Adriana Cavarero has argued, by the experience
of vulnerability that characterizes what is always on the verge of dying. In
situations of extreme violence—torture, for example—the sophistries of
necropower transform the subject's natural vulnerability into a defenseless
state that dramatically limits its tasks and its agency; that is, its very humanity. In this way, it is no exaggeration to conclude that in times of aggravated
neoliberalism, times when the law of profit-at-all-costs has created scenar-
ios of extreme horrorism, the body text has become—like so many other
once-living organisms—a corpse text. Certainly, both psychoanalysis and
formalism (to name two major lines of twentieth-century thought) have
elaborated, in great detail, on the mortuary nature of letters, the aura of
melancholy and mourning that doubtlessly accompanies any text. Seldom,
however, have the relationships between text and cadaver been as close as
they are now. Juan Rulfo's town of Comala, the liminal land that so many
have considered the cornerstone of a certain kind of fantastical Mexican

literature, is no longer a mere product of the imagination or of some formal exercise. Instead, it has become a true proto-necropolis, generating the type of existence (not necessarily life per se) that characterizes today's textual production. There are shortcuts between Comala and Ciudad Juárez or Ciudad Mier. And the roads go up or down, liberate or ensnare, depending on whether you're coming or going.

Any genealogy for the corpse texts of necrowriting must include at least two points: the exquisite corpse that the surrealists were playing with in the mid-1920s, and the death of the author as ascribed by both Roland Barthes and Michel Foucault to romantic literature—which still viewed, and views, the author as the owner of the language he uses and as the axis or ultimate judge of a text's meaning. Both critical proposals, which incorporate the mortuary experience into the very titles of their arguments, privilege an assembly-based form of writing that is both anonymous and collective, spontaneous, if not automatic or even playful. It may be more than a lugubrious coincidence that Nicanor Parra and Vicente Hudibro used the word *quebrantahuesos*, "bone-breaker," for what was otherwise known as the exquisite corpse. Within the "co-incidence," defined as the magnetic field that attracts fundamental pieces of culture, are the dead bodies identified by the Argentine poet Néstor Perlonger amid everyday conversations and holes in enunciation.[27] What we find there, everywhere, are unattributed citations; open phrases; the construction of sequences shaped more by sound than by logic; excavations; recycling; and ellipses that serve, as in the epigraph introducing this section, to indicate what isn't there or what can't be enunciated, among many other textual strategies that serve to secure the "con-fiction" of texts.

It isn't entirely by chance, then, that language's proximity to death (or to the experience of the cadaver, which is the same thing) should spotlight a materiality and a textual community in which authorship has ceased to be a *vital* function per se, or in itself, ceding its space to the function of reading and the reader's own authorship as an ultimate authority. Only texts that have died are open or can be opened. Only dead bodies, apparently open, come back to life. As a cadaver and in its condition as a cadaver, the text can be buried and exhumed; the text can be dissected for forensic analysis or forcibly disappeared by the aesthetic or political brutality of the times. The text can lie underground or rise into the air as ash, but because it exists beyond life, it escapes the dictates of originality, authenticity, and coherence that dominated twentieth-century's notions of authorship.

In *El cadáver del enemigo*, an essential book to our understanding of relationships between death and writing in the early twenty-first century,

Giovanni De Luna argues that the medical examiner is the quintessential writer of today's world. Only the medical examiner manages to "get the dead to talk." And only medical examiners can interrogate the dead "in order to delve into what their lives were made of, in everything that made up their pasts and has been entrapped in their bodies" (my translation).[28] In this way,

> through their notes and reports, doctors prepare the bodies of the dead, offering them as documents to historians [writers]; during a process in which marks and wounds become literary texts (anamnesiac index cards), cadavers cast off their silence and begin to speak, which causes irreplaceable documentary fragments to flower.[29]

Roque Dalton was right: "The dead are getting more restless every day. . . . These days they get ironic / ask questions. / I think they've started to notice / they're outnumbering us" (my translation).

Writings produced amid necropolitical circumstances are "anamnesiac index cards" of culture. "There are cadavers," Néstor Perlongher repeats at the end of every stanza in his poem "Cadáveres," signaling their absence.[30] There are cadavers, he maintains, that force us to remember every anamnesiac index card. At the end of Perlongher's poem, however, in response to the question asked by the Paraguayan woman ("Isn't anyone here?"), someone or something offers a different rejoinder: "There are no cadavers." The line interrupts the repetition and concludes the poem. In doing so, it evidences the disappearance of the dead bodies—and, paradoxically, it makes those bodies visible and audible as they fill the country and as they have filled the poem's prior lines.

Writers don't "give birth" to dead bodies. On the contrary: serving as medical examiners, writers read them carefully, interrogate them, dig them up or exhume them by recycling or copying them, prepare them and re-contextualize them, determine whether or not they've been reported missing. Ultimately, if they're lucky, they bury them in the reader's own body—where, according to Antoine Volodine, exemplary post-exotic that he is, they may turn into the dreams that will never let us sleep or live in peace. And if this doesn't radically disturb our perception of and experience in the world, then what does? They're hardly exquisite, and perhaps they won't drink the new wine of the twentieth or twenty-first centuries. Yet these bodies-made-of-text, these suitably dead texts, are what configure our contemporary screens: the rectangles in which we see ourselves, and see ourselves seeing ourselves, while a cursor pulses incessantly and letters appear and disappear like faith, sometimes, or like fireflies.

Since at least the fifteenth century, textual production has been transmitted through the interface of the page. But the page that continues to organize the twentieth-century interface of the computer is endowed with functions that have taught us, gradually but perhaps inexorably, to reconsider each of these narrative elements in profoundly different ways. As conceptual writing has already emphasized, the frequent use of copy-and-paste not only eliminates the significance of differences in scale (you can copy and add a pixel or an image fragment or a video) and literary genre (you can copy and add a verse or a moving image or a block of lines). It also questions the author's originality and the more general issue of language-ownership. Evoking pastiche and collage, the routine and widespread use of copy-and-paste has turned the most widely disparate authors into textual curators for readers who see the narrator/author distinction—or respect for verisimilitude—as minimally relevant to the effectiveness of their creative process or the resulting object of their exploration. Sam Shepard's *Motel Chronicles*, or Michael Ondaatje's *The Collected Works of Billy the Kid*, were seen as unclassifiable works in their day. *Dictee*, by the Korean American author Theresa Cha, received a similar reception. They can now be perceived as precursors of a certain kind of book—one whose critical interpretation requires, for starters, a terminology that includes concepts like juxtaposition, real time, and alternate forms of the narrative "I." Perhaps these were some of the books to demand the eyes we have today.

According to Lev Manevich in *The Language of New Media*, while the story of the computer interface is relatively brief, we (as its users) have gotten used to the direct manipulation of objects onscreen, the constant superimposition of windows, the representation of icons, and tiny menus, among other things.[31] We text-producers (the post-Fordist workers of immaterial capital) have been facing a peculiar screen-based reality since the 1980s, in conjunction with a financial crisis that would make Taylorist industrial capitalism obsolete. Why, then, should we be ordered to obey twentieth-century textual principles, or even older ones? Today's necrowritings confront this question, too. And, as Celan always reminds us, confrontation means confronting death.

IMMATERIAL WORK AND RESISTING WITH WONDER

If post-Fordian theorists are correct, ours is an age in which immaterial labor—based on informal education, imagination, and inventiveness—has replaced physical labor as the producer of surplus value.[32] Linguistic capacities have become essential both in the production of goods and in how such goods are assigned value. The emergence and survival of cognitive capitalism (also known as biocapitalism, post-industrial capitalism, or semio-capitalism) increasingly depends on its ability to incorporate, subordinate, and exploit a series of skills once considered common (in the sense that they were seen as part of the common good) to the human experience: language, the faculty of socialization, vivacity, spirit. The predominance of immaterial work, and the blurry line it draws between the work of production and the work of producing *oneself*, can easily yield a society in which everything, from babbling to kindness, is susceptible to commercialization. This would unquestionably be Adorno's private hell: total commodification.

Franco "Bifo" Berardi, the Italian theorist of post-operationism, points out another hazard. When the relationship between work and value is broken, when financial capital has little bearing on the real economy, a void is created that can only be filled with the purest violence or the most cynical simulation: outright deception.[33] In the language of Mbembian postcoloniality, this void is produced and filled by the war machines of necropolitics. And yet also emerging in that vacuum—perhaps as a reflex, but also as energy of resistance—are the anamnesiac index cards of today's cultural criticism. In other words, necrowritings.

Like Gorz or Marazzi, Bifo Berardi believes that we live in an age in which the value of goods no longer depends on the real labor invested in their production, but rather on the linguistic exchange through which this production is foregrounded.[34] Now, as financial capital and economic production operate in separate spheres, the chief conflict isn't waged between the proletariat and those who own the means of production. Instead, it plays out between the cognitariat (intellectual laborers who produce semiotic goods in accordance with a system of permanent availability) and the administrative class, whose only skill is competence, preferably lethal. If this is true—and the economic crisis of 2008 appears to confirm that it is—then this phase demands a critical reconsideration both of the role of the linguistic work required for text-production and of the distribution of those texts.

While Bifo Berardi has called attention to the particularly dangerous relationship forged between language and simulation (a relationship that, in terms of contemporary *financialization*, produces and leads to deception and lies), a critical analysis of today's conditions of textual production doesn't have to overlook its subversive potential. Far from serving as a mere tool of representation, language has become, effectively, the primary source of capitalist accumulation: "Speculation and spectacle intermingle, because of the intrinsic inflationary (metaphoric) nature of language. The linguistic web of semioproduction is a game of mirrors that inevitably leads to crises of over-production." But language isn't a one-way street. Language— Bifo notes this, too, in *After the Future*—is the practice "thanks to [which] we can create shared worlds, formulate ambiguous enunciations, elaborate metaphors." In this way, as other critics who see cognitive capitalism as a form of capitalist crisis have warned, the hazy distinction between the work of production and the work of producing oneself can lead us directly away from the powers-that-be and their designs. And they can lead us into the creation of autonomous communities, organized from the ground up, beyond capital's governing eye. More than ever before, what happens on the page and what happens beyond it have a direct, concrete relationship with the production of social value. What will writers do with this power? What is the role of writing, both in cultural and political terms, at a time when immaterial work—work with and through language, invention, knowledge—is the fundamental factor in value-production? Waist-deep in the age of semiocapitalism, can writers envision and produce a linguistic practice capable of producing a world that isn't completely dominated by capital—and that speaks truth to power? "Only the conscious mobilization of the erotic body of the general intellect, only the poetic revitalization of language, will open the way to the emergence of a new form of social autonomy," states Bifo Berardi in *The Uprising: Poetry and Finance*, one of his most recent books. Echoing the performative turn evidenced in much US-American poetry of the post-conceptualist age, this stance tends to emphasize the notion of presence and the body's materiality by valorizing the voice. However, as David Buuck has pointed out, the risk that this response poses to anti-expressive or highly mediated forms of writing is the nostalgia for something labeled as (or desired to be) authentic. Or, in the worst-case scenario, an acritical return to the very idea of the Author.[35]

#WRITINGSAGAINSTPOWER

On the occasion of the public protests that arose in Mexico after the 2012 presidential elections, I asked the following questions on Twitter: do you find yourself saying that the past has taken power, but do you keep talking about originality as a bastion of literary merit? Do you worry about the state of things, but do you also worry that aesthetics coexist with ethics when you write? Do you enjoy writing like a crazy person or a child, but do you call this activity an "exercise" or "note-taking," never "literature"? Are you a social media pro who does a lot of copying and pasting, but are you single-mindedly concerned about authenticity when you write fiction? Do you challenge authority but bow down to authorship? In short: are you against the status quo, but do you keep writing as if there were nothing wrong on the page?

With these 280-character texts, gathered under the hashtag #escrituras-contraelpoder (#writingssagainstpower), I wanted to express some of this book's core ideas in a conversational tone. In the future, surely, not all writing will be sheltered by disappropriating poetics that destabilize the dominion of what-is-one's-own. Surely, too, conventional and unconventional books will continue to be produced at the same time—just as books printed on paper now share space and readers with electronic books. It would be wise, however, for contemporary commentators to incorporate the strategies that configure and restructure today's necrowritings into their own critical arsenals. Perhaps, once we've learned to read them in context, both carefully and critically, necrowritings will be able to show us how to see and experience the world with the wonder celebrated by Kathy Acker.

ANAMNESIAC INDEX CARDS

"They're a social thermometer. Cadavers let you analyze what's happening in their societies," said the contemporary artist Teresa Margolles in 2012. The occasion was the opening of an exhibition that showcased her work on death, especially on dead Mexican bodies. Born in northern Mexico, a region particularly hard-hit by violence associated with the Calderón War, Margolles has built a body of work inextricably associated with death and the dead: their bodies, their stories, their expectations, their motives. Working less through them than with them, Margolles hasn't only conducted a live autopsy of Mexico, informing people of the contexts that radically affect both the living and the dead; she has also created, to borrow a term used earlier, anamnesiac index cards of Mexican and global culture in the necropolitical era of post-industrial capital. *The Restless Dead* is driven by a similar impulse. If, as Giovanni De Luna has argued, the anamnesiac index cards are the terrain in which the cadaver's marks and wounds are turned into writing, then the following pages seek to receive those "irreplaceable documentary fragments" through which cadavers forgo their silence. They analyze not the living organisms of Taylorist capitalism, but rather the signs that culture has managed to inscribe on the textual cadavers of necropolitical semiocapitalism, over time and through space. And so this book is a set of comparative necrographies in which the contexts of production—or, to be more precise, of post-production and distribution—are as relevant and influential as the specific written operations of each textual object.

The opposite of globalized authorships, which seemingly seep through borders without migratory obstacles, aren't local authors, but rather planetary writers. I open *The Restless Dead* under the influence of Gayatri Chakravorty Spivak, who emphasizes the embodied nature of planetary creatures vis-à-vis the smooth abstraction of the global agents of contemporary capitalism. In "My Journey through Transkrit," I write as a migrant of color on the Mexico-US border, fixing my attention on the slippery, awkward, politically charged scenes in which foreignness interrogates—sometimes comically, sometimes painfully—a territory as it becomes more and more xenophobic. In doing so, I explore the politics of my own exophony, my own experience with "the disquieting linguistic disorientation of migration," and my growing attachment to the critical operations of what Aymara thinker Silvia Rivera Cusicanqui calls *chi'ixi* language.

I continue with the series of essays I wrote as I developed the concept of disappropriation. My comments on a series of Western authors writing on community and belonging are presented alongside the ideas of Mesoamerican thinker Floriberto Díaz who, from the highlands of Oaxaca, trained as an anthropologist, wrote piercingly about the political importance of communality. Díaz wasn't thinking about writing—much less creative writing—while he elaborated his views. Even so, much of what he wrote on communality as a material experience that enables the survival of indigenous communities pertains to writing—to critical writing—in fundamental ways, especially when it comes to the fraught relationship between work and writing practices. Again and again, *The Restless Dead* invites its readers to examine the material contexts of production and distribution of texts, as well as to consider the practices of communality that may constitute and subvert them. My goal, among others, is to embrace a poetics and a writing practice that, in Jean-Luc Nancy's terms, is "offered to us" as "happening to us," helping us experience a "being-in-common." Or, as feminist and activist thinker Raquel Gutiérrez so aptly put it when describing the relevance of the assembly: "a dissemination of power that allows the reappropriation of words and collective decision over matters that concern us all because they affect us all."

While writing is certainly a practice of otherness, documentary writing may display this practice more explicitly. In seeking connections with the public discourses of culture, writers have also questioned the aesthetic and political relevance of how the altered voice—the other's voice—is created, distributed, and archived. Hence the pages of this book that lead us away from the conventional configurations of historical novels and into the challenges— both ethical and aesthetic—entailed by the material incorporation of others' practices into texts now rightfully presented as belonging to a plural "us." This inevitable communality is what gives them meaning, air, and life itself.

As language experimentalism, the work of the late David Markson inspires a series of reflections on the use (and abuse) of the autobiographical in contemporary literature. I am especially interested in the prominence afforded to death, especially the death of the author, both as subject and as writing strategy in a couple of his novels. I briefly revisit what Roland Barthes and Michel Foucault argued with respect to the death of the author for a 1960s audience, comparing and contrasting their views to Markson's: an author grappling with what appears to be the return of the dead. In Spanish, the verb *desvivir*, which incorporates the verb "to live" as a negative, may be reasonably translated into English as "to die for." Could it be that Markson's late work confirms this "undying" of the dead—and, even more specifically, the undying of the dead author?

Twitter may be a waste of time—or a laboratory for contemporary writing. I suggest that today's tweets, both in structure and in content, are good examples of what Josefina Ludmer has characterized as present-producing writing in an era of post-autonomous literatures. Indeed, these rectangles of words materialize less to make a claim about Twitter's literary status than to manifest what writing does, and can do, collectively. Here, I pay particular attention to the early, generative responses that emerged among young writers using Twitter in Mexico—and what their practice can tell us about their subjectivities, their humor, and their critical approach to language. While digital activism has rightfully—and at times successfully—overtaken Twitter platforms, I have chosen to focus on language experimentation in this chapter.

As a rule, writers speak little about their book advances or their jobs. Since writing is usually perceived as a vocation or a gift, not work, writers have been able to evade crucial questions about the materiality affecting both the production and the distribution of texts: an opacity that has exacerbated the perpetration of gender and racial hierarchies that therefore remain unchecked. I start this chapter by taking a look at some love letters written by the legendary Mexican writer Juan Rulfo—who referred to them, not incidentally, as business letters. This singular conflation allows me to interrogate the way in which making a living informs (or deforms, depending on the case) a range of writing practices and the history of literature as we know it. Writing, and art more broadly, is often presented as a recipe against violence. But is it? Writing workshops, specifically creative writing workshops, emerge in violent worlds, not outside them. I offer some thoughts about my own cross-cultural experiences in and with

US models of creative writing workshops, turning my attention, too, to their gradual expansion throughout the Spanish-speaking world. Much comes into view: the relationship between writing and academia; the various pedagogies at play; the gender and racial inequalities that so often go unseen; the marginalization of writing in languages other than English in the US (or other than Spanish in Mexico). I still believe that, when we are paralyzed with horror, when we are stripped even of the human condition that makes us both others and ourselves, writing communities can offer the kind of *shareng* (see the chapter on disappropriation) that engages these fundamental forms of being-in-common: dialogue, collective work, critical imagination.

I warn you, as I finish this book, about the dangers of unfounded optimism, but wholeheartedly support the call to be stubborn. Not determined, but stubborn. Not single-minded, but stubborn. As the powers-that-be strive to present this world as the only one available to us, even the only one possible for us, stubbornness is a tool—a state of being—that insists on the existence and benefits of alternative worlds, both in our midst and in our imaginations. Amid increasing fascism within the US and abroad, let's be stubborn and create together, piece by piece, word by word, the world we want to live in.

My Journey through Transkrit

Planetary, Sporadic, Exphonic

THE RITES OF PANGAEA: PLANETARY CREATURES
ON AN EXISTENTIAL EARTH

A "cloudofwords" is passing over this page. Through the window, you can see the "monumental M" of the mountain. The approaching storm will undoubtedly be "a rain of fundamental words." The peninsula is a tumor. Later, when it's all over, what's left will be the "stain on the pavement. Out of focus / it greases the mechanic's vision." Above, the firmament; below, the fragrance of certain gardens; in between, the mental state that releases vision with rash conclusiveness: "the distance between Liechtenstein and Uzbekistan is a sea."

> From here to there: the gaze in the telescope.
> From there to here: the gaze in the microscope.
> Between one and the other: the technology of sidereal language.

There is nothing accidental about evoking poetry to start a chapter on the challenges of planetary writing in a globalized world. Poetry—the language we use to investigate language, as Lyn Hejinian would say—remind us that writing is tied to the Earth. The vocabulary of necropolitics fans out once again: writing is in-terred, in-earthed. For example, from the continental waistline to the craters' fingerprints registering "the lunar soul," *Transterra*, by the Guadalajara-born poet Gerardo Villanueva, embraces the globe in its most majestic and most human breadth.[1] His words engage the eye, it's true, but they're destined mainly for our feet. Rise and walk, murmurs his private Lazarus. Touch. Perceive. Rise up and then sink here, swim. Variable cloudiness. Survive. This is a crack. A private cartography opens up. This is how you spell the meridian of anxiety. Altitude. Wind. Borders. Can you feel the geography pulsing under the palm of your hand or in the corner of your eye? More than a globalizing agent, this Lazarus, crawling iconoclastically along through Villanueva's trans-terring pages, is, to borrow the term coined by the theorist and literary critic Gayatri Spivak, a planetary subject; the emphasis is on the contested interaction of bodies rather than on the swift circulation of commodities.[2] And the same is true of *Los planetas*, a poetry collection by Mexican poet and environmental activist Yaxkin Melchy. The difference between globalizing agent and planetary subject is certainly an aesthetic one, but it's also political. The difference, in any case, exceeds terminology itself. It involves the ties—through melancholy or silence, celebration or movement—that connect a range of materialities: territories and languages, history and cosmos, human and nonhuman agencies, and the body right in the middle of it all.

In *Transterra*, the great driftings and shiftings aren't abstract. Here, history is written with the upper-case letters of stellar dimensions and the lower-case letters of knees and knuckles. Simultaneously telescope and microscope, the planetary subject understands that otherness "contains us as much as it flings us away" from ourselves. The subject subjects herself: to the Earth's surface, to the evolution of history, to personal memory, to the other. A being is a carnal creature here. The force of gravity. Divine and earthly all at once, in constant feedback with her surroundings, the planetary subject slips along, with exceptional powers of perception, across that "existential Earth" (as the social critic Mike Davis has deemed it) "shaped by the creative energy of its catastrophes."[3]

Attuned to the Earth's surface and both its animate and inanimate phenomena, Villanueva's and Melchy's poetry echoes the postulates of a contemporary geology, one that is based on an exacting reappraisal of catastrophe. Unlike the isolated, predictable universes of Newton, Darwin, and Lyell, the Earth as imagined by a handful of scientists known as neocatastrophists (such as Kenneth Hsu in Switzerland and Mineo Kumazawa at the University of Nagoya) is hardly immune to astronomical chaos. Quite the contrary: as a singular part of a historical solar system that doesn't seem to overflow with life, Earth is the crust on which terrestrial events and extraterrestrial process continually converge, albeit on various timelines. The most dramatic evidence of such convergences takes the form of the monumental impacts that cause catastrophes.

In *Transterra*, Gerardo Villanueva produces the words of this geocosmology: a colossal space, a nearly scientific precision, a laughing wink, a constant flow. His castaways "reach the Galápagos Islands, / encounter a native / with no language to celebrate / the welcome." His voyeurs meditate: "The globular clusters, glimpsed from a distance, / look like supernovas. / Could it be an electromagnetic knot, a love triangle, or / an irrelevant galaxy? It's all the same. / Here, Kepler's laws entangle, while pornography continues / on the TV set." His radio listeners (Castilian, or Pan-American, or simply American in the continental sense) prompt him to invite Severo Sarduy to visit. As far as I'm concerned, Antonin Artaud went to the Sierra Tarahumara to listen.

From a certain corner of the Pacific (Tijuana) to the center of the continent (Oaxaca) to the fini-secular metropolis (Mexico City) to the Polynesian Triangle, the planetary subject trans-terrs, which is just another way to say that "she moves around in the deepest place, which is here." Beyond the abstract discourse of globality—and, by contrast, rooted in the very most concrete of all errant locations—this trans-terring is a migration that travels through and invents a nervous, wounded planet, furrowed-browed, undermined. Alive.

On this planet, among its planetary subjects, myriad instants reproduce what Juliana Spahr calls "the disquieting linguistic disorientation of immigration."[4] Linguistic insurgency is not alien to the long, deep-rooted Chicanx literary traditions in the United States. They didn't cross the border, but the border crossed them on a fateful day in February 1848, when the signing of the Guadalupe Treaty ended the Mexican-American War with the victory of the US army. As the Recovery Program (Recovering the US Hispanic Literary Heritage in the United States) of Arte Público Press has documented so well: Spanish remained a language of artistic inquiry in the newly annexed territories, and, little by little, both Spanish and English helped express the experiences of exploitation and struggle, dignity and survival, of innumerable border communities. Some—such as Tomás Rivera, author of *Y no se lo tragó la tierra*, a jewel of a book—wrote in Spanish and thus inaugurated a tradition some of us are still carrying on today. A generation of powerful Chicanx women writers write mostly in English, but they use Spanish words or phrases to interrupt, and thus to question, the hegemony of English: from Sandra Cisneros to Vanessa Angélica Villareal, from Ana Castillo and Cherry Moraga, to Carmen Giménez Smith and Sara Borjas. Gloria Anzaldúa, who knew from borders and migration (and long walks, for that matter), always kept Spanish close to her arguments and her sentences. No one seriously interested in the Mexico-US border, and borders in general, can afford to miss her *Borderlands/La Frontera*: a theoretical treatise, a confession, a manifesto, a cross-genre round-trip map.

Yoko Tawada, the Japanese novelist who lives and teaches in Germany and who writes in her second language, emphatically asserts that "today a human subject is a place where different languages coexist by mutually transforming each other and it is meaningless to cancel their cohabitation and suppress the resulting distortion."[5] In this context, as we trans-terr each other, to speak always means to speak in translation—with someone else, on someone else's terms, or with someone else's help. Anyone who passes through, who comes and goes, is well aware of this. No one writes in a mother tongue anymore. Did it ever exist?

Trans-terring helps us open a door: let's push it in, let's cross to the other side. This is a writerly journey that began a long, long time ago, when the earth first sent messages we were too busy to acknowledge, much less heed. Territories write on our backs; Anzaldúa was right. And we leave our own traces on them. Remember: this place is full of mass graves. The air is alive with the hum of bullets and the death rattle of someone at rest. Without peace.

PLACE MATTERS

a. Noble and brutal

TRUE CONFESSION: I'm used to going away.

It's a noble custom, going away. And it's also a brutal one. You get used to lifting your hand and erasing, with a cautious oscillatory movement, what you leave behind. You forget, always methodically. The wedge that spoils the tangerine's completeness. The fist that transforms itself into five fingers. The piece that, by its absence, forces machines into imperfection—or the piece that, by its absence, lets a stream of water flow freely. You promise. You stare out at the landscape on the other side of the window and discover, right then and there, the exact meaning of the verb *to miss*, the noun *nostalgia*, the subjunctive *if there were*, the conditional future. Later, in the anonymity of somewhere else, you fail to act. You invent an origin and a past; if possible, you invent what is to come. Afterward, all that's left is the detonation sometimes triggered by this tree bark, that mountain, this piece of city, that light.

Something reverberates.

The subject's founding gesture, recalls Žižek in *The Parallax View*, is to subject itself.[6] To "voluntarily," he adds, subject itself *to*.

Leaving, which is noble and brutal, and which always means leaving somewhere in particular, is very much like writing. This bit I know to be true.

b. The imaginary relationship

"Materialism," Žižek also argues, "means that the reality I see is never 'whole'—not because a large part of it eludes me, but because it contains a stain, a blind spot, which signals my inclusion in it."[7] Could this be why place is the only thing I'll never truly be able to see? Is this why place subjects me? Is this perhaps why I insist on *objecting* it with my subjectivity?

Above all, a place is a relationship. It isn't a geography, but rather an approach to that geography; not a city, but rather the way in which the body moves around the city; not a book, but rather the irreplaceable reading of the book; not a birth announcement, but rather the birth itself. The sky. We describe our relationship with a place as *landscape*. Because it's human, this relationship is material: it's a connection to body and sweat and sex and class and race and poverty and inner thigh and saliva and fingernails and even fingernail-grime. The farther in we go, the denser it is, which means the more opaque it gets. The deeper, in fact, the more adjectival. The more *here*. Therefore, in being human (and nonhuman), the relationship that constitutes every place is also—perhaps on principle, but perhaps also in the end—an imaginary relationship. A place is pure writing.

c. Being from a place

A rigid, conservative vision dictates that the relationship between subject and place is, or must be, unambiguous—and monogamous. A subject, it is said, must be from a place, ideally but not always her place of origin. Everything else, it is said, is betrayal. Or worse, a loss of identity. But not everything in life, whether unfortunately or thankfully, is unambiguous or monogamous or pure loss. One ultimately passes through many places, and one roots herself in them if she truly passes. Appropriation magnifies. Wild Arabic tree. Boneshaker. Armstrong. "No one is born just once," asserts the Canadian poet Anne Michaels in her magnificent novel *Fugitive Pieces*. "If you're lucky, you'll emerge again in someone's arms; or unlucky, wake when the long tail of terror brushes the inside of your skull."[8] *Time is a blind guide*. Passing through a place always has consequences. Founding it, for example, among many others. This is why a place is actually *places*. Something plural, if you're lucky. A matter of good fortune. Sometimes.

For the person who's leaving, the place is everything. For the person who's leaving, the place is nothing. Both declarations contain a measure of truth. In any case, for the person who's leaving: the place. Better put: the places. After all, how many times have we not already been born? Another way to pose this question: how many times have we not already died? A while ago, in the valley traversed by a river some call Bravo and others the Rio Grande, I heard my first childhood stories. The voices came from afar, barely audible echoes of my paternal grandparents, landless peasants who left the high arid plateaus of San Luis Potosí for the coal mining regions of northern Coahuila—only to continue their journey and finally settle around the cotton fields that ringed Anáhuac, an agricultural border town in Tamaulipas. The voices, the soothing voices of these stories, also belonged to my paternal grandparents, who had lived and worked in fields and cities of the United States—only to be deported after the 1929 crash with the enactment of then president Hoover's anti-immigrant policies. Expelled, pushed back across the border, directly into the cotton experiment and land reform implemented by Mexican president Lázaro Cárdenas, my grandparents became owners for the first time in generations: owners of land and owners of words. And so, I was born there, it's true. In their words, on the plot of *eijido* land where they labored and dreamed. Held in the lap and the lullaby of cotton, transformed into sorghum fields decades later, and even later into assembly plants. Belonging fastened a belt across my sternum. And then let me go.

And I was born again nearby: in Cola de Caballo, a pond with fish and ducks in the middle of a university campus, polluted air. Monterrey, Mexico, the industrial city where my immediate family became a sovereign republic of four in permanent flight. Can we be born out of place? In between places, on our way toward—and, more often, on our way out afterwards. Migration, which grows out of need, also becomes a habit. We moved from town to town, from north to south, knowing that we carried a border with us. This knowledge, which is a treasure, is also a place of birth.

One is also born, sometimes, looking out at the sea, alongside a wall originally built with material designed to prevent the free passage of bodies. All brown. Pieces first brought from the war on Iraq. Rage is a place of birth. Happiness, a poet once said, lingering at the table after a meal, is only available to those whose existence depends on the radical overhaul of it all. Happiness, too, is thus a place of birth. Born with a built-in critical eye (and critical I). Born in Tijuana, on the other side of San Diego, right on the most dynamic crossing of our contemporary world.

I call all of these constant cycles of national and transnational migration, this entire mass of interwoven roots, What Is Contrary to the Universal: the Benjaminean constellation that, in its most concretely material form, as a saturated object, affects and is affected by everything else. When I'm in motion, and always including the perspective of the human and nonhuman eyes watching, the place marks me. But always in ways I'm not consciously aware of.

SPORADIC

a. Negative definition

They're not sedentary. This is clear from the get-go. They're errant, clearly: they move away and they make mistakes at the same time. We have to agree on this from the beginning, too. But, strictly speaking, they're not vaga- bonds. Or, at any rate, they may be a certain type of intermittent vagabond, given that one of their known habits involves remaining for periods of time (sometimes long ones) in specific places. Some take the time to make friends, acquire desks, chairs, beds, even build their own houses. Some, driven more by necessity than by convenience, secure forms of employment that they will later list on their imaginary resumes as "all kinds of work." They're not wholly rootless, because they tend to form communities in the territories they pass through. Their faces are familiar, for example, in cer- tain bars or cafés, in the aisles of certain silent libraries, on the rooftop ter- races of certain gloomy buildings, or in the guestrooms of certain friends. They're not exiles, at least in the political sense that the twentieth century assigned the term, because they come and go more or less as they please, civilian passport in hand. They could be professional migrants if they were willing or had the time to spend hours and hours waiting in line in differ- ent government offices to sign the documents that would confirm such a status. They could be members of a diaspora if the official definition (the dispersion of human groups who leave their place of origin) were to omit the word *origin*—so that it would then describe human beings who leave places, *of origin* or otherwise.

b. Passing through, passing for

I'm referring to writers. I'm trying to walk with and think through the work of various writers who have passed through territories known as Latin America during the twentieth century. And "passing through" is a verbal dumbbell I've taken a long time to select. These writers aren't from Latin America, but passing through Latin America doesn't eliminate the possi- bility of having been born there. These writers haven't traveled through Latin America, although, in order to pass through this region, it's necessary to em- bark on more than one journey. They could be Malcolm Lowry or Graham

Green or D. H. Lawrence, but they're more likely to be Witold Gombrowicz or Leonora Carrington or, indeed, Roberto Bolaño. They certainly aren't Vladimir Nabokov or Joseph Conrad or Samuel Beckett, known, among other reasons, for their versatile use of a new language. Rather, they're Gerardo Deniz and María Negroni and, indeed, Roberto Bolaño—all writers who, in having passed through Latin America, continued to write in one of the forms of language they grew up in. Careful: even when they live in the US, a territory in which much of today's Latin American literature is being written in both Spanish and English, they might not fit the labels of *US Latino writers*, or *New Latino writers*, or *US writers*. They are writers who pass through Latin America while also passing for many other things, thus opening the door both to dis-identification and to de-territorialization—which is simply another way to express the definitely fluid, permanently unfinished nature of contemporary identities. Here's the thing: they are the kind of writers who sporadically (not diasporically) inhabit sites and languages with which they forge a relationship of dynamic resistance rather than one of pleasant accommodation.

c. *The quid of the matter*

The translation from Latin to Spanish is, according to the RAE (the authoritative dictionary of the Spanish language) the "what" of the matter. It was late spring, but the afternoon slid along gray and slow outside the windows. Suddenly, "out of nowhere," as is usually said, a deafening and intensely white hailstorm unleashed itself from somewhere within that gray sky—so thunderous that it made me lift my eyes from the book I was reading, only to think, literally out of nowhere, about how sad it would have been, how truly sad, or at any rate vaguely disturbing, for Roberto Bolaño to know and witness the wild success of his books in English translation. I suspect that the late-spring grayness and the abrupt apparition of the hailstorm had something to do with this morbid thought, which then reminded me of an article written by the academic Sarah Pollack in which she explains the series of cultural and political puns that—behind the scenes, but not so much—help explain the swift and sudden "normalization" of Bolaño's texts on the market (and that's exactly how it should be said: the book market in the US).[9] Anyone else would have been happy, we can assume. But Bolaño, who by all appearances liked presenting his books as the weapons of a brave (*brave* is a word he often summoned in assessing literary works) and restless writer— crepuscular now, but no less passionate about "true," "authentic" literature— would have responded with at least a little incredulity, and then with some compulsive anger, and then even (why not?) with an age-old repudiation. Of course, we'll never know what he would have done, and it's certainly almost better this way. But on that gray spring afternoon, darkened by the startling emergence of the dazzling white hail (can something so white truly "darken" a spring afternoon?), I could only wonder how a book can possibly be protected—the true book, the book that is at least two books, both with a serrated edge—from the market's normalization and the maddening cheerfulness of fads and the vulgar avalanche of praise that is, ultimately, more of a grimace or a glut than real praise. I'm not entirely satisfied with the answer I reached there, staring out the bus window at midday (because it was, besides late spring, a little after midday), but it was this: we'd have to see Bolaño not as an exotic (and concentric) exception, but rather as one among the long saga of wandering writers sporadically passing through sites and languages in Latin America. Developing, meanwhile, in the same trance of passing-through, a relationship of dynamic resistance more than of pleasant accommodation with that heap of things that, for lack of a better term, we generally resort to calling *the environment*. Is there truly a thread running from those twenty-four years that Witold Gombrowicz spent in Argentina to, for example, Lina Meruane, the Chilean writer living and producing Spanish-language work in contemporary New York? Is there a thread, aesthetically speaking, that connects the books of Horacio Castellanos Moya (a writer born in Honduras who has spent long periods of time in both the US and Europe) with, let's say, Eunice Odio, a Costa Rican poet who died in Mexico? Do they constitute Units of Dispersion, these writers of a lineage as diverse as, say, César Moro (Peru) and Rodrigo Rey Rosa (Guatemala)?

EXOPHONIC ALPHABETS I: ADOPTING A NEW LANGUAGE

In a recent issue of the magazine *Granta*, the South African writer Elizabeth Lowry recounts the personal and intellectual experiences that led her to choose English as her writing language. Lowry, born and raised as an Afrikaaner in Pretoria—as well as in other major capitals across the world, due to her father's work as a diplomat—communicated in Afrikaans, just like her countrymen, ever since she could talk. After spending some time studying in London, however, and despite her family's criticism, she took up the English language as her own. "It is impossible," the author states in her brief testimony, "to adopt an entirely new language as a child without also becoming a new person. There is a sense in which the language we speak, with its compacted accommodations with history, its nuances of meaning and underlying cultural assumptions, speaks us."

She also says that "J. M. Coetzee once characterized South African literature in the era of apartheid as 'a less than fully human literature, unnaturally preoccupied with power and the torsions of power.' This was not the sort of book I wanted to write."[10]

If Lowry were analyzing why she had chosen English over French, say, or even Italian, her remarks would continue to resemble many others that have been made and are still made lightly, in an increasingly globalized world where cases of bilingualism or multilingualism may indeed abound. But Lowry, in an English utterly devoid of sentimentalism, in an austere and even contained English, knows very well that she's talking about Afrikaans, the language of apartheid, and she also knows that she's talking about British English, the language of an old empire. And in this context, her phrases—"adopt an entirely new language," "becoming a new person," "this was not the sort of book I wanted to write"—don't acquire new *meanings*, because the author holds onto those, abstaining from explicitly political comments. But they do bear new echoes that resound with tremendous weight, if not with gravity as such. Lowry knows that the decision to write in a language other than Afrikaans, being herself an Afrikaaner, is a matter of life and death.

Extreme conditions also drive Jakob, the main character of *Fugitive Pieces*, Anne Michaels's 1996 novel, to take up English not only as his language of everyday communication, but also and above all as a writing tool. Living in the US as a Holocaust survivor after his miraculous rescue by a Greek scientist, the future poet thus describes his ambivalent contact with this other language, the language that would gradually become his own: "The English language was food. I shoved it into my mouth, hungry for it. A gush of warmth spread through my body, but also panic, for with each mouthful the past was further silenced." In one of the most meticulously human logs of the microscopic actions carried out when one "decides" to write in a language other than that of one's birth, Michaels adds: "Language. The numb tongue attaches itself, orphan, to any sound it can: it sticks, tongue to cold metal. Then, finally, many years later, tears painfully free." And then, as Jakob himself finally acknowledges, a discovery occurs: "And later, when I began to write down the events of my childhood in a language foreign to their happening, it was a revelation. English could protect me; an alphabet without memory."[11]

But how do we "decide" to speak or write in a language in which we weren't born? As Mixe linguist Yásnaya Aguilar has persuasively argued in regards to the dying of indigenous languages in Mexico, communities don't decide to prevent younger generations from speaking a language out of contempt or in freedom. Linguistic discrimination targets and affects not only languages as such, but also bodies speaking languages deemed minor or nonessential or threatening to national unity. Demographically, Mexico was an indigenous country in 1810, when Mexican independence took place. And yet, just two centuries later, the Mexican state has achieved what the Spanish invasion could have only dreamed of: it has imposed Spanish as a de facto official language onto a pluri-linguistic population organized into distinctive nations. Did indigenous writers "decide" to speak Spanish in schools that forbid them from, and punished them for, communicating in their native language?

The widespread lynching of Mexicans after the Mexican-American War, and corporal punishment in US schools well into the mid-twentieth century, compelled Mexican families to adopt English as a means of communication. As in many Mexican-American families, Chicanx writers vividly recall the violent context in which English became *their* language. Spanish retreated to the domestic realm, where it conveyed the solidarity and endurance of intimate relationships. Meanwhile, out there in the public arena, as Mexican-American workers faced increasing discrimination and outright exploitation, Spanish became stigmatized as the language of labor. When and how do we "decide" to write in Spanish or English in the United States?

My maternal grandfather spoke English as he looked for work in the Houston construction industry and as he became a member of the Mutualist Society of Mexican Workers in the Second Ward. He had to. His livelihood depended on it. Having been born on the Texas-Tamaulipas border, English was never foreign to me. When I arrived in Houston in the late 1980s, I adopted English as my academic language but continued living and writing in Spanish. Houston, one of the most diverse cities in the United States even today, made that possible. I led an accented life. Some thirty years later, however, English has spilled over, tainting my accent and tampering with my vocabulary both in my everyday affairs and in my writing. When did I make this "decision"?

People often emphasize, with varying degrees of conviction and rage, the limitations imposed by using a language one didn't grow up speaking. There are numerous images: the speaker who moves only tentatively around the house of the second language; the listener who treads on unsteady ground, perpetually about to be swallowed up by utterances either nonsensical or inappropriate; the speaker who, in longing to express something, only manages to part her lips and feel the dry rush of air leave her mouth. I have been that speaker all too often. It's much less common to point out—in the respective ways of Lowry the writer, or Jakob, the other writer's character—that this uncertainty, this lack of confidence, this unerring attempt at mastery that is doomed to failure, also entails a paradoxical element of protection. And another pinch, perhaps even more intoxicating, of freedom. There it is, utterly whole: the chance to rebuild oneself from scratch. There it is, also whole: the chance to hear the other way in which a language "speaks to us" and therefore invents us. An accentuated life. It is not an alphabet without memory, as Lowry argues, for it contains, in my case, the expulsion of my grandparents from a country they used to call their own. It contains every single humiliation suffered by my parents and family members when crossing border lines. It contains thirst, and terror, and mass graves. It contains death, and cages to which death is summoned. And yet it is my language. I claim it as my own—for it too contains the labor that entire generations before mine put into it, reshaping it, subverting it, making it whole. This alphabet with a memory of its own has also enabled me to become this other person, this other writer. Look at her—she just turned the corner and disappeared for a while.

EXOPHONIC ALPHABETS II: THE SECOND LANGUAGE

a. The number two

I've always felt that second place is better, more comfortable. I also tend to believe that what's most important, both in books and in life, occurs with staggering frequency in the second-to-last paragraph, chapter, scene, floor. Between the ostentatious beginning and the frugal final conclusion is, thankfully for everyone, the number two: the entryway for postponement or prolongation or interruption or doubt. Perhaps this is why I prefer to speak about (in? for?) my second language rather than my first. There's a certain air of freedom about it. The smell of open things. An overcoming.

b. After

Strictly speaking, of course, every language is a second language. Strictly speaking, the language that embraces and envelops us in the womb is already a stepmother tongue. I know it's true, but this is what I like to call it: The Second Language. There's a certain sense of strangeness and a successive sense of unimportance that make me feel good about it. It's not my house, certainly, nor any other house. The Second Language means you are there with me, out in the open, exposed to the elements. It isn't responsible for keeping up appearances (of being original or primal or natural). Its responsibility, rather, is questioning everything (what is original and primal and natural) by the sheer fact of its existence. It's the one that talks with an odd accent and asks tough questions. It's the one that doesn't fit in, which means it doesn't take over. The one that showed up late, which is what allows it to announce that there may be more to come. If the mother tongue achieves an effect of intimacy through familiarity, The Second Language produces intimacy by way of hypervigilance. A state of alertness that knows no end. No respite. It's not home, but it's the road that brings me closer or takes me away, depending on whether the hill rises or falls—as Juan Preciado had already noted on his way to Comala—toward home.

c. Misunderstanding

There's an echo in my head. A faint buzz. A wheeze. For years, I called all of this The Second Language. Dirty noise. A slight dizziness like a vital levitation. The name I gave the veil that prevented me from seeing things clearly. Or that, once I'd looked at them, invited me to see things differently. Indeed, a distortion. An altered alteration. The imminence of a misunderstanding, which is another name for invention.

d. The other way

It's usually like this: everyone is speaking a certain language around a table, and then, unplanned, unthinking, The Second appears. Sometimes it's only the subtle wink of the suddenly untranslatable word; sometimes it's the silence lining the quick process of translation. Sometimes it's just a slight stammer, or, even more often, the accent sealing what's come from far away. It's there (I tell myself then) to remind me that always, in all situations, even in the happy ones, it's important to talk in *another way*. It's there to assure me there are always, at least, two of me.

e. Not the same, but equal

I once thought I knew which was which. I lived for many years in the country of The Second Language, and there, as it should, surrounded by nostalgia and mothballs and a dogged craving for The Great Narrative, the myth of The First Language emerged. There (which at the moment is Here, by the way) I carried out my earthy affairs in The Second, and my divine affairs, which are the most intimate ones, in The First. A question of symmetry. A matter of clarity. And everything would have been fine if it weren't for the proverbial night of the proverbial day when I had the proverbial dream in The Second Language. I don't remember what I dreamed about (although I'm almost certain there was a train involved), but I remember, with incredible specificity, how suddenly I woke. So then I wondered, is The Second now The First? It was terribly sunny outside. And everything would have been fine once again if I hadn't moved to the country of The First, where The Second returned—not without reluctance, not without that sudden whinny that tends to jolt me awake on dreamless nights—to its own place. Except that, according to the symmetries that have the misfortune or the virtue (depending on how you look at them) of being structural, I began to carry out my earthly affairs in The First— leaving, therefore, everything private (which is, as I've already said, the very closest thing to a concept of the sacred) in the hands of The Second. A matter of divinity. Ever since then, I've only spoken of love in a language I wasn't born in.

e. The freedom of The Second Language

In The Second Language, I can curse freely, truncate sentences wherever I feel like it, make scandalous declarations, rearrange sentences at will, avoid things (which is nearly the same as lying), err at great length, lower my voice until my voice reaches its own zero grade, assert myself and un-assert myself with the same solitary conviction, offer condolences, and promise the impossible, which may be just another kind of kiss. As if The First and I were overcome by a sudden fit of modesty when we're together, there are things I can't even conceive of in its presence. As if all the rules we'd learned by heart were getting in the way. As if we'd been through too much. As if everything hurt us. But with The Second, I can tell off-color jokes, utter words of love, release a long-kept secret, say goodbye, expound on politics.

f. Popular manifesto

No matter what language it's written in, all writing happens in The Second Language.

EXOPHONIC ALPHABETS III:
MY JOURNEY THROUGH TRANSKRIT

The scene is repeated outrageously often, although each time, to be fair, it incorporates slight variations that make it interesting or at least recognizable as a varied repetition of something else. The basic script involves two speakers participating in an everyday dialogue, the flow of which is interrupted by the appearance of The Accent. For a spectator outside the two speakers' shared context, I should clarify that both of them have an accent. That is, both pronounce words with a tone of voice and a rhythm and a speed that are *peculiar*. For a spectator more familiar with the context producing the dialogue between the two speakers, however, one of them clearly has an accent. And this accent, in its resemblance to the speech of the many others who surround them, has become transparent, and therefore goes altogether unnoticed, while the second speaker's accent is marked by elements of volume, rhythm, and diction that make it stand out. This dialogue is more noticeable when it is conducted between speakers of two different languages, although it also occurs between speakers who share one. Let's take a look.

SPEAKER 1: States *something*.

SPEAKER 2: Doesn't understand the statement and therefore makes an interjection that halts the dialogue.

[http://en.wikipedia.org/wiki/Interjection]

SPEAKER 1: Reacts to the interjection and therefore repeats, quickly, perhaps without thinking, the *something* stated before. From now on, we will call this *before* "the origin" or "the original."

SPEAKER 2: Doesn't understand the statement and therefore expressly and literally requests its repetition.

SPEAKER 1: Repeats the *something* stated originally, but now at a much slower speed.

SPEAKER 2: Doesn't understand and therefore requests the statement to be spelled out.

[1. v. i. To individually pronounce the letters of each syllable, the syllables of each word, and then the entire word; e.g., *u, t, ut, t, e, r, ter, utter.* 2. v. t. To separately and individually pronounce the letters of one or more words. 3. t. r. To guess; to interpret what is obscure and difficult to understand.][12]

SPEAKER 1: Spells out the *something* stated at the origin. Image: upraised lip-gestures, hands, and eyebrows incorporated into the exchange.

SPEAKER 2: Remains silent; listens to each letter as it's stated; watches all the letters literally file along before her eyes as they introduce themselves very slowly into her ears. She *reads*. This much is certain. She reads in this way, and then, only then, she responds.

SPEAKER 1: Continues the original conservation until the scene, which is this scene, is repeated once again.

TRAGIC CONFESSION: I have an accent, it's true. What's more: I have at least two accents. None of what I've recounted here would make much sense if the migration process that led me from Mexico to the United States some years go hadn't marked my habits of enunciation in the two primary languages I use when I talk, work, and write. I never tried to *not* have an accent, but neither did I imagine that I would eventually acquire two. At this point, I don't know what it would be like to live an unaccented life. I don't know how I'd feel if the way I talk didn't put everyone else on the alert: *she's not from here*. By now I have few memories of when my accent was indistinguishable from so-called normality. As Yoko Tawada explains in a text that hasn't yet been published in Spanish translation, but the title of which would correspond, I've been told, to the term *exophony*, "To pursue one's accents and what they bring about may begin to matter for one's literary creation."[13]

In her journey from Japanese to German, having also written poetry and novels in the latter language, Tawada says:

> People say my sentences in German are very clear and easy to hear, but still they are "not ordinary" and deviant in some ways. No wonder, because they are the results of the sound that I as an individual body have absorbed and accumulated by living through this multilingual world. . . . Today a human subject is a place where different languages coexist by mutually transforming each other and it is meaningless to cancel their cohabitation and suppress the resulting distortion.[14]

Let's go back to the original scene. We know that something has happened between Speaker 1 and Speaker 2 because the conversation, whose nature is to flow, has stopped. Surely, a strange or unrecognized element, like the repetition of something else, has been integrated into the conversation and prompted the unease. After all, the passage from one shore to the other is generally slow. Perhaps Speaker 1 and Speaker 2 have stumbled into something. Let's ask ourselves: when Speaker 1 doesn't understand something, why does she feel the need to hear it spelled out? What does it actually mean to pronounce the letters, paraphrasing the RAE, "separately and individually?" What's more, how is it that "spelling-out" also means "to guess; to interpret what is obscure and difficult to understand"?

The last time I took part in a scene like the one I've described, I realized something that I'd never noticed before, probably because it's obvious. As I watched my interlocutor making an almost palpable effort to see the letters I was spelling out, "separately and individually," in his language, I realized that he wasn't hearing me; he was *reading* what I was saying. Spelling-out is a way to read in mid-air. The interlocutor was transcribing my speech. As I spelled, he transformed the sound of my voice into silent letters, assuring himself that the distorting effect would diminish in the shift from the oral to the graphic. When he managed it, when he was finally able to understand and therefore to actively participate in continuing the dialogue, his pleased expression had nothing to do with the content of our exchange, but rather with the successful process of transcription.

It occurred to me then that we were both speakers of a language in a clear process of anti-extinction: Transkrit.

[http://en.wikipedia.org/wiki/Sanskrit]

And so it is: a ceremonial language used particularly by readers of multi-lingual screens who are used to copy-pasting and juxtaposition, readers for whom listening and aural functions pose a risk. Or, more often, a *beyond* from which it's impossible to ever return. It is, in some cases, the last bastion of the silent page, the final victory of eye over ear. It's practiced on the Cyber-ian tundra, of course.

SECOND TRAGIC CONFESSION: All I know is that I want to write a book in Transkrit.

THE STRANGEST CASE

a. The revelation

It wasn't until a couple of years after I'd accepted a new job in Creative Writing at UC-San Diego's Department of Literature that I grasped the peculiarity of my situation. There I was—a writer who was born and raised speaking Span-ish, and who writes to this day in her native language—meticulously reading and commenting on texts, both poetry and fiction (although, increasingly, texts that defy any strict distinction between genres), written in English by young students for whom that language was and is their mother tongue.

b. What fricatives did for me

Like all revelations, mine burst forth rather violently. I began to question everything. What am I doing here? I asked myself more than once. And I plunged, as they say, into a state of thoroughly childlike if not altogether adolescent perplexity. The bookshelves in my office are full, it's true, of similar quantities of books in Spanish and in English (with a small collection in French and another in Italian that, I must admit, I tend to pass over). I've written in English, yes, but mostly as part of my academic work, during the part of my life when my professional identity was primarily that of a historian. And although it's mainly a playful desire, if not an adventurous one, that has prompted me to write a few pieces in English, I'm not especially concerned with publishing them, nor do I have any intention of leaving Spanish behind when it comes to writing my books. On top of everything else, since in my workshops I always assign an immoderate amount of required reading, I'm rarely able to draw from the most contemporary writers in my native language, for translations, as we know, take time to arrive. In short, and to explain myself more clearly: I teach writing workshops (not literature classes) in my second language to groups of predominantly monolingual students who have (at best) minimal contact with literary traditions beyond the US. In writing these words, I feel that only a strategic distraction or something even more perverse could have so thoroughly postponed the emergence of the question *What the hell am I doing here?* They weren't easy years, I'll add, for anyone who's wondering. But they were interesting years. Rewarding years, even. Not everyone has the opportunity (the privilege?) to not-know herself so radically in the middle of her life. That's what I'd tell myself to compensate.

What can the speaker/writer of a second language actually offer a speaker/writer of a native language? This question (which is, strictly speaking, a much more productive one than the first) arose on the proverbial day when the discussion of a manuscript led me, "naturally," to a conversation on the aesthetic and political nature of fricatives, both in spoken and written discourse. And what can we say about the comparative analysis of adjectival functions in both languages? And how can we describe the long conversation (this one occurred in a thesis defense) on speed and space as entailed by the use of the semicolon in both Spanish and English? I know I'll never approach my second language with the familiarity I feel in moving around my first. Yet I also understand that I know my second language with a painstakingness and a state-of-alert that I rarely dedicate to the first. I've been learning about a linguistic intimacy that isn't based on familiarity, but (quite the contrary) on strangeness. It's a cautious intimacy, one that

doesn't necessarily eliminate the exact distance involved in intense observation. Aren't we truer when we're more vulnerable, and aren't we more
vulnerable when we're more out of place?

c. The many combinations

It's neither common nor unheard-of for a writer to end up writing in a second
language. The most famous cases include, of course, Joseph Conrad, Vladimir Nabokov, and César Moro, among others. Nor is it strange that some such
writers end up teaching at universities in their new places of residence. Usually,
though, they teach literature classes, not writing, and they teach these classes,
as is to be expected, in their native language as a means of communication.
Here, for example, I'd mention the case of the Bolivian writer Edmundo Paz
Soldán, who has taught literature in Spanish at Cornell for a good number of
years now. The establishment of at least two programs devoted to creative writing in Spanish has allowed people like Luis Arturo Ramos, the Mexican fiction
writer, and María Negroni, the Argentine poet, to teach writing workshops
in their native language at the University of Texas at El Paso and New York
University, respectively. As far as I know, the workshops that Mayra Santos-
Febres offers at the Universidad de Puerto Rico are taught in Spanish. There
are also numerous cases of Spanish-speaking professionals who, after finishing
a PhD in the US, end up teaching in English in their area of specialization at
US-American universities. Yoko Tawada, who writes both in her native Japanese and in her adoptive German, lives in Berlin and teaches in German—but,
again, these are literature classes, not writing classes.

d. The strangest case

Even stranger are the cases of those writers who, while continuing to write
in their native language (Spanish, for example), teach writing workshops
both at the undergraduate and the graduate level in a post-mother tongue
(English, for example). In short, this is my case. And I'm recounting it here,
like this, in such a denotative way, in hopes of collecting information on
other writers who have found themselves in a similar situation. Is there
anyone out there who writes in Turkish and teaches creative writing in the
German university system? (Are there creative writing classes in the German university system?) Are there any Chuvash writers who offer creative
writing workshops in Russian at some university in Moscow? I assume, perhaps over optimistically, that such intersections are more frequent than I
can imagine. But maybe not.

CODA 1: THE POETICS OF "OR" (A COMPARATIVE LOOK)

It's hard to begin an essay on the word "or" without thinking, even in passing, about *Story of O*, that unique and uniquely well-written erotic novel published, to the horror of many, by the French writer Anne Desclos under the pen name Pauline Réage. And this would immediately place the Or within the terrain of sexuality and the body. It's equally difficult to avoid this marvelous paragraph from *The Gate of the Sun*, by the Lebanese novelist and critic Elias Khoury:

> So, you want the beginning.
>
> In the beginning, they didn't say "Once upon a time," they said something else. In the beginning, they said, "Once upon a time, there was—or there wasn't." Do you know why they said that? When I first read this expression in a book about ancient Arabic literature, it took me by surprise. Because, in the beginning, they didn't lie. They didn't know anything, but they didn't lie. They left things vague, preferring to use that *or* which makes things that were as though they weren't, and things that weren't as though they were. That way the story is put on the same footing as life, because a story is a life that didn't happen, and a life is a story that didn't get told.[15]

The word "or" and the letter "o" (which in Spanish are both expressed by the single character "o") lend themselves to play, to error, and especially to divergence. It's a challenge to pass through their opening (which is ideally on fire) or get to know them "by their roundness" (my translation),[16] like López Velarde's legendary bird of prey. Like other words, "or" has its own semantics—even its own politics, if we exaggerate a little. Christian Bök and Óscar de la Borbolla, both of whom have devoted books to each and every vowel in two different languages, have perhaps *naturally* arrived at two poetics of the O that gesture toward human maps—high-contrast maps if not directly opposing ones. And I write *naturally* in skeptical italics because I'm not sure if these divergent notions organically correspond to the Anglo-Canadian English of Bök, the experimental poet, or to the Mexican Spanish of De la Borbolla, the fiction writer and philosopher. But while Bök's O, as Marjorie Perloff aptly notes in "The Oulipo Factor: The Procedural Poetics of Christian Bök and Caroline Bergvall,"[17] is solemn and scholarly, concerned with *books, provosts, dorms*, De la Borbolla's O chatterboxes its way into a scene in a mental facility where, clearly, *los locos somos otro cosmos* (we crazy people are a different cosmos). It's difficult to infer immediately, then, whether this divergence is the product of the writers' personal temperaments or the result of what a language can (or can't) do with a vowel.

By all accounts, 2001 was a good year for vowels. This was the year a Canadian press published *Eunoia*, by Christian Bök, and the year Mexico's Editorial Patria brought De la Borbolla's *Las vocales malditas* into readers' hands. (It had been previously published by Joaquín Moritz in 1991 and self-published by the author in 1988.) As Bök himself explains, "eunoia" is the shortest word in English that contains every vowel. It means "beautiful thinking." Nothing could be farther from the adjective *malditas* (damned), which, in plural and in the feminine (is there anything more marginalized or worth mistrusting than those two words together?), modifies De la Borbolla's vowels. Perhaps this is the origin of the disparity, the divergence, between two texts otherwise based on similar rules. Like De la Borbolla's, Bök's book consists of lipograms: that is, texts in which the author has systematically omitted a letter. Or various vowels, as in these two cases, in order to keep only one in operation. Following the great Oulipian principle that "the text written in accordance with a limitation will describe that limitation," both Bök and De la Borbolla have composed, then, single-vowel texts that have been generally well-received by critics in their countries of origin (the Canadian book, in fact, was awarded a prestigious national poetry prize in 2002). The Mexican audience calls these texts "stories"; experimental poets call them "poems."

Besides referring us to exotic destinations, Bök's letter A directs our attention to *grammar, law,* and *bans*—spheres of power safeguarded by Marx or Marat or Kafka. By contrast, E is *genteel* and I is *light*. As for the letter U, English's grandiloquent vowel embedded in words we should usually avoid exclaiming in public, we find not only Jarry's *Ubu,* but also the *truth*. Meanwhile, De la Borbolla's A leads us directly to sin and carnal pleasure. In "Cantata a Satanás," one of the first words is the verb *amar* (to love). Unlike the urbanity of the E in Canadian English, the Mexican-Spanish E shows us a *rebelde* (rebel) *que se vuelve hereje* (who becomes a heretic) *porque es aquí que brota la ley y el regente* (because this is where the law and the regent spring forth). The I isn't merely *ligera* (light) but also glum (*gris*) and even exotic (*I Ching*), even if Mimi is going around *sin bikini* (without a bikini). And perhaps here it would be worth pausing to acknowledge Mexico's great vowel-master: Cri Cri, the beloved composer and performer of children's songs (memorably, "The March of Letters," in which each vowel takes part). De la Borbolla followed the same rules for the U as for the other vowels, which is maybe why we run into *vudú* (voodoo) and a *gurú* (guru).

The most obvious contrast between the semantic ranges of verbs in Spanish and English emerges, however, with the letter O. In English, the O takes on a low, solemn tone, intensified in book-knowledge and provost-power; in Spanish, it leads us straight away to the world of madness and mayhem. There, in its entirety, is Khoury's *once upon a time there was*—or wasn't.

Pain and horror pass through the opening of the O, it's true. But just once, as they reach the other side of reality, so do *olorosos olmos hondos* (deep, fragrant elms).

Disappropriation

Writing with and for the Dead

DISAPPROPRIATELY: THREE EXAMPLES FROM
CONTEMPORARY MEXICO

Originally published by Sur+, an independent press established in Oaxaca, Mexico, *Antígona González*, by poet Sara Uribe (Querétaro, 1978), roared into the world in 2012. This documentary poem gives words—broken, merciful, full of rage—to the low-intensity war waged in Mexico for over a decade. Fierce, urgently political, and human to the core, Uribe's book summons the dead and invites them to sit at our tables. And it reminds us that on the day we stop sharing our memories and language with them, we ourselves will become loss, vanished signs, mere oblivion. Drawing from the words of actual victims of the armed conflict, and feeding off the many Antigones rewritten throughout an already long, venerable Latin American tradition of reading and recycling Sophocles's original play, *Antígona González*—now pristinely translated by J. D. Pluecker and published by Les Figues Press in 2015—may be the poem of an entire generation. This Mexican Antigone is looking for her brother, Tadeo, in order to honor his body and his life. One vanished person among many, Tadeo eludes her grasp as she, curator of words collected by journalists and Twitter accounts alike, attempts to apprehend him. Like many history books, this slim poetry collection ends with a bibliographical note in which the author dutifully (and beautifully) acknowledges her references and provides brief explanations of how she both researched and wrote the entire piece.

Antígona González is, as Uribe states in her endnote, a conceptual piece. This, too, is a disappropriative work. Here, the voices and traces of others emerge as such, as voices and traces authored by others. The poet is not "giving voice"; she is paying close attention to existing voices. Material voices. Voices that occupy space and deserve company. Even amid unfathomable pain and hardship, these voices are unwilling to dispense with their agency, their own versions of events. When we read *Antígona González*, we come close to the decisions made by Uribe as a curator of someone else's words; to her rhythms and cadences; and to the tumultuous, wounded presences of those invoked when she cites them. Reading this poem makes us participants in a larger communion. The triangle formed by author, reader, and text has been broken. We are more. We have always been more, and Uribe, as a disappropiationist poet, knows it.

Gerardo Arana (Querétaro, 1987–2012) published electrifying prose and poetry over the course of his short life. *Bulgaria Mexicalli*, his brilliant remix of the canonical civil poem *Suave Patria*, by Ramón López Velarde, and *September*, a poem by Bulgarian author Geo Milev, is both an update and a deterritorialization of both original works. Juxtaposing cartographies, languages, drawings, literary traditions, and historical and demographic data, Arana fundamentally transformed both poems while also allowing them to remain utterly familiar. Indeed, anyone who attended public elementary schools in Mexico (and was therefore made to learn *Suave Patria* by heart) will recognize some of the words and much of the weight of the original poem in Arana's rendition. Eerily, though, a strange wind will blow in all the way from both Bulgarian landscapes and present-day Mexico, distorting syntax and diction just enough to make them new. While López Velarde, writing in 1921 in celebration of the new nation that had just emerged from the 1910 Mexican Revolution, stated:

> I will say in muted epic:
> the homeland is impeccable and diamantine.
> Gentle Homeland: permit me to wrap you
> in the deepest music of the jungle
> with which you modeled me
> entirely by the rhythmic blow of axes,
> amid laughs and shouts of girls
> and birds of the woodpecker trade.[1]

Arana's contact with both present-day Mexico and the tradition of resistance of Bulgarian poetry allowed him to write otherwise (the translation is mine):

I will tell the sardine epic:
The homeland is darkness and fog.
Grave Fatherland:
Strangled in the famished jungle.
Just before the ax-blows,
Girls shout, scared to death.

The laughing girls of 1921, shouting mischievously as the music of the jungle envelops both the poet and the poem, have become the terrorized women of the early twenty-first century. Victims of femicides and subject to myriad forms of violence perpetrated by both state and patriarchy, these women's shouts are a far cry from the prior rejoicing at the birth of a nation. These are, unmistakably, the shouts of terror. Axes, once metaphorical, are now real. Welcome to the so-called War on Drugs.

Dispensing with bibliographies or footnotes, Arana's dexterous use of blank space and italics, as well as his effective selection of key words from the original poems, allows the reader to experience the mediated nature of language. We might not know for certain which word belongs to whom, but we must know that they're reaching us from far away. These words are someone else's materials. All this, he seems to be saying, belongs somewhere else. All this, he seems to be insisting, is also mine. Profoundly personal and deeply rooted in the experience of entire nations—known or unknown to the reader—this poem may be the best remix ever attempted of *Suave Patria*. And this exemplary early twentieth-century Mexican poem has never been so close to political poetry from Bulgaria.

Eugenio Tisselli (Mexico City, 1972) is first an activist and then a poet. A programmer in his own right, Tisselli has used digital technology to generate pieces that question the very tools with which we come in contact with language in our contemporary world. Occupied as he became, for example, with agricultural projects that connected Tanzania and Oaxaca, Tisselli programmed software that could produce and translate poems he no longer had the time to write or any interest in writing. Uncannily reminiscent of mid-twentieth-century avant-garde poems, the series collected in *El drama del lavaplatos* was developed by his program in conjunction with "language seeds" fed into it by the poet himself. Co-authored in the strictest sense of the word, this poetry isn't his—and yet it contains nothing that isn't.

Acutely aware of the uneven geopolitical and linguistic contexts where he works, of their rigid racial and economic hierarchies, and of the violent incursions of state and capital in their midst, Tisselli's pieces become political commentaries almost immediately. But they do more than that. An ardent supporter of open code, Tisselli has studied and participated in digital projects that allow for practices of mutual care. Take, for example, his rendition of the case of Salvatore Iaconesi—an artist, engineer, and hacker who, after receiving a cancer diagnosis, promptly hacked the information in order to make it available to worried friends, other doctors, and health practitioners. A disappropriationist at heart, Tisselli works with different platforms, languages, and genres, creating the conditions in which the materials he invokes—someone else's materials—are both aesthetically and ethically accounted for.

Community and communality

We are assured that community will take shape, that being-in-common will happen to us. That, according to the French philosopher Jean-Luc Nancy, is writing.[2] By defining it in such terms, by placing the act of writing and the experience of community into a tense and imminent relationship, always dependent on someone else ("we are assured"), Nancy joins a long conversation in a singular way. Through this conversation, readers and authors analyze and question the ties that bind them together—and therefore make them possible. Flesh and bone. Presence. In the end, as Nancy argues, "The most solitary of writers writes only for the other. (Anyone who writes for the same, for himself, or for the anonymity of the crowd is not a writer.)" He insists: "Being as being *in* common is (the) being (of) literature."[3]

Many contemporary authors are concerned with the relationship between writing and community. In fact, this interest is not optional for authors who are most aware of the necropolitical context in which they work, and it also emerges among those attentive to the changes triggered by the digital revolution of our times. However, expressing concern is only part of the task. The challenge is to engage with the writing processes that embody this fraught relationship, or that contribute to the radical revision of our shared contexts. One thing is certain: contemporary authors no longer talk about the "committed art" versus "art for art's sake" dichotomy that dominated—and calcified—much of this conversation throughout the twentieth century. The discussion has increasingly moved to critical considerations of the relationship between writing and community. In doing so, neither the defiant materialities of writing processes nor the making of concrete communities have remained untouched. What do we mean by community when we don't want to leave our dead behind? Are communities based on mere affinities or similarities, or on contested production processes involving reciprocity and labor strategies that are not optional? If we say that writing is a community-making practice, does it mean, too, that writing is labor? How can we write in and through communities in a world sundered by war and changing notions of territoriality, a world in which belonging and loyalty often become spectacularly violent inscriptions onto vulnerable bodies? In what follows, I move discreetly from European-based notions of community to the Mesoamerican understanding of communality, for which shared labor, material reciprocity, and a relationship of mutual belonging with the earth are basic components of survival. I have come to believe that writing with and through others, that writing as a practice of disappropriation, is writing in communality.

The very definition of communality in relation to writing, though implicit in many discussions, requires both exploration and definition. There is indeed a line of argumentation that extends from Anderson and his *Imagined Communities* to Agamben and *The Coming Community*; from Maurice Blanchot and *The Unavowable Community* to Jean-Luc Nancy and *The Inoperative Community*. Authors engaged in this conversation have rightfully abandoned the notion of the individual and have in turn emphasized various practices of dis-identification as a basis for the production of alternative subjectivities, as Rancière argued. Here, being-in-common is a taut, dynamic, and ultimately unfinished process. Thinking about community, which means thinking about the beyond-oneself and the emergence of the between that renders us ourselves and others at the same time, is certainly among the tasks of writing. Perhaps this is its true task, if it has one. Its raison d'être, if it has only one.

This philosophical discussion of community and its relationship to writing rarely includes critical analyses of the historical and cultural processes through which concrete communities are produced. Yet this is a key concern for thinkers of communality: a concept coined and widely used by indigenous communities throughout Latin America, but especially relevant to daily life and theoretical references in the Mexican state of Oaxaca. I am bringing the Mixe conception and experience of communality into this brief review of Western European brushings with community because I want to underscore the role of labor in the production and reproduction of the sensible world, writing included. An essential link in Mesoamerican peoples' production of communality is labor—the material creation and recreation of the world—and especially *tequio*, a form of free, obligatory, and collective labor that benefits the community at large. More generally, it also connects nature with human beings in contexts of mutual belonging that radically oppose notions of property and dominion (of what-is-one's-own) in today's global capitalism.

Something similar occurs, I argue, in certain contemporary writings that seek to participate in ending the dominion of what-is-one's-own, using strategies of disappropriation to evade or directly impede the text from circulating (often in book form) within the economic and cultural cycles of global capitalism. These are politically relevant means of conceiving the writer's work as such, as work. I insist: not as employment, but work. A form of labor that, having been in close contact with everyday language, sets out to produce and reproduce both signified and signifier. The idea is, then, to understand the writer's work as a practice of being-in-common in which or through which, to borrow from Jean-Luc Nancy, the finite singularities that constitute it are exposed. Writing, in this context, is always rewriting, a going-back to what others have put into words and sentences, a practice that delays and belabors the finished version of any text. An exercise in unfinishedness. Could this be akin to the material being-in-common embedded in communality? Perhaps it is a first step. Perhaps a mere first gesture.

Being-in-common: Community and communication

Like the communality of Mesoamerican peoples, the community Nancy addresses in *The Inoperative Community* is not a simple accumulation of individualities (the individual, as he emphasizes from the beginning, is "merely the residue of the experience of the dissolution of community"),[4] nor is it a historical combination of territory and culture. Community, at least in its modern definition, is "the spacing of the experience of the outside, of the outside-of-self."[5] Closely following Bataille, but distancing himself from the idea that community is reduced to a community of lovers, Nancy hurries to create an axis connecting community and communication (through the concept of ecstasy); from communication to sharing (through the text); and from there to the interruption of the myth that constitutes all writing. Between one thing and another operates, of course, the inoperative.

Because community is made of singularities—that is, of finite beings—Nancy rejects the possible fusion present in communion. Instead, he emphasizes the place of communication—not viewing "communication" as an intrasubjective social link (as Habermas does, for example), but as the site of "sharing." Sharing "consists," he says, "in the appearance of the *between* as such: you *and* I (between us)—a formula in which the *and* does not imply juxtaposition, but exposition."[6] The experience of community is thus an experience of finitude: "Finitude compears [comparaît]," writes Nancy; "that is to say it is exposed: such is the essence of community."[7] In other words, the communication that makes a community is its sharing: which is to say, its means of interrupting and interrupting itself, its means of suspending itself. Its inoperativeness.

While Nancy treats the words "writing" and "literature," "speech" and "orality" as stunningly interchangeable—all elements with which Mixe thinkers have been far more careful in their own practice—the link between writing and community is neither random nor insignificant in *The Inoperative Community*. In fact, writing would "*inscribe* the collective and social duration of time in the instant of communication, in the sharing."[8] Therefore, what writing communicates is none other than "the truth of being-in common."[9] This is an inscription of being-in-common, of being there for the other and through the other. And thus, he adds later, "undergoing, in whatever manner, the experience of community as communication: it implies writing."[10]

Shared work: Communality and writing

On several occasions throughout his book, Nancy insists that community isn't *produced*. Community, he says, isn't a "work" in and of itself. Community is experienced: it appears at the very limits of its being, which is being-with-others. "It is not a matter of making, producing, or instituting a community," he states; ". . . it is a matter of incompleting its sharing."[11] Turning to Marx's *Capital*, Nancy asserts:

> What Marx designates here . . . is community formed by an articulation of "particularities," and not founded in any autonomous essence that would subsist by itself and that would reabsorb or assume singular beings into itself. If community is "posited before production," it is not in the form of a common being that would preexist works and would still have to be set to work in them, but as a being *in* common of the singular being.[12]

In Nancy's discussion, communication and interpretation, which are the basis for his idea of community as inoperative community, expose the finitude of the singularities it distributes. Interestingly, Damián Tabarovsky explores his argument in *Literatura de izquierda*, in which writing becomes a negative community that keeps its distance both from institutions (the academy) and from circulation (the market), exclusively addressing "language" instead. In his re-enunciation of Nancy's inoperative community,

Tabarovsky comes to privilege books "without an audience," a term that seems to treat the reader as a client, located in a non-place beyond the community—a circuit far removed from the finite singularities of the interrupted community and in the suspense that is the inoperative community.

Anthropologists of communality, who are interested in writing but even more interested in oral tradition, reconstruct community as "something physical." That is, "the space in which people carry out acts of recreating and transforming nature, insofar as the primary relationship is between the Earth and people, by means of labor" (all translations of Díaz are mine).[13] In addition to having and reproducing a means of material existence, the community also attends to spiritual existence, thus forming horizontal axes (1. Where I sit down and stand up; 2. in the portion of the Earth occupied by the community I belong to in order to be myself; 3. the Earth, as all living things) and vertical axes (1. The universe; 2. the mountain; 3. where I sit and stand).[14] The community becomes communality in a relationship that Díaz calls immanent: a relationship with the earth based not on property, but on mutual belonging. A mutual belonging that is based, moreover, on work, defined as "a labor of materialization, which ultimately also means the recreation of the created."[15] Since the common good is what determines rights and obligations, the labor that nourishes the production and reproduction of the community as communality is the aforementioned *tequio*: free, collective, obligatory work. Its variations include "direct physical labor, reciprocal help, participation in festivities (where the sharing of the community is at stake), and intellectual labor."[16] Each and every form of this collective labor may be akin to what Nancy depicted as inscribing the "being-in-common, being for others and through others." In the highlands of Oaxaca, where Mixe communities reside, participation in *tequio* ensures a place in the community, which in turn generates respectability, and, eventually, the opportunity to fulfill important positions of service to the community, for example, as "communal work heads" that carry out organizational tasks and contribute to the justice system.

Governed more by mutual belonging than by property, and supported by the collective labor on which its production and reproduction relies, communality is suspicious (logically, perhaps) of writing's ability to inscribe what Nancy calls communication and its sharing. In fact, Díaz maintains that "a society with a spoken language appears to be more open to change, less authoritarian and dogmatic, with a capacity for critique," simultaneously arguing that "not all feelings can be expressed [in writing], since written language is cold and each individual reader determines whether a text will or won't make sense." He then adds: "Written language is what reinforces and expresses a high degree of dogmatism, authoritarianism, and loss of control, since its use and comprehension has always remained in few hands."[17]

Nonetheless, after long and passionate debates in Mixe community, it was necessary to accept that the writing of indigenous languages

> increases the possibilities for communication among a language's inhabitants . . . it can strengthen identity as a basis for unity; that is, the orality of our peoples can be fortified through writing, which they can use to better exchange our ideas and questions . . . thus overcoming atomization.[18]

This discussion on the production of Mixe as a written language illuminates the communal work contained in the production of writing. Indeed, it wasn't until 1983, in the seminars called Vida y Lengua Mixes [Mixe Life and Language], conducted in Tlahuiltoltepec, that there emerged "the project to write all variants of our language in the same way. To do so, we would have to agree on the broadest possible alphabet."[19]

This is, of course, a practice involving many, as Díaz would say.

It's also a practice in history and with history in which eighteenth-century missionaries and speakers occupy a privileged place beside the cultural promoters and translators of religious books, especially the Bible, in more recent times. And it is, then, the work of the community's own speakers and the connections they forged with anthropologists, linguists, agents of the state, and independent organizations that enabled them to create an alphabet, as well as the concrete and locally determined forms of its transmission and instruction. It's the long, dynamic, cacophonous, communal path that the written language travels as it becomes an everyday activity, with its own practice and rules of collective use. This activity is then presented—in the societies already deemed so by written culture—as a teleological process. And an individual one at that.

This disassociation, which is historical and political in nature, lies at the very heart of a writing process that perceives itself as outside the community: an ivory tower from which a privileged observer peers down at the past and the future. Such a separation—generated by the impression of individuality, of authorial genius—may be the same one that Ulises Carrión attacked in the 1970s, when he set out to remind writers of their responsibility to and in the "whole process" of book production. That is, the process of producing written language. "In the old art the writer judges himself as being not responsible for the real book," Carrión asserts, placing special emphasis on the division between manual and intellectual labor at the root of class and gender hierarchies that this decision entailed and still entails: "He writes the text. The rest is done by the servants, the artisans, the workers, the others. In the new art writing a text is only the first link in the chain going from the writer to the reader. In the new art the writer assumes the responsibility for the whole process."[20]

Rewriting, especially disappropriated rewriting, displays and actually problematizes this "whole process," this "responsibility."

Disappropriation: A poetics of communality

I have heard the questions so many times: What is the subjectivity at work in this text? What kinds of subjectivities, or even inter-subjectivities, emerge or take shape in this line or through these characters? Valid as they have been in probing rigid or essentialist takes on identity (which is so often attached in overdetermined ways to class, gender, race, or generation, among other factors), such questions still eschew, albeit more carefully, the aesthetic and political realm of communities and language. How do we ask these questions when subjective capture is not a given—and, when, in fact, it is the very challenge that propels writing in the first place? Are concepts of disidentification vivid enough, ample enough, to tackle the complex dynamics of material struggle and resistance beyond notions of identity, even when they are oppositional?[21]

A disappropriative poetics invites us to ask these and other kinds of questions. A disappropriative text flaunts the marks of other people's presence and work: the labor of production and distribution carried out by entire communities. Language is not a raw material or an instrument, much less a natural resource, but a fraught relationship involving bodies in tense, volatile contact with other bodies as they partake of the creation and re-creation of our material worlds. There are layers of collective work behind and beneath each word we employ; there is history, strife, tragedy, loss, blood, and hope. Fingernails. Saliva. Words, and writing strategies, reach us already charged with a history we participate in and share, knowingly or unknowingly, when we adjust our desks or switch on our laptops.

When I read a text, and when I attempt to contribute to the making of one, I am less interested in the subjectivity at play than in the set of material practices that have made it possible, even imaginable, to begin with. If, instead of asking the question about subjectivity, I ask the question about the communality underlying the existence of a text, I am asking a question about work—and about bodies at work. More generally, I am asking a question about accumulation. I am acknowledging that writing is not a unique form of inspiration or a particularly troublesome "calling," but a form of labor that involves whole communities. Communities, moreover, that have been able to survive through a range of material relations, including but not limited to practices of reciprocity based on forms of unpaid, obligatory service labor known as *tequio*. This collective work—work that often becomes invisible and goes unnoticed in interactions of capitalist exchange—is what rewriting exposes when undertaken in a disappropriative mode. That's why I claim that rewriting, not writing, is the first step of disappropriation. First times do not exist. We are always stepping into someone else's footprints. Someone dreamed this dream of ours: someone else failed, and then failed better, before we had the chance to do the same. Our bodies occupy spaces from which others have been expelled—which is what makes the apparently innocent "YOU ARE HERE" signs on contemporary maps into political insinuations. Who is *not* here where I am? Who will be here when I am forced out? There is no originality. There is only an ongoing writerly conversation, an exacerbated system of layered quotations, that may—or may not—help us reconfigure the labor of whomever paved the way beforehand. Disappropriation, which is what I am now describing, forces us to discern the material traces of those who were *there*, and those who are *here* as I write: specters, apparitions, memories, accompaniment. There is no solitude in writing. Disappropriation haunts the closed hierarchical systems of literary production that live and advocate for privilege, prestige, and an upper hand in the market. Disappropriation does not want us to take part in fair capitalist exchanges, but to question the very exchanges and the very system that justify its existence. It is not a matter of giving away work for free, but of bringing our writing into connection with practices of labor and life that interrogate the naturalization of processes that define them both: commodification, extraction, and devastation.

It would take another book to run with the consequences of such views. But I'll offer what I can imagine here. For one thing, truly answering questions about the communality of a text will avoid mere authorial intellectual biography (the books read by the author, the universities or gatherings she attended, the music she considered most influential, the names of her most distinguished friends) and focus instead on the material practices that linked the making of an author's life to the text. Ricardo Piglia once drily suggested that the true history of literature was not to be found in books, but in the history of jobs held by writers as they wrote them. This alternative history of literature, which is the history of writing, would have to pose questions about the making of a life, the writer's "livelihood"—the "how-to" of her everyday work—and link these answers to the personal system of aesthetic and political decisions that allowed her to create this book instead of a different one, this cultural artifact instead of another. I imagine that the questions won't always seek to illustrate the specific relationships of the writer's material body in her being-with-others—the identity-focused data on class and race and gender and age, among other things—but will go farther: they'll reach into the depths of where their communal brew is concocted. The first such questions will have to address the communal labor (mandatory, in-service-of, through language-in-common) that structures and gives life to the text beyond itself.

This will involve a history of reading, indeed—but we're actually already talking about something else, as Volodine would say. If reading, as is so often said, is not an act of passive consumption, but rather a practice of mutual "shareng," a miniscule act of collective production, then what's at stake here aren't just the books people read. So too, and most importantly, are the books people interpret, reactivate, and bring back to life: the books rewritten by others, whether in their own imagination or in conversations (which also constitute, of course, a practice of our collective imagination).

What has become clearer and clearer over time is that book-writing in communality will have to welcome the challenge and explicitly address—and embody—the staging of plural authorship. Will the figures of the narrator, point of view, and narrative arc remain the same when bearing witness to the generative presence of others in the very existence of writing? Which platform will best adapt to the continual evolution of the palimpsest and the juxtaposition intrinsic to every writing process produced in communality? What sort of so-called critical apparatus will we use when every sentence, even every word, would have to be accounted for?

Maybe it isn't outrageous to start imagining books solely or mostly made of acknowledgments pages—the place heretofore designed for recognizing other people's participation in the making of a book. Acknowledging will take up more space, in terms of both content and form, in the communalist books of the future. Perhaps, in the writing that overcomes the fluctuations of necropolitics through communality, it won't be impossible to envision books that are just that: sheer recognition, which means sheer critical questioning, of the dynamic and pluralistic relationship that enables their existence in the first place.

And what is recognition if not pure gratitude?

COMMUNALIST WRITINGS

It's become a cliché for poets to put in their bios all the menial jobs they've had. I'm not sure if this is because poetry seems like non-work, or that poets want to seem relatable. Nevertheless, poetry is work, too, and that becomes one of the jobs of the book. The meta-job.

Rosa Alcalá[22]

In sum. Recapping. Disappropriation is a practice that, in recognizing writing as labor, endeavors to unveil the different forms of collective work that structure and constitute a text.[23] Drawing largely from the concept of communality as formulated by the Mixe anthropologist Floriberto Díaz—a concept centered on an understanding of labor as production and reproduction of the material world, through vertical and horizontal axes that unify specific communities' spiritual and material experiences—I concluded the previous chapter with a prediction both outrageous and rigorous. It went like this: the writings of the future, those truly critical writings that some might call avant-garde, others would describe as experimental, and still others may simply call daring or innovative, will eventually become an act of "pure gratitude."[24]

With this statement, I was not referring to the merely paternalistic act entailed by the formal acknowledgment of an other's or others' participation in specific writing practices (the dedication of a book; the moment in which authors offer explicit, public thanks to those who have participated, perhaps silently, in the elaboration of said book). Nor was I referring to the soft policing that so often demands information about the sources employed, safeguarding some other author's rights rather than fostering shared work in noncommercial circuits. I wasn't defining disappropriation, in other words, as a component of the gift economy, the realm of bestowals. I argued in the prior chapter, and I'll repeat it here, that this act of gratitude was a way to materially recognize (that is, to make it visible for and before others) the plural roots at the core of every act of writing as both an aesthetic and a political practice. It's hardly gratuitous, then, that the authoritative dictionary of the Spanish language defines the act of thanking as (in my translation), "3. Said of something: To repay labor undertaken by ~~preserving or improving it~~." Unlike Literature—which conceals the collective work of language behind the authorial bulwark and endeavors to produce commercial objects still known as books—communalist writing "does not generate the object (the commodity), but rather the world in which the object exists. Nor does it generate the subject (worker and consumer), but rather the world in which the subject exists."[25] So it

could be said, or confirmed, that these writings are engaged in constructing another world: the world in which both the writing and its production
process exist and will continue to exist. Instead of being passive, isolated
consumers, readers will necessarily become part of that assembly in which,
as Gladys Tzul Tzul has said, it is decided how the community itself will
produce and reproduce itself.[26]

On this subject, as in so many others, art history and its various modernisms may be able to offer us some relevant lessons. Jacques Rancière isn't
alone in pointing out the popular roots of many fundamental works of
modern art, but he has documented the negotiation, and often the outright antagonism, that permeated this process. Just as Literature has ob-
scured the tense, dizzying exchange between life and textual production as
it transpires under the armor of authorship, Rancière states that what we
call the emergence of art as a field also means the concealment of social
conflict, the collective tension that configures and constitutes certain works
dubbed "masterpieces." Simultaneously, John Roberts has studied modern
art in terms of the fraught, dynamic relationship between skilled and un-
skilled labor amid the growing hegemony of immaterial labor that characterizes the post-Ford economy—or, in other words, the financialization of the
economy.[27] Carefully distinguishing between artisanal and technique-driven
work, Roberts manages to step back from the charges against modern art as
works empty of specialized labor. Aside from its natural unfolding toward
contemporary art, this argument may prove equally useful in analyzing writings that employ digital technology and are developed within a citationist
aesthetics dominated by resources like copy-paste, collage, excavation, and
recycling. What these two perspectives—material, historically determined,
and based on theories of collective labor in concrete contexts of increasing
financialization and precariousness—invite us to examine in a new light is
the dissociation, which some see as natural, between avant-garde art (or
writing) and radical politics. This is the subject of what follows below.

Art is a dis/appropriation (of what isn't art)

A certain elitist, self-indulgent view of art history locates its own begin-
nings at the very origins of humanity, as if it had simply emanated along
with the human condition itself—that is, as if the art regime were ahistorical and therefore almost natural. Any survey of artistic masterworks,
organized in varying but always-ascendant degrees of perfection, more or
less adheres to this perspective. When the topic is restricted to the history
of modern art, the situation varies little. Generally speaking, the different

modernisms (or avant-garde movements, as they are often denominated in Latin America, so as to distinguish them from Modernism as such) are presented as the triumph of art's growing autonomy. In other words, the triumph of specialization over interdiscipline and exchange, and of the separation of artistic production from everyday experience. In his counter-narrative of modernism, Rancière is ready to present an opposing view of art history—or at least of the history that spans, in his book, from the late eighteenth to the early twentieth century.

In *Aisthesis: Scenes from the Aesthetic Regime of Art*, an English-language translation by Zakir Paul that was published by Verso, Rancière presents and painstakingly analyzes fourteen scenes that show how interaction and contact with non-artistic experiences marks the onset of what we call art today.[28]

Step by step, the book argues that "a regime of perception, sensation and interpretation of art is constituted and transformed by welcoming images, objects and performances that seemed most opposed to the idea of fine art."[29] Hence the author's interest in exploring not only the eminent milestones endorsed by official and officialist history, but also those subtle moments when interest, seduction, contact, and eventually incorporation occurred. From the instant in 1764 Dresden when the antiques dealer and historian Joachim Winchelmann decided to present the mutilated statue of Hercules as an irrefutable example of a new art until a wildly committed and passionate James Agee compiled astonishingly detailed descriptions of the objects marking the lives of poor Alabaman farmers in 1936 for his now-prominent book *Let Us Now Praise Famous Men*, Rancière seeks out the books that no one read when they were published, the performance pieces that everyone criticized as too commonplace or tacky, the paintings that most people disliked for their naiveté or lack of skill. And then, one by one, he illuminates the scenes that constitute the form of experience we call art.[30] It's a material argument, certainly, in the sense that he analyzes the means of production and distribution of all this work. Yet it's also an argument about "the modes of perception and regimes of emotion, categories that identify them, thought patterns that categorize and interpret them."

While Rancière asserts his reasoning with clarity and even kindness, he goes directly against many interpretations of twentieth-century modernisms: "The movement belonging to the aesthetic regime, which supported the dream of artistic novelty and fusion between art and life subsumed under the idea of modernity, tends to erase the specificities of the arts and to blur the boundaries that separate them from each other and from ordinary experience."[31] In a word: contamination. Constant exchange. Appropriation. A process of circulation that travels from the basic tasks of everyday working-class life to the hallways of what, in scholarly books seeking self-affirmation, will later be called art. In this way, social conflict and collective tension are concealed in a series of pieces later recognized as works of rupture: that is to say, as exemplary.

Here's an example. Rancière studies Mallarmé, modernist par excellence. But instead of analyzing (yet again) those dice that play with chance and representation, he takes up a text of singular if lesser importance that focuses on a peculiar dancer: Loïe Fuller. Like various other cultural critics of the time, Mallarmé had approached the Folies Bergère cabaret music hall, "a place that they had disdainfully left until now to a 'vulgar' audience,"[32] like someone approaching an aesthetic awakening against all odds. By engaging with and incorporating activities that few at the time accepted as properly artistic, Mallarmé's article reveals how his own concepts of figure, site, and fiction were constructed. "The figure is the potential that isolates a site and builds this site as a proper place for supporting apparitions, their metamorphoses, and their evaporation. Fiction is the regulated display of these apparitions."[33] Seen this way, the history of symbolism (and, in an adjacent chapter, of transcendentalism) is in fact a history of the appropriation of activities and ideas that were initially shaped both by the working classes' everyday lives and by their forms of production and entertainment.

Because he believes that the rise of the arts in the West occurred precisely when the hierarchies established between the mechanical arts (handicrafts) and the fine arts (the pastime of free men) began to shift, Rancière searches for that moment, or its echo, in every scene he analyzes. This isn't the vision of someone pursuing the marginal or the strange for its exotic value, but rather that of someone who wants to place it back where it belongs: right where it was decided—gradually, and amid contexts of great social and cultural tension—what defines art and what kinds of practices and knowledge would be so classified over time.

"Vulgar figures of genre painting, the exaltation of the most prosaic activities in verse freed from meter, music-hall stunts and gags, industrial buildings and machine rhythms, smoke from trains and ships reproduced mechanically, extravagant inventories of accessories from the lives of the poor":[34] all of this attracts our attention not as odd examples of what remained in the past, but as moments when the experience of sensitivity—the ways in which we perceive and are affected by what we perceive—are challenged and transformed. This is, indeed, an alternative history. An alternative history that, as Benjamin would say, can't tell us what really happened, but can illuminate what happened as it matters to us now, in this moment of danger.

Work and the readymade

Among the simplest (and most common) ways to question the aesthetic value of contemporary art includes questioning the quantity and quality of the labor expended in its production. Indeed, anyone who has ever visited a museum and exclaimed the proverbial "Even I could have done that!" before a work of art—which is valued in a way that isn't based on the implementation of manual skills associated with artisanal labor—has already joined this vast contingent, whether she knows it or not. What are we actually saying when we say that an art employing montage, literal reproduction, or quotes and recontextualizations of other people's texts or images doesn't involve *work*?

According to John Roberts, the author of *The Intangibilities of Form: Skilling and Deskilling in Art after the Readymade*, we're saying that we don't understand the role and function of work, especially with respect to artistic work as *productive* work in its mode of immaterial labor that generates art. Or that we haven't understood it at least since Duchamp's readymades invited us to consider artistic work not as a reflection of a certain individual's manual skill, but instead as the meeting point (his famous concept of the "rendez-vous") between the limits of artisanal labor and the expanding use of technological techniques and processes that are particular to capitalist production.[35]

We're saying, then, that despite centuries of domination by industrial production (and, at least since the 1970s, by postindustrial production), we still believe that the only form of valid work, when it comes to the realm of art, is artisanal labor. We're saying that we are willing to deem "artistic" only work that, under the pretense of authenticity, escapes the possibility of reproduction by technological forms—forms that, since at least the mid-nineteenth century and increasingly throughout the twentieth, have become hegemonic forces of production. We're saying, too, that we're willing to ignore the fact that art, as productive labor, establishes material and practical relationships with its communities of origin and reception, especially with respect to transformations in the labor relations through which we produce value, aesthetic or otherwise.

Thus, in asking what a viewer in 1913 saw when Duchamp placed a bicycle wheel atop a kitchen stool and called it art, Roberts refuses to accept that, though clearly fueled by a playful and rebellious spirit, the show was simply yet another witticism, a joke devised by a smart aleck who wanted to plant a time bomb among the establishment ranks. He also refuses to see, there amid the maze of objects produced by the alienated labor of Taylorist production, a mere consumer seduced by the absolute power of commodities and the never-satisfied desire they provoke. What the spectator saw in

1913—and this is what Roberts puts forward in accordance with the Marxist theory of labor—was "the absence of palpable artistic labour, the presence of the palpable labour of others, and the presence of immaterial or intellectual labour."[36] And it's precisely within this triangle, which moves in three directions simultaneously, that Roberts locates Duchamp's most radical proposal: "First, the readymade obviously deflates the privileged place of the artisanal in artistic production; second, it reveals the place of productive labour in artistic labour; and third, it discloses the capacity of commodities to change their identity through the process of exchange."[37]

The early Duchampian readymades, in which hands and manual labor aren't yet preponderant as participants (as they would be, later, in *The Green Box* and *The Large Glass*, both made in the '30s), show, and with radical transparency, the process by which a commodity (the result of alienated productive labor characteristic of capitalism) becomes another kind of commodity (productive artistic labor).[38] And they do so both as explicit acknowledgment of the material transformations affecting the environment that produces the work of art (the increasing disqualification of artisanal labor) and as a critical, potentially liberating reading of those conditions, marked as they are by exploitation and inequality.

In this way, just as the readymade questioned the empire of manual skills in the production of art (Duchamp would ultimately declare the death of painting, for instance), it also implicitly called for the consideration of a new skillset, one in which the relationship between eye and hand wouldn't respond to imitative or mimetic principles. The age of mechanical reproduction—and then digital reproduction—came with its own series of practical processes, which in turn required and valued new artistic skills. These skills are specific to immaterial labor. It is in this realm, according to Roberts, that the process of re-qualifying artistic work transpires. And in response, it is possible to examine entire movements, such as contemporary art itself, starting from their most material roots: the labor that makes them possible and affords them cultural significance.

Contemplating the political economy of artistic practices allows us not only to move beyond assessments grounded in individual taste when it comes to aesthetic matters. It also invites us, at its most critical moments, to engage in a radical reconsideration of artistic work, as well as of the salaried/productive work with which it is both politically and aesthetically interwoven in relevant ways. Hardly a minor gesture in 1913—and no less significant now, over a hundred years later.

A radical modernism

Jacques Rancière recounts how, in 1939, the *Partisan Review* rejected a text by James Agee, a US-American journalist with communist convictions—only to publish, in the following issue, the article that would catapult Clement Greenberg into renown as a leading art critic of his time. Greenberg's text (in which, just as Agee had done, he answered a series of questions on the dominant conditions of art and its relations with capitalist society) is the now famous "Avant-Garde and Kitsch." This article assessed the double movement by which a certain form of contemporary art was constantly distancing itself from its relationship with direct experience while simultaneously engaging in self-reflection; that is, reflection on its own resources and supports. It isn't for nothing that Greenberg is generally recognized as the creator of, rather than as a commentator on, abstract art.

According to Greenberg, however, difficult art, highbrow art, and art for the highbrow had a great enemy to vanquish: kitsch. Kitsch was the cultural output that industrial capitalism and mechanical reproduction had put in reach of the semi-educated masses, passing itself off as art and making them, the masses, pass themselves off as citizens capable of recognizing art. A double farce. A wary Rancière interprets Greenberg's declarations as the moment when modernism not only turned its back on the working classes, but also declared them its chief enemy.

In competing for the ruling classes' riches (Greenberg's words, not Rancière's), it was already clear that "popular, commercial art and literature" was winning the match. Overwhelmingly. Indeed, both then and now, it spanned a range from Hollywood movies to romantic ballads—and, according to Greenberg, "chromeotypes, magazine covers, illustrations, ads, slick and pulp fiction, comics, Tin Pan Alley music, tap dancing." What Greenberg—a Marxist critic of his time, by the way—sees as an almost natural solution is "to turn the page on a certain America—the America of itinerant and politically committed art of the New Deal, and more profoundly, of cultural democracy stemming from Whitman" (now in Rancière's interpretation).[39] Rancière, for his part, interprets this shift as the moment when modernism betrayed its historical legacy; namely, "the idea of a new art attuned to all the vibrations of universal life: an art capable both of matching the accelerated rhythms of industry, society and urban life, and of giving infinite resonance to the most ordinary minutes of everyday life."[40] The irony, of course—and this is the line that concludes

Aisthesis—is that "posterity gave the very same name to this will to end as to what it was trying to destroy. It would call it modernism."[41]

This profound ambivalence and brutal struggle, waged in all aesthetic regimes on the fields of perception, sensitivity, and interpretation, is particularly evident in the chapter Rancière dedicates to James Agee and his *Let Us Now Praise Famous Men*—a feature that would soon become a bold, mad, thrilling book. The story is well known. Initially, *Fortune* magazine had commissioned an article for a section, titled "Life and Circumstances," devoted to exploring how average US-Americans lived. In 1936, Agee and the photographer Walker Evans traveled to Alabama, where they probed into the lives of poor sharecroppers in an area especially hard-hit by the Great Depression. The result was an unclassifiable book in which Agee questioned the capacity of a text to critically, radically communicate the experience of lives lived at the limit. Influenced by an objectivist poetics drawn as much from Whitman as from Proust, Agee—meticulous to the point of near-insanity—not only describes the objects, and other sensory elements, that characterize the homes of these men and women whom capitalism had so brutally exploited. Indeed, he also manages this without succumbing to the temptations of sentimentalism or condescension, instead employing peculiar syntactic strategies within a book structured with very little consideration for conventional notions of either narrative or reporting. And he did so because, in the opinion of the communist Agee, he was ultimately recounting

> the attitude of the gaze and speech that are not grounded on any authority and do not ground any; the entire state of consciousness that refuses any specialization for itself and must also refuse every right to select what suits its point of view in the surroundings of the destitute sharecroppers, to concentrate instead on the essential fact that each of these things is part of an existence that is entirely actual, inevitable and unrepeatable.[42]

James Agee died in 1955, at the age of 45, in a New York City taxi. The dilemma he confronted is the most human and most political one to be found at the heart of modernism. His defeat—as Rancière's interpretation of his essential work appears to indicate—is the defeat of the legitimacy of an aesthetically relevant and politically engaged art. Both at once. What followed is what Greenberg ushered in with his profoundly elitist argument in favor of highbrow art *vis à vis* that false (read: popular) art he called "kitsch." What followed, in other words, is the conservative version that still upholds endless debates on art's autonomy and "natural" separation from everyday

popular (read: political) experience. Which is precisely—and I'm with Rancière on this one—where it originates.

*Speech that is not grounded on any authority and does not
ground any authority*

Hence the following question: can communalist writing be formally bold
and aesthetically radical while simultaneously demanding an organic
connection with the community that has grounded it and gives it meaning? My answer is another question: how can it possibly be otherwise?

I think of communalist writings as they make their way along the route
traveled by James Agee so many years ago. They are political—that is, linked
to their communities of production and reception—but without resigning
themselves to transparency or directness. They are daring and open, but
so that they may touch more people, not fewer. They aren't cult writings or
texts of acritical devotion. Even if the literary establishment managed to
sunder these two energies in order to neutralize the emancipating power
of art and writing, the contexts of horrific violence in which the contemporary world is discussed (writing included) demand both their interweaving
and their dispersion.

When a writer explores largely untraveled formal paths, perhaps she
doesn't do so to escape reality or to embark on an internal journey, but
rather to forge a concrete connection with the collective work—the work
of life and language that constitutes specific communities—which will give
meaning to her practice. Perhaps what drives a writer, investigating the
routes followed by alternative traditions, isn't the simple capitalization of
prestige or the commercial investiture of what she's challenging, but rather
the search for ways in which her writing can connect organically with the
languages that produce it—only to scatter it later throughout the social
whole. And how can we be sure of this? Many have contemplated the com-
plicated link between literary work and everyday life, and this material
connection emerges quite clearly in the "Coda Manifesto for the Autobiographical Novel" (my translation) with which Michael Onfray ends his
Théorie du corps amoureux: Pour une érotique solaire.[43] "A philosophical
life needs, and even demands," Onfray argues, "the autobiographical novel;
when a work shows interest only if it causes effects in the immediate, visible,
and reparable real."[44]

As disappropriated writings, communalist texts aren't part of the economy
of gifts and bestowals. Rather (as labor, and, what's more, as productive
and collective labor) they are part of the economy, period. A writer doesn't

"return" "something" that she "took" from the community. No: she herself returns to it as an organic part of the community itself, as yet another component of the complex system of labor—productive or unproductive, cognitive or service-related, but always collective—that, with all the language of the commons' power and vigor, might finally contribute to the production of that other world for its new language. If, as Saúl Hernández Vargas argues, communality isn't an essence at all, millennial or otherwise, but rather a technology employed by precarious present-day communities to assure their own survival, then it's possible to see writing as one of the tools that allow us to connect technique with discourse. And thus, too, with critical practice.[45]

DISAPPROPRIATION: A MANIFESTO

And we move forward, however zigzaggingly. We find the crack on the wall of the present that may allow us to peek into the now. What follows is a collection of short texts summarizing the main components of an evolving idea. As is true of all cultural entities, disappropriation shifts and encompasses, discards and evokes allied concepts in order to complete and fulfill its own trajectory. Hence the need to both compile and clarify. While I have insisted, since the very beginning, on the labor-based and labored nature of writing, I will now list the geological aspects of disappropriative analysis, "shareng" as a connective tissue that enables an alternative distribution of writing materials, and the assembly as the horizon where writing and reading converge as critical practices.

Writing is work

Writing is not the product of some inexplicable individual inspiration, but rather a form of material labor undertaken by concrete bodies in contact—tense, volatile, unresolved contact—with other bodies at specific times and in specific places. Writings, in other words, are bodies in contexts. As these bodies engage in contact with the common good that is language itself, the work of writing participates in different processes that produce and reproduce social wealth. In this sense, a writer doesn't represent reality. Rather, she presents it (that is, she produces it) in relation (or not) to literary traditions for their future reproduction through reading.

Other people's materials

Even if we talk about ourselves when we write, the very act of writing means we're already talking about others. There is no account of *I* that isn't, simultaneously and necessarily, an account of *you*, as Judith Butler reminds us in *Giving an Account of Oneself*.[46] Not only is it true that the language we write with contains both history and conflict; not only is the language we access, and which accesses us, already charged with experience and time. Indeed, it is also true that the stories told with that language (or, better put, embodied by it) are the stories of others: from grandmothers' famous tales and anecdotes we overhear to the accounts contained (and author-ized) in other books. The solitary figure of the author has helped conceal the complex relations of exchange and "shareng" (see below) that generate, in turn, the different forms of writing that he—with support from entrenched hierarchies of capital-L Literature—has generally claimed as his own. In this way, the appropriating author is a cover-up-er in the literal and not necessarily moral sense of the term. Disentangling the materialities immersed in those authorial claims is the work of disappropriation.

Geological writings

Disappropriation makes visible—better yet, tangible—what authorial appropriation conceals. In doing so, disappropriation spotlights the work undertaken by practitioners of a language when some among them turn it into writing. Thus, disappropriation exposes the plurality that precedes individuality in the creative process, opening a window onto the material layering so often concealed by appropriative texts. In other words, disappropriation reveals the communal work of a language's practitioners and marks it as a source of creative work itself. In turn, it shows us the forms of self-production and the stories shared by collective subjects of enunciation. More than denouncing appropriation by means of an opposite discourse (often based on the same appropriative logic), disappropriation announces it; that is, it cracks it open, manifesting it in aesthetically relevant ways. Far from serving as a police force that hunts down any instance of appropriation in sight, the disappropriative aesthetic produces writing strategies that embrace, welcome, and ultimately incorporate—in open, playful, and nonconformist ways—the writing done by others.

In producing layers upon layers of connection to language as mediated by others' bodies and experiences, disappropriative writings are geological writings.[47] As a result, disappropriation's way of "appearing" is usually attained by means of many different re-writing strategies, including excavation, recycling, and juxtaposition. While academic protocols make use of quotation marks and the bibliographical framework to account for its discourse-appropriating relationships through textual citations, disappropriative aesthetics draw from broader and more varied resources—linked, or not, to specific literary traditions, and also and more often linked to digital technology.

The unpayable debt

Debt is the foundation of the post-financial capitalism we inhabit. The debt that made us social, according to Nietzsche, lies in wait around every corner like a hungry dog. We are born with a debt. Over the course of our lives, it only increases. If the universe and its expenses have anything to teach us, especially in the United States, it's that the debt never stops growing. When we demand payment, the debt ties us down, determining every decision of our adult existences. From our clothes to our cars to our homes, the objects that render us indebted subjects therefore imprison us. Which is why, instead of covering the debt, Fred Moten and Stefano Harney propose exactly the opposite in *The Undercommons*. They propose increasing it: making it so enormous that it becomes impossible to pay.[48] When disappropriation sets out to expose the links of debt that bind writing to a language's practitioners, what it actually does is default on the debt. A writer has no responsibility to others (which is optional); she is indebted to others (which is structural). This isn't a moral debt; it's a material one, because writing is labor. More than proof of the debt, writing, in its disappropriative form, is the debt in and of itself. The greater, longer, and more outrageous the writing is, the greater, larger, and more outrageous the debt is, too. When we write disappropriatively, we say: we will not (un)cover the debt; we will crack it open.

The communalist book

Floriberto Díaz's theory of communality is driven by the energy and effort of the labor that produces and reproduces social wealth. This isn't the salaried work through which bodily energy is exchanged for money, but rather that other kind of mandatory service-work known as *tequio*. In this way, in order to exist and be enunciated, Díaz's *I* doesn't only call for the *you* as referenced by Butler, but also for the *we* embodied by a communality in which *tequio* and the assembly are inexorably linked.

Constructed along vertical and horizontal axes, an account of the *I* in a communalist mode—a communalist book—would have to be located materially along the horizontal axes that Floriberto Díaz described earlier in this chapter:: "1. Where I sit and stand; 2. On the portion of the earth occupied by the community to which I belong in order to be myself; 3. The earth, as for all living beings." The communalist book of the *I* would return, then, along vertical axes: "3. The universe; 2. The mountain; 1. Where I sit and stand." Like other theorists of communality, Díaz approaches the community "as something physical"; that is, "the space in which people carry out activities of recreation and transformation of nature, insofar as the primary relationship is between people and the earth, through labor."[49] Allow me to recapitulate Díaz's description of how community becomes communality: through an "immanent" relationship with the earth defined not by property, but rather by mutual belonging based on labor. He defines the latter, again, as "a labor of materialization, which ultimately also means the recreation of the created."[50]

In this way, what is "common," or in-common, isn't the book-object, the book-thing, but rather the process of production, re-appropriation, and disappropriation through which the book itself is generated, in constant bodily contact. The communalist book bears a signature, but not that of the author-appropriator who conceals the text's process of production. Instead, it is signed by the indebted author, the author who defends the textual decisions that constitute the fabric of the work being presented. The disappropriative author doesn't hide behind the mask of anonymity, either. That is, she doesn't conceal, through anonymity, the shared labor and desire that make up the text and give it life.

What is up to us because it affects us

The disappropriative writer works on what Raquel Gutiérrez has called internal horizons: "the most intimate content of the projects undertaken by those who struggle." Components, too, of the unstable horizons marked by conflict and de-totalization, these inner horizons are "contradictory; revealing themselves only in part, they are found, sooner than in positive formulations, in the set of discrepancies and ruptures between what is said and what is done, between what isn't said or done, in how the available desires and social capacities are expressed."[51] The disappropriative writer emerges through this popular/communalist contact, working with pieces-of-language that unveil a world, layer by layer. In doing so, she must then return her text to its context, now transformed into the reading-assembly where everything is of concern to us all because everything affects us all. In this way, even if the disappropriative text falls into the hands of Literature's tenacious employees (critics, specialists), it will continue along its path until it reaches its true addressee: the reading-assembly. If an assembly "scatters power where it enables the re-appropriation of language and collective decision-making on subjects that are up to all of us because they affect all of us," then, in reaching the assembly, the disappropriative text is actually reaching its own birthplace.[52] The dialogue it sparks, the controversy or debate it triggers, only constitutes the book's continuity in others, in other sources, and by other means.

"Shareng"

According to the anthropologist Jaime Luna, *compartencia*, which we could translate as "shareng,"[53] secures the horizontal production and distribution of knowledge among equals.[54] Far from imposition, and going hand in hand with resistance, shareng (which is present both in a classroom and at a village celebration) is also a fundamental element of reading. The disappropriative writer must not only decide on production strategies for her texts in relation to others; she must also settle on and participate in their reproduction and distribution processes. Just like Ulises Carrión, maker of books (not only a writer of texts), the disappropriative writer must fuse intellectual work with manual work, actively participating in those books' processes of production, reproduction, and distribution. There are many decisions involved, and not all of them are structured vertically, following a logic by which what's above determines what's below. Publishing a text with an independent press to subvert the merely commercial circulation of books? Publishing a text with an independent press whose readers are already persuaded by its content? Publishing a text with a commercial press as a provocation to expand the scope of the conversation itself by reaching new interlocutors? Not publishing at all? These and many other combinations are possible, even desirable. As it begins its journey within the channels of capital, the published work (whether published by commercial or independent presses) doesn't necessarily need to limit itself to them or subsume itself within them. When the distribution of books published this way is connected to *tequio*, for example, subtle but important reversals occur. For one thing, the book-as-merchandise escapes or is diverted from its ultimate end, which is to generate a surplus—and, essentially, to earn money for the few. Instead, as a text, it participates in strategies focused on the common good. Creative Commons licenses offer myriad possibilities that guarantee the shareng of a text beyond monetary interests—while still enabling fair commercial exchange among authors, publishers, and readers.[55] The book, however, is only one way to momentarily capture the experience of reading—a way station where appropriative writers often remain, and where disappropriative writers pass through en route to the reading-assemblies that are their final destination. In this context, what matters most is how the participants make their decisions. The path along these inner horizons that accompany unstable horizons, beyond state-centric axes, is always marked by the footsteps of those who came before. The disappropriative or communalist writer places her own feet in their tracks. And so, as José Revueltas once wanted, they become inhabited footsteps.

APPROPRIATION AND DISAPPROPRIATION ON THE BORDER: KATHY ACKER IN TIJUANA

A synonym for a cure

Before it became the capital of borderland sin, before La Coahuila and Bar Zacazonapan and the red-light district tour, long before the Arellano-Félix brothers put it on the map of the so-called War on Drugs, Tijuana was a ranch renowned for the healing properties of its hot springs. Located a few kilometers from the former customs facilities and the present-day Universidad Metropolitana de Agua Caliente, the hot springs made this border ranch a prime destination for medical tourists. In the late nineteenth century, as Arturo Fierros Hernández describes in *Historia de la salud pública en el Distrito Norte de la Baja California 1888-1923*, US-American investors often published ads in the *San Diego Union Tribune* to invite people suffering from diverse afflictions to soak in the springs' restorative waters. Tijuana "was synonymous with a cure for different illnesses for many Americans who traveled to California from far and wide and then crossed over by wagon to Tijuana, seeking remedies for their ailments."[56]

After it became the capital of borderland perdition, after La Coahuila and Bar Zacazonapan and the red-light district tour, long after the Arellano-Félix brothers put it on the map of the so-called War on Drugs, Tijuana continued to attract sick US-Americans in search of cheap medications, budget dentists, and affordable plastic surgeons. Lacking a public health system that guarantees medical care for most of the population, many are pushed to seek treatment in a city that, despite its sordid reputation, still offers numerous cures for an increasing range of ills.

Appropriation in San Diego

In Chris Kraus's account, after she married Bob Acker in New York, Kathy Acker moved to San Diego, California, in 1966, where the couple rented a large Victorian house on C Street, right in the middle of the coastal city.[57] Acker finished her degree at the University of California, San Diego (UCSD) in May '68, and although she took a few graduate classes in literature, she never formally went back to school, which had never interested her much. She did, however, study with David Antin, who had accepted a job as director of the university gallery and professor of several creative writing and art classes. The UCSD campus had opened just eight months prior, on land that had belonged to the Department of Defense. In the process of defining its identity within the UC system, it pursued avant-garde figures both in the sciences and in the arts. It was hardly odd, then, that the university also hired intellectuals such as Herbert Marcuse and Jerome Rothenberg in addition to Antin himself.

Antin's classes were essential to Kathy Acker as she got her start as a writer. While she was already a consummate graphographer, Acker would find the seed of her appropriative aesthetics in his teachings. Reluctant to read hundreds of terrible student poems, Anton urged them instead to steal everything they could. "'Go to the library,' Antin would tell his class, 'find someone who's already written about something better than you could possibly do at this moment in your life and we'll consider the work of putting the pieces together like a film.'"[58]

The results were immediately apparent. Instead of submitting poems based on their short-lived personal experience, Antin's students started producing pieces that juxtaposed disparate materials—for example, Aeschylus and a plumbing manual—in bold, imaginative ways. More than a simple, random copy-paste or a senseless mishmash, the idea was to seek out "the connections between divergent realities," explained Kathy Acker, who always acknowledged the influence of this pedagogy on her own work. Released from the burden of authorship—especially a fixed, narrow kind of authorship—Acker began working with singular fury on the books that would stamp appropriative aesthetics with her own defiance of the status quo: *Politics*, in 1972; *The Childlike Life of the Black Tarantula: Some Lives of Murderesses*, her first novel in 1973; and *I Dreamt I Was a Nymphomaniac: Imagining*, in 1974.[59] These books would also make her a heroine of US-American counter-culture:

In *The Childlike Life of the Black Tarantula*, for example, Acker tried to dynamite the old compact-identitied, fissureless God associated with conventional notions of authorship and literary genre. This is how she described her working method to Barry Alpert in a 1976 interview:

I was very interested in the use of the "I." So I went to the UCSD library . . . and took out whatever books about murderesses I could get. . . . Basically I just copied . . . only I changed the third person to the first person, so they'd seem to be about myself. And then I set up sections within parentheses what were just diary sections . . .

So there were two I's in the book . . .

Gradually what happened was the two I's started playing games with each other, becoming one.[60]

Indeed, Acker tended to replace the "he" or "she" in her source texts with an "I" that could henceforth be transformed into something else. This shift, which corresponded not only to the character or narrative voice but also to the entire concept of literary genre as a whole, became her signature. Likewise influenced by the cut-and-paste methods practiced in New York and by William Burroughs's cut-up experiments, Acker was ready to become the superstar of antiestablishment punk feminism. Since its inception, then, the literary appropriation that emerged in the distant 1970s SoCal, practiced by a group of white authors with no intention of questioning English-language hegemony on the border, had an aura of rebellion and opposition against a rigid, oppressive literary system. These radical San Diego writers—who lived in small, sleepy coastal towns like Solana Beach, a place originally established to accommodate migrant workers—never glanced south to Tijuana, the city that switched on its lights after dark on the other side of the border.

Disappropriation

Many years later, facing the small audience of a poetry reading at Brown University, the appropriationist gesture that allowed the poet Kenneth Goldsmith to present the autopsy report for Michael Brown—the young black man killed by local police the summer before—sparked wildly disparate reactions. Gone was the radical halo emanating from what was already known as conceptualism, the pulse of which Vanessa Place and Robert Fitterman had so deftly taken in *Notes on Conceptualisms*.[61] It was 2015 when Goldsmith read at Brown, and a new generation of writer-activists and a wide array of POC writers vehemently denounced the colonial mechanism and subjective exploitation that allowed a white man of indisputable privilege to recite words that so painfully exposed the deadly outcomes of racism and classism in US-American society—only to leave them intact in the field of experimental literature. Similar criticism met the work of Vanessa Place, who, in a provocative gesture, had decided to copy out every sentence of *Gone with the Wind* on her Twitter account. In this contentious novel, Margaret Mitchell had reproduced degrading stereotypes of the African American community, especially those of slavery during the Civil War; many argue that such stereotypes are presented as justifications of racism. The fact that Place made her Twitter avatar the image of Mammy—the domestic worker who appears, in the novel's perspective, perhaps too comfortable in her role as a slave—triggered an unrest that soon expanded into outrage. It is no exaggeration to say that conceptualism, and especially the aesthetic and political operation known as appropriation, had met its end.

Those of us writing in the United States, especially in the southern area of the West Coast, couldn't ignore the interventions that called—with relative clarity, with relative vehemence—for new poetries, new writing practices, and a new society. Students at UCSD, where Antin had launched the appropriative strategies of his era, participated with particular enthusiasm in discussions that in my case, as a creative writing professor who taught at the same institution for eight years, led me directly to the concept of disappropriation. My position as a bilingual writer, a Latinx, an accented woman with brown skin, an immigrant with her gaze permanently fixed on Tijuana, propelled me directly into discussions of experimentation— but without forgetting the disparities of race, gender, class, immigration status, and mother tongue that constantly shape the task of working with the materials of others. Which is to say, the task of writing. Rendering visible and even tangible the words that compose our texts through others and with others, and doing so in aesthetically and ethically relevant ways, may be the starting point for anyone who engages in disappropriation.[62] While Kathy Acker's name was conspicuously absent from these long discussions, her specular presence in classrooms where she had set foot, raised her hand, and expressed opinions fluttered invisibly over our heads.

Fulfilled expectations

The photographs of Kathy Acker do justice to her fame. With her hair cut short, staring directly into the camera, flaunting her tattoos and sporting her customary leather jacket, Acker looks like the rebellious punk writer she always was. Her reputation as a writer to be taken seriously grew when Printed Matter Books, the prestigious imprint founded by Lucy Lippard and Sol LeWitt, decided to publish two of her books—*The Childlike Life of the Tarantula* and *Toulouse Lutrec*—and it was solidified a couple years after that, with the publication of her best-known book, *Great Expectations*, in 1983. By then, her legend was walking on its own two feet from New York to London to San Francisco and back again. How did it all happen? Chris Kraus relates how, after she left San Diego, Acker famously moved back to New York, where the challenges of finding steady work and her decision to devote as much time as possible to writing prompted her to spend four months working in a sex show with her boyfriend, Len Neufeld, in a club called Fun City on 42nd Street. Much of her subsequent work—novels, essays, performances—was influenced by this formative experience, both in the personal stories it yielded and in terms of her critical reflections on the ruthlessness of capitalism, which had always struck her as reproducing the mechanisms of sexual exploitation. For example, when the police shut down Fun City and arrested her, the experience inspired "The Whores in Jail at Night," which appeared in *New York City in 1979*.[63]

Books aren't written in isolation, and Kathy Acker's are no exception. Just as Antin played a key role in the start of her career, her connection to the Language Poets, who have left an indelible mark on UCSD, accompanied much of her early work. Jerome Rothenberg and Ron Silliman, for example, were close readers of *Politics* and *Toulouse Lutrec*, respectively. Although they shared intellectual interests and a taste for a certain experimental aesthetics, Acker, who "wanted her thoughts to be manifested in a compulsively readable prose," shifted gradually toward the novel, the genre in which she achieved her greatest triumphs.[64] Her relationships with the art and performance world, relationships that evolved alongside her shows and publications, soon brought her new travel companions: the British writer Paul Buck accompanied the writing of *Great Expectations*, as did the filmmaker Peter Wollen as she wrote *Don Quixote*.

Kathy Acker thus continued to fulfill, and often exceed, her own expectations of herself as the twentieth century moved toward its end. In 1978, however, she had her first encounter with cancer. A routine exam revealed a small lump in one breast, and while the biopsy came back negative, the shock was great enough that it led her to marry Peter Gorden, her partner of six years, although they were no longer living together by then. In the years that followed, her medical check-ups continued to turn out negative, but breast cancer stayed with her, following the rise of her career and accompanying her into fame.

The gift of disease

Getting sick in the United States is no simple matter, especially if you don't have a job with health insurance. The small minority that does can go to the doctor and have surgery by paying a fraction of the real cost. But for the vast majority of the population, a disease, especially a serious or chronic one, is a death sentence. It is no accident, then, that when Kathy Acker was diagnosed with breast cancer in April 1996, her first words addressed the precarious working conditions that kept health insurance out of reach for her:

> At that time, I was working as a visiting professor at an art college and so did not qualify for medical benefits. Since I didn't have medical insurance, I would have to pay for everything out of my pocket. Radiation alone costs $20,000; a single mastectomy costs approximately $4,000. Of course, there would be extra expenses. I chose a double mastectomy, for I did not want to have only one breast. The price was $7,000. I could afford to pay for that. Breast reconstruction, in which I had no interest, begins at $20,000. Chemotherapy, likewise, begins at $20,000.[65]

First terror, then trust, made Acker take a "leap of faith" toward other means of facing cancer. She had already shown interest in Tibetan Buddhism, and she frequently consulted nutritionists and astrologers. But it wasn't until after her double mastectomy, and amid her increasing frustration with what she came to call the cancer industry, that she began to systematically explore the world of alternative non-Western medicine, from ancient Incan cultures to North American shamans to Chinese herbalists. Kathy Acker never subjected herself to chemotherapy.

To the growing concern of her friends, not only did she turn her back on the US-American hospital as an institution; she also placed herself in the hands of a psychic, Frank Molinario, and a past-life regression specialist, Georgina Ritchie, in a quest to locate the root cause of her illness. Leaving no stone unturned, investigating any method that might leap out from the others, Acker met all kinds of people who invited her to confront herself. She wanted to live, and, unlike what the cancer industry had offered her, she wanted to believe in the possibility of healing. That was, in the end, the gift of disease: to believe in a cure. And, above all, to believe that she could cure herself, without having to entrust the process to someone else. Returning to health was her own responsibility. Facing cancer was a way to confront her own self, her past, her body, her story. When she wrote "The Gift of Disease," she was convinced that the cancer had vanished from her body.

A clinic in Tijuana

A naked woman running down the side of the street. A pack of white dogs, panting, tongues flapping. A man in a wheelchair offering typed poems in exchange for coins. Buy: 18:30. Sell: 18.53. All I need to do is peek out onto the streets of Playas de Tijuana and the city comes crashing down over me. Behind me, the ocean, iridescent; in front of me, Tijuana unfolds with a languidness that betrays its singularity. There's no other city like it in the world. Along one side of the most heavily trafficked borders on Earth, Tijuana is many Mexicos, many Central Americas, many Africas, many Caribbeans all together. The immigrants who come in hopes of crossing over to the other side are often forced to stay here, and here they rebuild their lives. A man talking to himself. A squad of bicyclists cruising down the pier. A *quinceañera* poking her head up above the sunroof of a black Hummer limo. Buy: 18.05. Sell: 18.56. Cacophonous, teeming with contrasts, Tijuana is a perfect city for the worlds created by Kathy Acker. I think she would have liked it. The saint with no left eye at the entrance to the cathedral. The stairs descending into the underground world of Zacazonapan. The Hong Kong strip club's sordid atmosphere of sex and commerce. The bar El Fracaso. All the Tacos Varios stands. The La Hermita tacos. Tacos from El Francés.

In any case, cancer brought her here.

It was her acupuncturist who'd told her about the Gerson nutritional method for curing cancer. She learned that "In November 1946, the American Medical Association openly attacked Dr. Max B Gerson. They subsequently destroyed his professional reputation and denied him malpractice insurance. Gerson was forced to move to Mexico; today the Gerson Institute, directed by Charlotte Gerson, his daughter, operates partly in Bonita, California, and partly in Tijuana, Mexico."[66] Acker had refused conventional hospitalization, but when the cancer spread to her pancreas, lungs, liver, bones, and lymph nodes, she asked, her condition severely deteriorating, to be taken to Tijuana. Her illness was so advanced that the Gerson Institute declined to admit her. But Viegener, one of her best friends, managed to get her admitted to another clinic near the Alianza Francesa, a block from the Hospital del Prado: American Biologics. Acker arrived on the Day of the Dead, and there she died on November 30, 1997, about a month later. Viegener hoped her friends in San Diego would cross the border to visit her, "though Tijuana seems to everyone there so far away, which it is—culturally."[67]

The Canadian poet Anne Michaels says that home isn't where we're born, but rather where our bones are buried. Kathy Acker's ashes were scattered in several places, true to her nomadic life across cities in the US and Europe. But her death certificate was issued in Tijuana, the border city that, while just a few kilometers from San Diego, had caught her attention too late. How fitting, though, that she came here not to run wild, like so many others do, but in search of a cure. Like her late nineteenth-century fellows who came to soak in the hot springs, and like those who continue to flee a bankrupt medical system, Acker, too, hoped to restore her body to health in Tijuana. I'd like to think that home is also wherever we stop breathing, that it's also whatever place saw our eyes open for the very last time, that it's also the language that heard our final whimpers. If this is true, then Kathy Acker—or at least the Kathy Acker who leapt into the void when horror and trust overwhelmed her, when she had nothing left to lose—is at least a little bit at home in Tijuana, too.

THE SIGNS OF HERE

In a famous essay on the work of Alberto Giacometti, the French writer Jean Genet maintained that a true work of art necessarily had to address the dead. If a sculptor or a writer's work had managed to peer into or even glimpse the solitude of beings and objects, that "secret royalty, profound incommunicability yet a more or less obscure knowledge of an invulnerable singularity," then its end couldn't be the past, nor even the future. Much less posterity. Artistic work doesn't move along in the direction of future generations, which Genet calls "the generations of children to come," but rather toward the innumerable dead—who, as they wait along their tranquil riverbanks, will recognize (or won't) the signs of *here* that constitute true art. According to Jean Genet, whom Jean-Paul Sartre would canonize in his monumental *Saint Genet*, art could only attain its greatest splendor, expand into "awesome proportions," if it was able to "come down through the ages and join, if it can, the immemorial darkness populated by the dead, who will recognize themselves in this work."[68]

Nothing rings truer in the terrible twilight of necropolitics. But can Jean Genet's aesthetic proposal really be translated through time and space? What could he have meant by "the innumerable dead" in 1957, the essay's publication date, in Europe? What could he mean now, in the second decade of the new century, in a land sown with mass graves and besieged by everyday horrors? Are we—the holy mid-twentieth-century thief, the terrified souls of today—even talking about the same dead?

Genet begins his essay, which Picasso would come to describe as one of the best writings about any artist ever, with a reflection on the nostalgia for a universe where human beings, stripped of themselves, could discover "that secret site within ourselves that would capacitate an entirely different human enterprise."[69] It was an adventure that Genet also considered a moral one. In such a world, art would fulfill its ultimate task: "ridding the chosen object or being from its utilitarian pretense," removing it, in other words, from the circulation of goods as organized by a capitalist system based on devastation and horror. Only then, only in this way, would art "discover this secret wound in each being and even in each thing, for it to illuminate them."[70] This vital wound, which defines us as a species, is solitude: the secret place, the refuge, a remnant of incommunicability, and therefore what opposes commercial exchange and the cheap transactions of utilitarianism.

According to Genet, to delve into the kingdom of the dead, to "[seep] through the porous walls of the realm of shades,"[71] artists must use the scalpel of personal solitude to direct someone or something's attention, separating them from the world—and thus preventing them, that something or that someone, from being mistaken for worldly occurrences or from disappearing "into ever vaguer meanings."[72] Aesthetic attention, which both starts with and multiplies the solitude of creative attention, must "refuse to be historical."[73] Aesthetic experience privileges, or should privilege, discontinuity over continuity. Which is why Genet argued that every object, every piece of art (and here we could also include, deliberately, the reality of a book), "creates its infinite space."[74] Art's operation, which is a moment of recognition, is also and perhaps especially a moment of restitution. "It is the solitude of the represented person or object that is restored to us, and for reality to perceive it and be touched by it, we viewers must experience the space not of its continuity [its historicity] but of its discontinuity [its infinitude]."[75] The innumerable dead are this infinitude.

Genet describes how, on one of his visits to Giacometti's studio, the sculptor told him that he wanted to make a sculpture just so he could have the pleasure or the privilege of burying it. What struck Genet was that Giacometti didn't want his buried statues to be found. Not then, and not later, when neither he nor his name would remain on earth. Genet's question in response was this: "Was burying it a way of offering it to the dead?"

Genet's dead, as he says in the same essay, "have never been alive"; or, on the contrary, "they were alive enough to be forgotten, and the purpose of their life was to make them pass over to that calm shore where they wait for a sign—from here—that they recognize."[76] They aren't an abstract concept, but they're infinite. They aren't historic, strictly speaking, but since they're an eternity, they are an *eternity that happens*. They're dead, certainly, but entire traditions of artistic and literary operations depend on their reactions. In any case, they are responsible for whether a work reaches its farthest limits, in its recognition and acceptance—where communicability and utility bear no more weight, and where the materiality of the object as such, where its communality reigns undisturbed. What is this sign? How can we be sure that when we experience a work of art—which is just an offering, after all—we are witnessing its journey to (its escape toward?) and from the innumerable dead? Perhaps the only sign is the way one solitude can touch another. That echo. A reverberation. That's how Genet described Giacometti's work: "an art of superior beggars and bums, so pure that they could be united by a recognition of the solitude of every being and of every object."[77] I'd like to think that the touching of these solitudes, this flickering material connection, this fleeting moment of recognition and gratitude, is too present in disappropriation.

The dead are getting more restless every day.

It used to be easy to deal with them:
we'd give them a stiff collar a flower
we'd praise their names on long lists:
the homeland's memorials
distinguished shadows
monstrous marble.

The corpse signed off in search of posterity:
it lined up in formation again
and marched to the beat of our old music.

But no
the dead
aren't what they used to be.

These days they get ironic
ask questions.

I think they've started to notice
they're outnumbering us.

Uses of the Archive

From the Historical Novel to Documentary Writing

EUPHORIC ARCHIVES

In an intriguing scene from Christopher Nolan's 2012 film *The Dark Knight Rises*, the heroine, Catwoman, confronts the evil of the archive. Her main problem is that she can't eradicate her past. The remnants of her own experience haunt her and hunt her. Literally. Since she's feverishly searching for an electronic program that can erase its own tracks, we assume that her past has been inscribed into an archive with unrestricted public access. All eyes that want to look at it will see it. In this sense, the record of her life has vaulted from the private confines of personal recollection into the public domain of memory. The archive, as Jacques Derrida has said, entails a domiciliation, the designation of an institutional space in which "law and singularity intersect in *privilege*." An archive consigns; that is, it collects signs. As Derrida states in his classic text on the modern archive, "*Consignation* aims to coordinate a single corpus, in a system or a synchrony in which all the elements articulate the unity of an ideal configuration."[1]

What life scatters, centrifugally, the archive gathers. Centripetally.

But "the archivization produces as much as it records the event," Derrida adds. "To put it more trivially: what is no longer archived in the same way is no longer lived in the same way. Archivable meaning is also and in advance codetermined by the structure that archives."[2] In this sense, Catwoman wasn't searching for a heap of dusty yellow papers belonging to a conventional archive. She wanted to destroy the electronic records of those other archives: detached from the state's storage schemes but still protected by the private companies that have gradually overtaken cyberspace.

Considering the fact that Nolan's film was released in 2012, how many places might have domiciled Catwoman's life experience? Apart from the civil registry containing basic identifying information (name, date and place of birth, address), it's entirely conceivable that the life of an outlaw like Catwoman would also be documented in the state's criminal archives. In the same way, it wouldn't be strange for a young twentieth-century woman to keep an electronic log, or a Facebook page, or even a Twitter account. In that case, the excess of inscription would make it easier to follow her trail through cyberspace. How many electronic missives might she have sent over her lifetime? Regardless of the quantity, and of their recipients, her emails are also prey to that artificial, media-generated environment. A person lived, people used to say, privileging memory's oral moment, to tell the tale. A person lives, it would now be entirely plausible to say, to inscribe that tale. To archive it. To produce it as an archivable event.

As an area to which specialists (especially historians, but librarians, too) have long devoted their attention, archives have also found exceptional readers among a broad spectrum of artists. In *Le Futur anterieur de l'archive*, for example, Nathalie Piégay-Gros analyzes the many ways in which the archive is "implanted in fiction." In a study that ranges from Sebald to Claude Simon, encompassing Pierre Michon and Annie Ernaux along the way, Piégay-Gros pinpoints the archive's proliferation in modern life. She particularly focuses on the miniscule archives of small-scale memory, the missing archives and archives-found-lacking in our disorganized lives, the irrelevant archives of everyday experience. In appropriating archives, she argues, "literature also modifies the representations and conditions of the archiving process."[3]

While the historian is often singled out as the figure behind a somewhat totalizing, homogeneous idea of archival material, many writers have contributed to this notion as well. Advocates of the so-called historical novel—who so often hide the work of archival seeking-and-finding and thus turn the archives into ghosts—tend to file down the rough edges of historical documents, normalizing them into linear narratives or incorporating them as just another plot point. These are the writers seeking juicy material, long-forgotten stories, tales too good to go untapped, which are swiftly and sometimes very effectively incorporated into plot-based narratives—narratives that seldom question the materiality of both the archives and the documents used along the way. These are the authors writing weighty, serious novels based on a range of events deemed to have national relevance. Even if they show interest in the archive's inlays of power, these books tend to move with ease within a highly limited orbit: the historically few members of the elites who author memoirs or sign official documents. The countless novels about dictators, presidents (one-armed, like the post-revolutionary Mexican president Álvaro Obregón, or otherwise), presidents' wives, rebellious and charismatic leaders, or wealthy mob bosses all certainly fit within this framework.

Little by little, though, as the objectives and methods of social history (the so-called bottom-up history) expand their sphere of influence, more and more writers seem willing to incorporate the archive materially into the very structure of their books. Emulating the archive's highly relevant role in the visual arts—which have come to treat it as a work of art in itself, rather than as a mere record-keeping system—some writers have not only employed unique or interesting anecdotes extracted from the archive, but have also taken the time and care to explore and actively interact with the porous, incomplete, gap-ridden, fragile structure of archiving as such. In this sense, an archive doesn't give rise to a novel; more accurately, a novel aspires to embody the fickleness of the documentation system itself. Derrida aptly called this phenomenon the political moment of archivization as event-producer. The archive isn't the novel's predecessor, serving as its instructional backup or source of legitimacy and prestige. No: in these works of documentary fiction, the archive is the novel's present. Or, as Piégay-Gros would have it, its previous future. The life of a Catwoman fleeing her past would unquestionably be improved, in any case, within these mobile, interrupted, traversed, dizzying structures that so keenly emulate the euphoric archives of the digital present.

HUMAN MATERIAL

In *El exceso de pasado: La destrucción de manuscritos como liberación del autor*, Patricio Pron, an Argentine-born author living in Madrid, undertakes a material history of his writing process. He doesn't only recount the different technologies he has employed to write over the years (from the pencil to the computer, from the legal-sized page to the notebook or the digital archive); he also elaborates on his complex relationship with manuscripts and his own archival process. When, one evening, he decided to burn documents he'd forgotten about but which remained stockpiled in the attic of his parents' house, Pron nonetheless took the precaution of digitally photocopying the pages to save them. Pron describes this process as such: "In some way, in doing all this, I recovered the past, but by deactivating it. That is, I didn't lose the past; I preserved it solely as a monument to something unrepeatable that I can't grab hold of in searching for the perfect text, which is similar to what happens with published books."[4]

Elsewhere, I have mentioned Bob Dylan and his idea of a record as something that "is just a recording of what you were doing that day." What collapses in both cases, then, is the very notion of the final or definitive edition, with its self-described teleology, its halo of transcendence, and its stairway up through the hierarchies of prestige. In both cases, too, the archive gains importance in emphasizing the procedural nature of any work. The value of the publication (or the album) lies simply in arresting time, no matter how fictionally. One register among many others. A moment multiplied. Nothing less, but nothing more.

Rodrigo Rey Rosa's novel *El material humano* is a good example of this second wave of Latin American authors who have decided to highlight the mediated nature of language and the representational trap to which books based on archival materials so often fall prey.[5] Unlike other novels grappling with documents from the late-twentieth century Central American civil wars (and its most evident opposite may be the novel *Insensatez*, by the Honduran author Horacio Castellanos Moya), Rey Rosa's advances tentatively, close on the trails left by words and sentences, the classification formats and systems of the entire archive. Instead of transforming the researcher/reader/writer into a one-dimensional hero, this reader enters the archive without knowing exactly what he'll find, hesitating when it seems like he may have found it. Between one thing and the other, he copies; that is, he transcribes. Entries from the archival log accompany more personal notes, which are more emotionally contained, that document the document-reader's private life. These are consciously selected reproductions, but not necessarily conscious of something else. What happens here, in any case, is artificially made: it has been read, chosen, and then written out. The book isn't reality, nor does it intend to be reality, nor does it try to pass for reality. That is to say, it isn't a historical novel. It's writing, and documentary writing at that. Even the oldest truisms have rarely caused such astonishment. The great advantage of emphasizing the mediated nature of the novel's universe (the language, the archive, the document) lies in questioning the widespread idea of language as a neutral vehicle that allows for the passing-through, the long voyage, of the story. Beyond the plot, then, albeit with various plots within it, writing emerges as a material process. And through fragile scribbles, stark discoveries, consequential coincidences, and the juxtaposition of an increasingly weakening sense of the present with an unceasing energy coming from the past, the book interweaves a steadfast, full-on critique of the mediation that has made it possible in the first place. This is, as Piégay-Gros asserts, an archive of the tiniest, most tremulous order. Not an archive that favors prestige and validation (whether of the right or the left), but an archive capable of embodying the human material it contains. Not the archive of nineteenth-century or journalistic realism, which seeks to account for *what really happened*, but the archive of extreme realism that occurs when present-day danger sheds light on it with the glow of flickering candles or utterly ephemeral lightning bolts.

THE MELANCHOLY OF THE FILE

As anyone who has ever set foot in an archive well knows, an encounter with a historical document can easily be described as a traumatic experience. I'd compare it to the minute, or rather to the lightning bolt, in which the author who has spent months or years struggling with a character, whether courting her with information or torturing her with constant questions, finally hears her "voice." In both cases, each with the particular tools of their particular trade and always for the first time, historians and writers confront the instant when everything that has kept them up at night—what has given them nightmares, triggered desires, incited their intuition with often-empty promise—takes on a life of its own. Or a death of its own. In this sense, both moments are points of arrival. But they are also, and perhaps more importantly, points of departure. From then on, both historians and writers will devote themselves to following the dictates of the voices they've run into. And they'll pretend, of course, that they're in control (total control, if possible) over the dense, malleable human material they've confronted.

Despite the epiphany that surrounds it, despite the sense of fulfilled destiny with which researchers and writers often receive the echoes of the distant voices they've stumbled into, an encounter with a historical document is also and especially a detour. Or, better put, an interruption.

I realize that this kind of claim requires some sort of explanation. So I'll explain.

To begin with, I should perhaps stress that when I say "historical document," I'm referring particularly to institutional papers that involve the participation of state agencies through questions organized in bureaucratic formats. In such papers, too, the state agent may interfere, even if obliquely or tangentially, with the answers or information produced by the citizens to whom such questions are posed. Dialogic in nature, this type of file addresses the institutional need to document an existence. Depending on the nature of the institutions, such an existence may be recorded according to a hegemonic series of achievements—or, as is too often the case in the archives of many hospitals or prisons, according to acts of rupture, lawlessness, and decay. In any case, archives don't suppress the voices they literally depend on—the voices to whom the institution is answerable—but, in adapting them to the interests of the record-keeping machine, they surely taint them, often disfiguring them, though seldom beyond recognition. There is always something left—an echo or a reverberation that, if we're lucky, we can open our ears to. This is the moment I treasure. Half knowing what is there, but still truly unaware of what, in its more radical sense, is to come. Receiving a letter or message from an unknown sender feels more or less the same. There is a sense of threat, even a trace of annoyance, but beneath this response lurks a question about the future: What kind of detour is this document inaugurating in my life? How will I be transformed by it, and where will I end up after receiving it?

Earlier, I mentioned the interruption brought about by the existence of the file. Here, I would like to clarify that this interruption is, more often than not, a radical one: participating in the dialogic missive exchange—through an encounter in the archive, with any luck, that is both coincidental and inescapable—turns us into someone else. Anyone who has ever spent time in a historical archive must have wondered more than once (the degree of distress in asking these questions is of course random and personal) who these documents were really intended for in their active life, changing hands over time, proving or refuting any number of arguments. Once the document is transferred to an institution's dead archive, once it joins the mountain of papers whose very volume makes them into an obstacle or a nuisance to the organizers of bureaucratic space, the intended recipient's identity becomes a growing enigma. Where are the documents really going when they don't seem to move? I suspect, and it's a suspicion that has only increased as I've continued to visit historical archives, that the true trajectory of the document I've found, and have therefore diverted, is none other than eternity or oblivion. In short: the innumerable dead.

Advancing without moving an iota toward the recipient who is actually awaiting it, the file places the reader (who has interrupted its course) in the wrong place along the eternity that is death itself. Euphoric or pensive, with the sense of meddling in something that is surely darker and more complex than what she initially suspected or believed, the reader of historical documents must then experience the most insidious possibility: a fragile but genuine connection with the otherworldly, unknown, and perhaps unknowable worlds of the dead. And right then, at this moment that is unquestionably epiphanic, there must be a creeping sense of melancholy: the melancholy of she who knows from the very beginning that her task is impossible (getting the dead to speak). The melancholy of she who keeps reading even as she realizes this impossibility. And the melancholy, too, of the file itself—which has maybe been forgotten for years, resting quietly on a dusty shelf, but which is nonetheless palpitating and real, ready to leap into the lap of the present.

A book related in some or various ways to the file must be able to embody these melancholies. It must contain them. Or, to put it in another, truer way, it must free them.

WHAT PHOTOGRAPHY KNOWS (AND NARRATIVE SHOULDN'T FORGET)

All factuality is already theory.

Johann Wolfgang von Goethe

Oscar Wilde said that the true mystery of the world does not lie in the invisible, but in the visible: in appearances. I'd like to revisit this implicit critique of a binary view that hierarchizes and separates (on the one hand) the invisible as something deeper and therefore superior from (on the other hand) the visible as something superficial and therefore trivial. In taking up this appraisal, I'd like to advocate for the peculiar form of realism that nurtures what has been sometimes been called the new historical novel, but which I call "documentary writing" here. I will use some of Walter Benjamin's ideas on photography as a method of historical knowledge: a way of both demystifying and re-enchanting the real. I will also integrate various observations on the ascent of social history and new cultural history. I'm interested, then, in examining certain interconnections between photography and fiction that go beyond the finished products (the specific artifacts that are assigned the names "photography" and "fiction") and which, by contrast, delve into the processes of knowing and representing the real as shared by both fields. If these notes are even minimally successful, I will at least manage to spark certain curiosities about the status of realism that is sometimes facilely and acritically ascribed both to photography and to the historical novel.

In our postindustrial world, characterized by widespread distrust of metanarratives and the very possibility of the real, it's easy to attack realism as a naïve representational strategy. The usual suspects include the division between subject and object of knowledge; the assumption that the subject has sensorial access to the object, and thus to the real; and the belief that the object's representation (which occurs within the subject's consciousness) is, generally speaking, direct and mimetic. Together, these accusations cast doubt on a rigid, often transparent notion of representation that, in social terms, contributes to the naturalization of progress. In turn, this effect fosters the elaboration of linear narrations in the Aristotelian sense (with a beginning, a crisis, and a resolution). By reflecting such "progress," these narrations confirm it.

In their desire to reproduce *what really happened*, some historical novels undeniably suffer from these or other shortcomings, and they multiply them as they go. Equally undeniable, though, is the fact that many documentary fictions have a realist vocation that problematizes and escapes (escapes because it problematizes) such assumptions. I'm thinking here of novels by Canadian authors Michael Ondaatje and Anne Michaels—the former's *Coming through Slaughter*, for example, or the suggestively titled *Fugitive Pieces* by the latter—in which the emphasis on concrete, sensuous details and the reliance on well-researched historical events don't necessarily conform to linear narratives or preconceived ideas of progress. These novels, which are based on a realism utterly saturated with evidence, yield more uncertainty than proof. And they achieve this because before they set out to tell a story as it happened, or instead of doing so, they look through the lens of the Benjaminean state of emergency affecting all matter that deteriorates and disappears. In other words, they find themselves behind the camera at the moment of danger that defines every flash. This way to narrate a state of emergency has sparked and increased reflections about narrative styles; about, to be more precise, what it really means to *tell*. To narrate. A story, a history. Would I be utterly wrong to approach Michaels's and Ondaatje's novels as experimental documentary fiction? Perhaps not.

I have always been intrigued by Benjamin's concept of utmost concreteness, especially his intent to read the language of objects—which in being objectual, as Goethe argues, was already theoretical. In conflating here the subject and object of study, Benjamin appears to question our connection to the real as resulting from the natural unfolding of an idea. On many different occasions, then, Benjamin used photographic metaphors to explain his way of producing knowledge. An explanation that was hardly foreign to Juan Rulfo, incidentally. Benjamin wasn't interested in getting to know the past, or the real, exactly as it had happened. Quite the contrary: he wanted to capture it—halt it, update it—in the moment of danger illuminated by the camera flash. In his studies of the mechanical reproduction of art, which privilege photography as the inaugural moment of modernity, Benjamin insisted (as Roland Barthes would later do) that a photograph wasn't a reproduction of what was there, but rather of what *wasn't* there. A photograph managed to capture, in fact, the not-being-there of things. In other words: the image was a long mourning; the image was an absence; the image was a longing. Scholars of Benjamin's work have called his knowledge-acquisition process an alternative hermeneutics: a process that doesn't seek out what lies beneath or behind what appears, but rather one that tries to pause there, on its taut, clearly objectual surface, even when or precisely because that *there* is the very place of its disappearance.

If a photo captures what isn't there (or, to use Benjamin's own terms, if it captures what we know will soon not be there); if, more than reproducing, it announces and even evokes the death and absence of what is photographed, then the image becomes the grave of the living dead. As such, it tells their story, which is a story of ghosts and shadows. In this sense, the copy of the real that is so often attributed to narrative realism and photography becomes the least "realist" task possible.

Here, Benjamin closely resembles the Michel Foucault of *The Archaeology of Knowledge*. He urges us to delve into discursive practices (on discourse treated as and when it occurs) instead of prowling around them and their mysterious origin in search of simplistic teleologies and totalitarian totalizations. And he also resembles what Susan Sontag once defended in her essay "Against Interpretation," where she asks us to stop searching for the enigmatic content of artistic work and pay a little more attention to form. Which is, after all, the most faithful proof of what an artistic work contains. The list of theorists could grow, but what matters here is to underscore the continuous problematization of the real as what appears, what is visible, and the ways in which some authors have anticipated access to it. If appearance is mystery embodied, then we don't need to represent it, but to present it—realistically—in all its glorious interconnection of surface and ghost, apparition and sensuousness. But this is a different kind of realism, then, isn't it?

AGAINST THE HISTORICAL NOVEL

In the lead-up to the festivities commemorating the bicentennial of Mexican independence, the publication of books on historical subjects positively ballooned. The increase was evident not only in academic monographs on great national figures or episodes; it also marked the so-called personal essays that, in the context of the anniversary, were dedicated to historical topics in which their authors had long specialized. Few genres, however, saw such growth as the historical novel. As if incentives were scarce, both specific presses and state- and federal-level cultural institutions created a plethora of awards specifically designed to produce and promote historical novels. The unusually high monetary amounts associated with these prizes only serves to emphasize the privileged position possessed by, or ascribed to, the historical novel in today's publishing world.

At a moment that combines official festivities with one of the worst-ever economic crises on the global level, both private and public initiatives in Mexico seem fixated on the idea of the historical novel as a champion that will rescue book sales and reading habits for the nation to come. Both entities seem to trust in the convening power that the historical novel has historically (forgive the redundancy) boasted.

These circumstances demand—what's more, they make it imperative, if not indispensable—that we discuss the historical novel and documentary fiction as two often-antithetical sides of the same coin. It is important, both for aesthetic and for political motives, to distinguish between those books published with the express goal of reaffirming the status quo and those books striving to question and sometimes subvert the status quo. This alone is the most basic difference between the two.

The reader of historical novels says it all when she confesses that she reads these kinds of books to "learn" something. Assuming that reading in general is a waste of time (which it is, essentially, or which at any rate it should be), the reader trusts that a book based on real events (as this close relationship with the referent is called) will offer her a series of facts, a certain form of information, that will inevitably transform her into a cultured person. Without becoming a boring intellectual, the "productive" reader may take advantage of her idle moments to become someone with whom others enjoy chatting around the dinner table, for example, or someone better prepared for the difficult if certainly pleasant initial phases of courtship. We must also consider the equally relevant figure of the "perverse" reader, who, in attempting to adopt more of a progressive stance, states that she reads historical novels in order to distance herself from Official capital-letter History and thus delve into the complex everyday life of important characters. This reader knows that dirty laundry isn't generally washed in public—but, as a dedicated viewer of talk shows or *Big Brother*, she approaches books as if she were slipping backstage in search of the whats and whys of other people's triumphs and failures. In this context, as in so many others, the strategies at work in fiction (e.g., an attention to detail, showing vs. telling, an appeal to the senses, multiple points of view) are a great service to a product that actually affirms the status quo instead of questioning it. Above all, the historical novel is concerned with faithfully reproducing a world it constructs out of information from documents whose materiality it typically conceals or plainly betrays. Remember that only the historian is obliged to record her sources and use those infamous footnotes as proof. Rather than basing her work on a document, then, the historical novelist bases it on the information contained in the document. Thus, she conceives of the document as atemporal and not historical, just like the information it produces.

But the past, as we all know, is always about to occur. "It is only partly the present time, or it is only partly here, because it is at the same time a part of past and future time, because there is more of the future in our past than in our present": this is how Milorad Pavić memorably phrases it in his remarkable novel *Landscape Painted with Tea*. And history, I mean to say with Pavić's help, is hardly a thing of the past. Yet history continues to serve as a mere contextualized interpretation of archival documents. The writers who "con-fiction" works of documentary fiction know this well, and because they do, they transform the document—the document's materiality, its language and structure, the process of its production and discovery—into the true core of their texts. Rather than concentrating exclusively on the information contained there, this kind of fiction (fiction-with-documents) questions, attacks, uses, recontextualizes, pimps, and transgresses the form and content of those documents. More than reproducing an era or revealing a series of preferably scandalous secrets, documentary writing (both in prose and in verse) brings into the present a past that is about to come into being. Here. Now. This is the goal of authors as diverse as, for example, Michael Ondaatje in *The Collected Works of Billy the Kid*, Theresa Cha in *Dictee*, and Marguerite Duras in *The English Lover*. In terms of plot, these books distance themselves from the great historical figures, whether men or women, opting instead for the nameless wanderers of everyday streets. Their intention isn't so much to recover voices, but rather to accept the authority of texts written by others. And better still: to work closely with that other authorship. This is, then, an exchange between authors and writing systems, representation styles, and margins. A far cry from the metaphor of the voice that travels through time to be "heard" (that is, normalized by writing), documentary fiction confronts writing systems in a present that pulls it out of time through an act of writing both political and playful. In this sense, documentary fiction doesn't recover voices; rather, it reveals (and produces by revealing) authors. Better put: authorships. Perhaps there lies the reason why documentary fiction is unable to confirm our present. In close relationship with both the form and the content of a document, making the document and its context into the very source of the interrogation that produces them in the present, documentary fiction exists to disrupt.

DOCUMENTARY WRITING

US-American writing has enjoyed a long tradition of documentary poetry. In the context of social activism that evolved in the 1930s (right after the crisis of '29 and the start of the Great Depression, when Roosevelt forged the pact that established state intervention in the national economy, better known as the New Deal), various poets distanced themselves from the intimate or personal lyric and instead devoted special attention both to their own social environment and to the available means of engaging with it. This poetry is eminently political without being conventional or simplistic. In the Latin American context, it would be more closely associated with Nicanor Parra than with Ernesto Cardenal, at least in temperamental terms. More with Raúl Zurita, though not in its style or its methods. These poets employed the practices and teachings of US-American modernism (such as the rupture in formal linearity) to include historical documents, textual citations, oral history, folklore, and even commercial ads in formulating hybrid texts characterized by a plurality of voices, and therefore by multiple subjectivities. According to Michael Davidson, what truly distinguishes the documentary poets from earlier Surrealist or Dadaist experiments with collage and pastiche is that the former remained interested in questioning the social record safeguarded by different public or governmental agencies. In this way, Davidson continues, the documentalists managed to redirect the modernists' emphasis "on the materiality of aesthetic language to the materiality of social speech."[6]

Well-known works translated into Spanish during the same period include the great social novels of authors like John Dos Passos. Also recognized, though less avidly distributed, are the texts and annotations and photographs comprising *Let Us Now Praise Famous Men* (translated by the Círculo de Lectores in 1994 with the title *Elogiemos ahora a hombres famosos*), the aforementioned book published in 1941 by the novelist James Agee and the photographer Walker Evans based on the eight weeks they spent interviewing poor white residents of Alabama. Lesser known in the Spanish-speaking world are Muriel Rukeyser's documentary poems *The Book of the Dead* and Charles Reznikoff's aforementioned *Testimony*. Far from the imperialist move of trying to supplant others' voices with the writer's own, these poets set out to document the suffering and struggles of vast sectors of the US-American working classes, incorporating their voices exactly as they appeared in official documents, oral interviews, or newspaper articles. Rejecting the role of the visionary guru-poet guiding the dispossessed, both Rukeyser and Reznikoff researched and/or interviewed those directly involved in the everyday struggles and tragedies of capitalism as they experienced it themselves, later integrating these people's testimonies into texts that were necessarily interrupted, disrupted, intervened.

Muriel Rukeyser (who once translated Octavio Paz, incidentally) was convinced that a true poem demanded a "total response" from the reader. In *The Life of Poetry*, a book that was out of circulation for over twenty years before its reprinting in 1996, Rukeyser asserted:

> A poem does invite, it does require. What does it invite? A poem invites you to feel. More than that: it invites you to respond. And better than that: a poem invites a total response. This response is total, but it is reached through the emotions. A fine poem will seize your imagination intellectually—that is, when you reach it, you will reach it intellectually too—but the way is through emotion, through what we call feeling.[7]

This type of poetics clarifies Rukeyser's interest in the tragedy that occurred during the construction of a hydroelectric plant in West Virginia, near the town of Gauley Bridge. There, underground, a group of miners contracted the debilitating lung disease called silicosis when they followed orders in breaking through the rock that obstructed the project. Vast numbers of them would die. *The Book of the Dead*, published in 1938, addresses this event. The book documents it, questions it, keeps it in mind, uses it; in sum, the book aches with it. What's more: it co-aches. Reznikoff, in the way of a new social or cultural historian, did something similar by making use of the language recorded in criminal court cases in order to interrogate the racial and class inequalities of the gilded age. The result was *Testimony*, published in 1934.

While some contemporary US-American poetry may seem dominated by a devotion to the intimate epiphanies of conventionality or by an adherence to the linguistic experimentation of the post-Language era, there is more and more room for documentary poetry. This modernist legacy may be most evident in the political and poetic work of Mark Nowak. In *Coal Mountain Elementary* (2009), Nowak joins forces with the photographer Ian Teh to document the extreme circumstances in which coal miners live (and die) from the US to China. Avoiding his "own" voice, acting as a sort of DJ, Nowak mixes newspaper texts that excerpt mourners' voices, paragraphs from official documents issued by the mining companies in question, and even school lessons included in a textbook on everyday mining activities. Thus, in a work of constant juxtaposition, Nowak manages to tear off the seal of "naturalness" from the public language of testimony or the press, deftly questioning the exploitative relationships that govern mining work today.

In *Memorial: An Excavation of the Iliad*, the British poet Alice Oswald stripped away seven-eighths of Homer's text to recover, like living fossils, the deaths of approximately two hundred soldiers, all killed in the Trojan War. It is, in the poet's own words, a re-writing that seeks to recover the *enargeia*, the "bright unbearable reality" of the Homeric poem. And so it is also, firstly, a kind of plundering. The poetry looks sidelong at history, scalpel in hand. From the stasis of information and anecdotes, poetry excises the incomparable, indivisible moment when a human being loses his life. In the end, this is what war is all about: how flesh-and-blood human beings lose their lives in violent ways. Armed, then, with the energy of poetry, Oswald wrests that loss, that death, from the accumulation of details or entrails that so often leads to indifference or insensitivity or speedy readings-in-one-sitting. If "grief is black," if it is "made of earth," if it "gets into the cracks in the eyes / It lodges its lump in the throat,"[8] what this long poem carries on its back—not on the sly so that no one will notice, but dramatically, to make it more visible—is death itself, death alone. The dark, anonymous, violent death of war.

There, in Oswald's poetic excavation, in the grief she invites us to engage with over time and space, forever iridescent, is the death of Protesilaus: "A focused man who hurried to darkness / With forty black ships leaving the land behind," he who "died in mid-air jumping to be first ashore." And there, too, in the gerund of eternity, is the death of Iphidamas, "a big ambitious boy / at the age of eighteen at the age of restlessness," who seemed "even on his wedding night / . . . to be wearing armor," the "[a]rrogant farmhand fresh from the fields / [Who] went straight for Agamemnon," and who "[s]imply bent like lead and he lost." And there's Coon, Iphidamas's brother: "When a man sees his brother on the ground / He goes mad he comes running out of nowhere / Lashing without looking and that was how COON died." His head cleaved from his body by Agamemnon's sword: "[A]nd that was that / Two brothers killed on the same morning by the same man / That was their daylight here finished."

One after another, the two hundred soldiers of the Homeric tales fall to their deaths. One after another, in tight verses, often crowned by the repeated song of the chorus, they die again. And again. Now in the light of a contemporary sun, right before our eyes. A memorial is also a plea. Was it necessary for them to die again? The answer is: yes. Was it necessary to rub our eyes and feel pain again? The answer is: yes. When we mourn someone else's death, Judith Butler argued in *Precarious Life: The Powers of Mourning and Violence*, we accept that the loss will change us, hopefully forever. Which is why, even if Protesilaus has "been in the black earth now for thousands of years,"[9] it is necessary to attend to. We must attend our appointment with death, and afterwards we must share our grief. It is necessary to re-read, for example, what Oswald has re-written in order to update the death that has already happened so it can happen again, before our eyes, onto our hands. So that, someday, it will stop happening. How many times a day do we forget that we are, from the very beginning and at the end of the day, mortal?

Incited by the Calderón war, Mexico's new political poetry takes up this and other urgent, agonizing, uncomfortable questions. Such questions are both aesthetically and politically relevant. They're present in Hugo García Manríquez's excavation of the North American Free Trade Agreement in his book *Anti-Humboldt*—a book in which the language of international treaties lends itself to the "magnetic fields" of poetry. Or where poetry, through a series of bold operations, constructs a critical stance on our immediate present. They're present in Mónica Nepote's *Hechos diversos* (unfortunately not yet translated into English) and in *Querida fábrica* by Dolores Dorantes (whose work has recently been translated by Jen Hofer). They're present in "Di/sentimientos de la nación," by Javier Raya, and in *Antígona González*, by Sara Uribe. They're present in many of the poems included in *País de sombra y fuego*, the anthology edited by the Guadalajara-born poet Jorge Esquinca. All of them are here, their *enargeia* alive in the air we breathe, shrouding us as if in embrace.

A CODA FOR HISTORIANS: THE ETHNOGRAPHIC WAY OF NARRATING HISTORY

Ever since I started writing history, which was years after I started writing novels, I've suspected that the general public doesn't read history books because the vast majority are written in exactly the same way, regardless of the subjects they address or the stories they try to tell. I'm referring here mostly to academic history books, which—while they generally explore deeply fascinating or frankly disturbing topics, and are full of otherwise entertaining or scandalous anecdotes—remain faithful to dull formats. Once organized according to principles long entrenched in academia (whether surreptitiously or obviously) by methodological manuals, many of these texts end up settling for (and thus confirming) a linear, Aristotelian narrative. Such a narrative namely includes three steps: the elaboration of a stable and duly documented context; the description, ideally in great detail, of the conflict or event that occurred in said context; and the production of a final resolution or lesson, ideally associated with theoretical language and encompassing major concepts. Arranged in a linear mode, this narrative appeals to visual sequence, ultimately downplaying the sense of impermanence and simultaneity that are so closely connected to empathic listening and bodily presence. Historical writing in an ethnographic mode, then, calls for narrative strategies that counteract this phenomenon and open up the text's dialogic possibilities. And here is where Walter Benjamin's notes on collage as a strategy for composing a high-contrast page come into play. Quoting and juxtaposing displaced materials was hardly a novel technique, but his idea that the goal of this operation was redemption, not mere knowledge, remains powerfully evocative.

Certain historical files are often structured according to high-contrast composition principles themselves—especially the medical files I consulted as I conducted research in the archive of the General Insane Asylum La Castañeda for *No One Will See Me Cry*, a novel published in Spanish in 1999 and translated into English by Andrew Hurley in 2004. The medical questionnaire, which included questions designed to bring up the patient's social and medical history, ended with a diagnosis signed by the doctor. Such a verdict, however, was rarely conclusive or final. Quite the contrary: a detailed reading of this textual material shows that the diagnosis, like the file and life themselves, remained a multilayered, poly-vocal, and often contradictory interaction between psychiatrists, patients, and patients' families. The file of Matilda Burgos (not her real name), who became the protagonist of the novel by virtue of her compellingly talkative nature, is a case in point. Two mental conditions were listed as the causes of her hospitalization, namely mental confusion and amorality, as well as hebephrenic dementia praecox. The first of these notes is conspicuously, heavily crossed-out. Like a palimpsest or a geological layer, the file flaunted this and other revisions, while keeping prior diagnoses still visible. Nothing, no word, was completely erased, nor—more importantly for the reader in the ethno-historiographical sense—were the new versions incorporated into the prior ones. They weren't normalized. Historical writing conceived fundamentally as writing would have to take up the challenge of embodying, right on the pages of the book, this sense of tense, competitive composition, this dialogic structure particular to (and internal to) the document itself. In this way, a collage as a means of representation isn't arbitrary or external to the document; it isn't a fad. Rather, it's a strategy that, in certain cases (like Matilda Burgos's), helps bring her story (her history) to the page, as well as the way in which that his/story was composed in the early twentieth century at the Manicomio General La Castañeda, the insane asylum where she was institutionalized. And so, it isn't enough to identify "all" possible versions and leave—and therefore reveal—just one, the final version; the whole contradictory, unfinished process as such must be exposed. The collage's role is to sustain as many versions as possible, for as long as possible, arranging them so close to each other that they provoke contrast, astonishment, pleasure. Knowledge here is not generated as a result of the random, externally imposed application of a high-contrast composition technique, but by honoring, so to speak, the compositional principles emanating from the materials themselves. Knowledge does not come from without, and it isn't formulated out of brainy explanations external to the materials, but through the unsettling experience embodied by the very display, the contrasting layout of the writing.

What this means in terms of the author's position within the text, especially at a time of experimentation with the death of the author, is important. A historian writing in an ethnographic mode according to the principles of collage can't preserve her hermeneutic role as a document-interpreter or sign-decipherer. This isn't a historian in search of the truth hidden in things. This other historian, and here I'll use a comparison from the contemporary music world, must fulfill the functions of the composer. Or, even better, of a gestural orchestra conductor à la Boulez. Quoting him:

> The conductor must be able to recall the layout of the players instantly and at all times, all the more so when the events that you wish to create do not happen in a prescribed order, or when this order is improvised and can change at any moment. You must really be able to "touch" the players, exactly as if they were the keys of a keyboard.[10]

To paraphrase: you have to "touch" the documents as if they were the keys of the piano. I have become increasingly convinced that both historians and writers of documentary books know this, or at least imagine it, to be true.

Undead Authors

The Autobiographical and
David Markson (1927–2010)

Given the dates when Roland Barthes and Michel Foucault introduced their
ideas on the death of the author, and considering their immediately colossal influence on the reading public, we could conclude that the author (at
least within a certain Western tradition) died more or less at the start of the
second half of the twentieth century. Barthes published *The Death of the
Author* in 1968, while Foucault delivered his lecture "What Is an Author?"
to the Société Française de Philosophie in February 1969.[1] Countering the
romantic notions of writing that hinged on an authorial figure who privileged the expressive faculties of a lyrical *I*, Barthes asserted, in close adherence to Stéphane Mallarmé, that "only language acts . . . not 'me.'" This
statement launched a devastating critique (lethal, actually) against the empire of the author. And in doing so, it launched the hegemony of the reader.
Because Barthes believed that the text "is made up of multiple writings,
drawn from many cultures and entering into relations of dialogue, parody,
contestation," he argued that the author's sole power consisted of mixing together these writings, which preceded her. In this way, she effectively translated what was always and inescapably already there. Untroubled by the
question of textual originality, which was and remains an inquiry into the
reliable expression of authorial interiority, Barthes insisted that the text is
"a tissue of quotations drawn from the innumerable centres of culture," with
a meaning revealed or forged—reconstituted, certainly—by the act of reading. Thus: "The reader is the space on which all the quotations that make

up a writing are inscribed without any of them being lost; a text's unity lies not in its origin but in its destination."

Some months later, before an audience that included Jacques Lacan, among others, Foucault asked "What is an author?" to interrogate the position from which the authorial role is carried out. Responding to a question raised in this case by Samuel Beckett ("What does it matter who is speaking?"), Foucault developed a critical analysis of the conditions—including the author's name and its meaning, the appropriative relationship between author and language, and the attributive relationship between author and text—that permits the figure of the subject to emerge as the "originator" of discourses, not as a complex and variable function of them. Ultimately, it didn't matter who was speaking. (It was to be expected that Foucault would reach this conclusion.) What did matter was, and is, to ask with respect to surrounding discourses: "'How, under what conditions, and in what forms can something like the subject appear in the order of discourse?' 'What place can it occupy in each type of discourse, what functions can it assume, and by obeying what rules?'"

David Markson—an experimental US-American author, an attentive reader of Thomas Pynchon and William Gaddis, and the author of (among other books) *Wittgenstein's Mistress*, was concerned with the death of the author.[2] Literally. In his latest novels—especially in the series comprising *Reader's Block*, *This Is Not a Novel*, *Vanishing Point*, and *The Last Novel*—the third-person narrator tends to be a character, too, perhaps the main character, and is sometimes simply called Author.[3] At other points, he responds to the name of Reader. Nevertheless, in each of these renditions, the Author dies. Reading his death, witnessing his death, perhaps even becoming an accomplice to his death, is what these books ask of their readers.

The question, then, is appropriate and urgent: if the author, who appears in the novel as a narrator or character called Author, dies, then who or what is actually dying? Another way of asking the same question is to wonder whether the author can in fact die twice, once as the author and again as an Author. And if the author dies twice, does this mean that the second death invalidates the first, somehow bringing him back to life and placing him in a state of, so to speak, un-dying? Or does this mean that the second death re-validates the first, now fostering true grief and, if possible, his final burial?

A great deal of time has passed since the author's death, and the basic elements of nineteenth-century fiction (the stuff of prose manuals, for example) haven't survived unscratched. The positions of the author, narrator, and character will never again be transparent or defined by their inevitability.

As David Foster Wallace said of *Wittgenstein's Mistress*, this book is "pretty much the high point of experimental fiction in this country."[4] Markson's work far precedes the rise of early twentieth-century conceptualisms, and emerged long before a group of poets and theorists, assembled on the pages of the journal *L=A=N=G=U=A=G=E*, united Marxism and French theory to dynamite official verse culture. He not only interrogates the basic elements of fiction—challenging, with singular effectiveness, both the author's and the reader's positions—but also employs an unusual and telling syntax. His language is strange, or, rather, is made to be strange, in the sense that poet Charles Bernstein favors opacity and artifice over transparency and communicability in experimental poetics.[5] Markson alters grammar at will and swiftly combines elements of a given genre in unexpected ways. For example, he works closely and actively with subordinate clauses, which often appear at the start of a sentence without preceding clauses, producing a vague sense of dislocation, a state of alert. While paragraphs are usually known as the basic unit of prose, Markson's are too short, sometimes as short as long lines in a poem or versicles, and they are not necessarily held together by the glue of plot. Grammatically thwarted, strong-armed into hybrid genres, the reader herself is left to determine the relationship between these units of language that barely resemble paragraphs. In this sense, the reader is conceived more as a producer than as a consumer of meaning. The fact that these brief paragraphs, especially in his later books, are built from other writers' words—in the form of textual citations, often apocryphal and sometimes including unclear or inaccurate information—only further reduces the author's already-diminished figure as the guiding axis of a book and its meanings. And in doing so, it further removes them from the dominion of what-is-one's-own.

If reading is where all the writing's citations gather together, then the author, who has died—who has already been dead for so long!—can certainly travel the road back home. The reading that summons others, especially the dead, spares little. It also summons the dead author. The authorial role is thus invited to occupy a liminal space between something that is no longer death as such and something that is no longer life as such. The author returns from among the dead—not to reclaim an empire he's lost forever in the territory of the text, but rather to continue questioning his ambiguous, dynamic, specular relationship with himself. The author returns from among the dead not to live, but to un-live. Or even, as paradoxical as it may seem, to *die for*—that peculiar expression of yearning and excitement.

In one of its final definitions, the Oxford Dictionaries tell us, the prefix *un-* (Old English, of Germanic origin, from an Indo-European root shared by Latin *in-* and Greek *a-*) can sometimes denote an affirmation, as in *unburden* or *unselfish*. In general, though, *un-* is a prefix that denotes "the absence of a quality or state: *unabashed, un-academic, unrepeatable*"; "the reversal or cancelation of an action or state: *untie, unsettle*"; or "deprivation, separation, or reduction to a lesser state: *unmask, unman*." Of course, the noun *unlife* doesn't exist, but the adjective *undying* does. Used especially to describe an emotion, it means "lasting forever," as in "promises of undying love." The word in Spanish, *desvivirse*, here taking the infinitive form of the verb, eloquently contains the root *vivir*: to live. In English, we might mistakenly infer that the act of *undying* (as a verb) is close to if not synonymous with *dying* as such. But grammar itself shows us how a prefix that usually takes something away can add something here. Someone *undying* is someone who clearly shows a deeply *living* interest: someone who is *dying for*. She who *undies* has been read.

As a subject and a formal concern, the Marksonian death of the author is certainly ironic. It's a wink, rather than a complete gesture, to much of the theory behind a series of texts only tenuously united by a narrative arc based on a fairly basic anecdote: the death of someone who writes. Structured as brief quotations, short enough to resemble versicles but placed in the text to resemble paragraphs, these Marksonian novels are initially presented as hybrid texts whose elements, even the most trivial ones, question and subvert the strict delimitation of the literary genres they summon. On pages 12 and 13 of *The Vanishing Point* (2013), the author declares as if out of nowhere: "Nonlinear. Discontinuous. Collage-like. An assemblage. As is already more than self-evident." He continues, "A novel of intellectual reference and allusion, so to speak minus much of the novel."[6] Later, as Author's body begins to decline, with his language following suit, the connection is forged. Author is dying right before Reader's eyes. Author and Reader participate in this death, positively dying to stay there, in a practice of reading that at least briefly revives them. This is how Author *dies for*. And so does Reader.

ABSOLUTELY AUTOBIOGRAPHICAL

Mirror makers know the secret—one does not make a mirror to resemble a person, one brings a person to the mirror.

Jack Spicer, *Admonitions (first letter),* 1958

Few would use the adjective "autobiographical" to describe *Wittgenstein's Mistress*. This novel by David Markson was published in 1988, after 54 rejections, by Dalkey Archive Press, which has also published authors like Gombrowicz, Sarduy, Stein, Luisa Valenzuela, Anne Carson, and other poets and prose writers known for taking risks with language. But that's the word, preceded by the adverb "completely," used by Kate—the protagonist of a story that begins some time after (neither the protagonist nor the reader can know exactly when) she becomes the only person on planet Earth—to describe the ultimate objective of her solitary writing. Kate, the very last woman on a literally post-human world, spends her days writing her autobiography. What might the word "autobiography" mean to the last survivor of our species?

After deciding not to write a novel (because "People who write novels only write them when they have very little else to write," and "Your ordinary novel is basically expected to be about people. . . . And which is to say about certainly a good number more people than just one, also"), Kate reaches the conclusion, near the end of the book, that she needs to write an "absolutely autobiographical" novel. This novel must be a meticulous account of everything that crosses the mind of a woman "who woke up one Wednesday or Thursday to discover that there was apparently not one other person left in the world. / Well, or not even one seagull, either." Referring to herself for the first time with the third-person singular *she*, and thus dissociating the narrative "I" from the authorial "I," Kate reflects on what the narrator of this completely autobiographical account might or might not know. She would know, for example, that

> one curious thing that might sooner or later cross the woman's mind would be that she had paradoxically been practically as alone before all of this had happened as she was now, incidentally.
>
> Well, this being an autobiographical novel I can categorically verify that such a thing would sooner or later cross her mind, in fact.

Her "completely autobiographical" account is a far cry from the schemas that begin a life's documentation right at the beginning (at birth, for example) and continue along linear, usually progressive strategies of accumulation, which eventually converge in the actual writing of the account as its moment of self-validation. Indeed, the completely autobiographical account has passed through the death and un-death of its author. The German philosopher Peter Sloterdijk, for example, uses the concept of nervous writing (marked by emotional tattoos, also known as engrams, that "no education can wholly cover and no conversation can wholly conceal"; my translation) to argue, drawing from Paul Celan's famous quote, that "Poetry does not impose itself; it exposes."[7] And exposing itself—at least for Sloterdijk, who wrote his lessons from Frankfurt under the title "The Tattooed Life"—certainly involves the self-baring gesture that brings the original tattoo into play. It is, from the beginning,

> a gesture of openness, a triumph over asphyxia, a step forward, a self-exhibiting, a self-manifesting, the raising of a voice, a sacrifice of intimacy in pursuit of publicity, a renunciation of the night and fog of privacy in favor of enlightenment beneath a common sky.

In art, Sloterdijk continues, testimony (expression) comes first, then creation (production). Otherwise—that is, without that primordial tattoo that sets language in motion, that "moves" language—art would only "be an example of transmission of a brilliant poverty." That is, an imposition. Ultimately, poetry exposes in order to renew a commitment against "the false sublime," and it exposes itself "against the know-it-alls on high, against self-complacency, against aestheticisim, against the ladies and gentlemen of culture, and against journalistic culture, with all its possessions and measuring tapes."

Michael Onfray, a philosopher from a very different lineage, seems to advocate for something similar in concluding his *Théorie du corps amoureux* with a coda titled "For an Autobiographical Novel."[8] Drawing from the work of Lucian of Samosata, the philosopher who wielded sarcasm against dogma, Onfray broaches two lessons, namely, that "philosophers teach virtues that they take great care to practice. They sell morals that they recognize are impossible to activate" (again, my translation). Therefore, the French thinker declares unequivocally that "an existence must produce a work exactly as a work, in turn, must produce an existence." In this case, then, providing an account of oneself isn't a superfluous act of personal exhibition, but rather a rhetorical and moral strategy that links (indissolubly, we could say) a professed idea and a lived life. Onfray argues:

> The lesson we can retain from the ancient doxographers remains important when life and work act as both sides of the same coin; when, in a fractal manner, every detail reports on the nature of the whole; when an anecdote recapitulates an entire trajectory; when the philosophical life needs, and even demands, the autobiographical novel; when a work shows interest only if it causes effects in the immediate, visible, and reparable real.

Providing an account of oneself means telling a story about the *I*, but it also (and above all, and for the same reason) means telling a story about the *you*. In *Giving an Account of Oneself*, a treatise on moral philosophy that compiles a series of her lectures at the University of Amsterdam, Judith Butler argues that the *I* is hardly a hermetic, unitary structure, part of a more or less static context it gravitates within, barely brushing against other similar entities.[9] Following Adriana Cavarero and in contrast to a Nietzschean view of life, Butler establishes that

> I exist in an important sense for you, and by virtue of you. If I have lost the conditions of address, if I have no "you" to address, then I have lost "myself." In her view, one can tell an autobiography only to an other, and one can reference an "I" only in relation to a "you": without the "you," my own story becomes impossible.

But being preceded by and thus constituted by the other doesn't only establish a link of inevitable dependency with the *you* (with you), but it also constitutes a testimony of the *I*'s radical opacity to itself. Thus, the *I* is less an entity than a rip, a rupture.

An autobiography, an account of oneself, must be enunciated in a narrative form that testifies relationally to human vulnerability. An autobiography, in this sense, must be the testimony of something unknown. An autobiography, in this sense, must always be a biography of the other exactly as she appears, enigmatically, in me. And this and nothing else must be an autobiography stripped of the dominion of what-is-one's-own. Three titles for our consideration: *The Autobiography of Alice B. Toklas*, by Gertrude Stein; *The Autobiography of My Mother*, by Jamaica Kincaid; and *Autobiography of Red*, by Anne Carson.[10] Bestselling autobiographies—those linear accounts that evolutionarily track the formation of an isolated, exceptional *I*—decisively escape this notion of writing, both intimate and foreign to the approaching stranger.

The autobiography-writer, the author of *I*-accounts that are actually refracted accounts of the *you*, faces aesthetic challenges. But these challenges are also fundamentally political ones, because they stem from the fantasy-forged connection between *I* and *you* that gives them form. For one thing, Butler argues, the rupture that is the *I* is impossible to narrate. It's impossible to give an account of this rupture, despite the fact that, or precisely because, it structures any possible account of the *I*. The norms that make me readable to others are my own norms, and their temporality doesn't coincide with the temporality of my life. In the same way, the temporality of the discourse with which, or within which, I try to enunciate my life doesn't fit into the temporality with which I live that life as such. This mismatch, which is more like an interruption, makes my life, and the account of my life, possible. Bringing this interruption into the narration of the *I*, to its account of itself, is certainly an aesthetic challenge. As Butler puts it: "a life is constituted through a fundamental interruption, is even *interpreted prior to the possibility of any continuity*. Accordingly, if narrative reconstruction is to approximate the life it means to convey, it must also be subject to interruption."

Furthermore, the account of the *I* wouldn't be an account at all, strictly speaking, if it didn't address an other. Indeed, the account is completed if and only if the other effectively disappropriates it. "It is only in dispossession that I can and do give any account of myself," Butler states. And if this is true, and I tend to believe that it is, then the narrative authority in this *I*-account relates in an opposite way to the *I* conjured by the narrative itself. Structurally impossible and alien, because it rightfully belongs to the other, every *I*-narrative essentially lacks an author. And this surrender to the *you*, ceding my opacity and my unknowing of myself, implies an interrogation of the account's authorial hierarchies. Which is just another way to interrogate the power dynamics that make it possible. Politics. In this sense, giving an account of yourself through an *I*-account ceases to be a narcissistic exercise focused on the authenticity of experience, and on the emotion of the experience, that provokes it (that is, the song of the lyric *I*). Instead, it becomes an "ex-centric" excursion through my opacity (that heart of darkness), which you are in me.

Kate's text, I must mention, shies away from the type of terse, explanatory realism so often associated with the autobiographical genre and that Kathy Acker attacked in one of the memorable essays compiled in *Bodies of Work*.[11] As Acker argued, true realism, radical realism, would have to document absolutely everything that happens around and within the subject in question. Realistic realism, then, would need to very closely approximate the experience of madness. And this noun, by the way, soon appears in Markson's novel, be it as a shadow or a premonition or something inevitable. After all, are we really ready to believe that Kate is truly the last living person on Earth?

David Markson doesn't bother investigating the possible reasons behind the disappearance of all-humans-but-one. Proving or rejecting the materiality of this hypothesis is neither a concern nor a central idea of a text that consistently turns its back on all the questions that drive most apocalypse tales. We could describe this one as a post-science fiction book. The protagonist clearly states the topic, if indeed there is one, right as she explains why she has decided to write a completely autobiographical novel: solitude. Kate isn't only a solitary person; she is also constituted, throughout her completely autobiographical novel, as The Great Loner. In this respect, in regards to the experience of solitude, the book doesn't narrate a specific event (although there are inklings here and there that Kate has lost a son, perhaps around seven years old, whose name she's nearly sure is or has been Simon, and whose grave she occasionally visits, or has visited, in Mexico, of all places) as much as the use of language itself. Solitude or loss, or solitude resulting from loss, is evident not only in how Kate organizes her autobiography (which, at the end of the day, is an account for herself), but rather and especially in how its sentences are written. Kate's syntax is, in a word, odd.

Structured as "messages," which are often "an invented writing that nobody could read," her completely autobiographical text is divided into small paragraphs that resemble verses. In any case, they are lines in which an entire universe slips along, and the line-breaks are frequently sudden, interrupting both the meaning of each phrase and the apparent inevitability of sequencing. In this way, it's hardly unreasonable to associate these constructions with what Ron Silliman, alluding to Gertrude Stein, has defined as "the new sentence."[12] Often introduced with relative adverbs (that which, in which, where), Markson's sentences are actually subordinate sentences that appear on the page, and in the text, without antecedents or separated from their antecedent, as if emerging out of silence, out of nowhere. These are the sentences generated by interruption, the sentences in which interruption reverberates and makes sense.

> Most items in cans would still appear to be edible, by the way. It is only foods packaged in paper that I have stopped trusting.
>
> Although two fresh sunnyside eggs are what I would give almost anything for.
>
> What I would seriously give almost anything for, in all truth, would be to understand how my head sometimes manages to jump about the way it does.
>
> For instance I am now thinking about the castle in La Mancha again.
>
> And for what earthly reason am I also remembering that it was Odysseus who found out where Achilles was, when Achilles was hiding among the women so that they would not make him go fight?

A NATURAL HISTORY OF CULTURE

So what is it like, the world after the world? What are our ruins, exactly? How is language dealt with when there's no one, literally speaking, to address it to? The interrupted, syncopated discourse of Kate, the sole protagonist of *Wittgenstein's Mistress*, seems to try to answer these questions in one way or another. Its references to the paradigmatic cities of the modern and post-modern world, as well as to its museums—institutions dedicated to the identification and conservation of cultural heritage—are wholly relevant in this sense. Kate begins her completely autobiographical account by stating:

> In the beginning, sometimes I left messages in the street.
> Somebody is living in the Louvre, certain of the messages would say.
> Or in the National Gallery.
> Naturally they could only say that when I was in Paris or in London.
> Somebody is living in the Metropolitan Museum, being what they would say when I was still in New York.
> Nobody came, of course. Eventually I stopped leaving the messages.

While she's never entirely sure how much time has passed between the period when she was still searching for some other survivor and the period when she stopped searching altogether (she eventually hazards an estimate of ten years), Kate knows she has traveled a great deal between one point in time and another. Kate's journeys, which take her from Turkey (the original location of Troy) to Paris, from Pennsylvania to Mexico, passing through Madrid and Rome, sketch a sort of post-human map of the world. Like all maps, this one isn't merely fortuitous, a scale replica of what's-simply-there, but rather a set of slippings-around. In Kate's case, such slips travel primarily in and through culture and its artifacts. This is how, in a completely empty world, with everything directly at her disposition, Kate chooses to live in museums. And eventually to live off of them—burning certain works, for example, to warm herself at night.

In *Wittgenstein's Mistress*, as in many of his books, Markson integrates a plethora of literary, artistic, and philosophical references ranging from the classical period to the dawn of modernity. The way Kate's mind works in absolute solitude, the riddle of memory that interweaves and often confounds, prevents these references to the Great Works of Culture from serving as mere evidence of the status quo or as a coarse reaffirmation of the Western canon. Kate not only easily confuses (and, in confusing them, questions) authors and works (Anna Akhmatova, for example, is now a character in *Anna Karenina*), or original pieces with their film depictions (she's quick to shift from Hecuba to Katherine Hepburn). In addition, and with great humor, she sets out to re-appropriate the West's fundamental narratives.

One such example is the *Iliad*. Not coincidentally, one of her first journeys in the post-human world brings her to Hisarlik, the contemporary name for ancient Troy. Equally telling is the appearance—here and there, over and over, sometimes like a narrative thread, although more often like an inter-ruption of a different one—of the names Helen, Achilles, Hector. In this way, when Kate summons Euripides, Orestes, Clytemnestra, Helen, Cassandra, and Agamemnon to re-tell the story of Troy, this time centering it on sub-jects like rape, kidnapping, and family dynamics, it's impossible not to make comparisons with similar exercises: *Homero, Iliada* by Alessandro Baricco, or *Memorial: An Excavation of the Iliad* by the British poet Alice Oswald.[13]

Reversible and grotesque, necessary but open, great cultural artifacts (without which Kate's post-human world is unthinkable) thus provoke more irony than astonishment, more guesswork and doubt than validation. Kate, as is clear from the beginning, is attentive to the occurrences of high culture. She pays attention, though, in accordance with their portrayal in dictionaries and on the back covers of certain books and the jackets of cer-tain albums. (If Markson had written this novel a decade later, Kate would have undoubtedly been a great internet-searcher.)

In *On Creaturely Life*, Eric Santner interprets the concept of natural his-tory as coined by Walter Benjamin:

> Natural history, as Benjamin understands it, thus points to a fundamental feature of human life, namely that the symbolic forms in and through which this life is structured can be hollowed out, lose their vitality, break up into a series of enigmatic signifiers, "hieroglyphs" that in some way continue to address us—get under our psychic skin—though we no longer possess the key to their meaning.[14]

In this sense, in the way Kate confronts cultural artifacts as enigmatic, hollowed-out forms that nonetheless keep giving meaning to what she thinks and sees and does, Kate is a sort of Virgil who leads us, both tentatively and comically, into the natural history of culture in a post-human world.

WRITING AS SCULPTURE

Toward the end of *Wittgenstein's Mistress*, when Kate decides to write a completely autobiographical account, the novel turns around and looks itself in the face. It's the moment, in other words, when the novel both ex-poses and mocks itself. Both at once. However, the novel begins with an explicit reference to the fact that Kate is, in fact, writing. "In the beginning, sometimes I left messages in the street," she says. She later states that she'd stopped writing them. And between one thing and the other, she'd written in the sand—and even tried writing in Greek:

> Well, or in what looked like Greek, although I was actually only inventing that.
> What I would write were messages, to tell the truth, like the ones I sometimes used to write in the street.
> Somebody is living on this beach, the messages would say.
> Obviously it did not matter by then that the messages were only in an invented writing that nobody could read.

Her problematic relationship with this writing that nobody can read, or which constantly fades into the sand, remains unresolved until Kate begins to press the keys of a typewriter. In Kate's post-human world, writing fundamentally means typing. This is the verb she uses again and again to describe what she does: ceaselessly, tirelessly, relentlessly. Kate types. The difference between writing (the creative activity that a romantic worldview might associate with acts of inspiration and genius) and typing (the mechanical activity that involves a specific relationship between technology and the body, and which romanticism can neither reduce nor expand) is by no means superfluous. Kate, an extreme typist, is recording mental processes. And through these processes she attempts, like Wittgenstein in his *Tracatus Logico-Philosophicus*, to heal language of its own illness: imprecision, which could easily be another name for its meanings. Kate corrects her writing on multiple occasions (adjusting verb tenses, for example, or the verbs themselves), and announces each time that "one's language is frequently imprecise in that manner, I have discovered." But the extreme typist doesn't only correct: she is also responsible for producing a reality that is a textual reality, both for the narrator herself and for the reader, through which her life in a world possibly uninhabited by anyone else may be, in the end, bearable.

Revising or making her own sentences more precise, Kate sets out to change their constituent parts, sometimes by removing certain elements and sometimes by adding new ones. Thus, in a novel teeming with cultural and artistic references, it isn't entirely anodyne for the narrator to explicitly state the difference between the process of creating a sculpture and that of creating a painting. "Sculpture," she writes, "is the art of taking away superfluous material, Michelangelo once said. / He also said, conversely, that painting is the art of adding things on." In Kate, David Markson has created a writer who, as a typist, works with a sculptor's methods. Indeed, all superfluous material has vanished from *Wittgenstein's Mistress*: conventional notions about, for example, what makes an anecdote, how a character is constructed, what defines "plot development," and even how to produce an ending. In this novel, what remains has remained: the ruin, and the question of what this might mean.

But the novel is also sculptural in the nearly physical care with which each and every line has been made. And here, *to make* is the precise verb. The syntax that embodies Kate's solitude, the echo of strangeness that still allows it to be read, is the result of constant and occasionally violent work with and against language. There, behind everything we're talking about, is a writer, Markson, who uses the keyboard like a chisel. Someone is touching these words. In this sense, and in the sense of how the novelist uses a sculptor's techniques, his sculptural novel is a form of what I have called colliding writing, also known in the US as cross-genre.

BODIES MATTER AT THE END OF THE END OF THE WORLD

Kate is a woman, as I've said. But in a post-human world, such a statement may cause more anxiety than relief. On a totally uninhabited planet, does the distinction between women and men even make sense? Kate's abundant references to her own body ultimately expand the range of these questions rather than answering them. Not far into the story, Kate confronts the indeterminacy of her age. She might be fifty years old; the spots and wrinkles on her hands suggest as much. But she still menstruates. And the appearance of her menstruation sometimes helps her, incidentally, to keep track of time. She might have other, more restrained reactions to, say, an accident that breaks her ankle, or at least causes a sprain, but hormones (no need to specify that they're female hormones) keep her from doing so. In each and every one of these scenes, her gender identity is revealed and erased, asserted and questioned. Even so, this fact is important. Kate says more than once: "There is naturally nothing in the Iliad, or in any of the plays, about anybody menstruating. / Or in the Odyssey. So doubtless a woman did not write that after all." Everything seems to suggest that, even in a world without women or men, being a woman (or not) matters. And it matters for the simple or complex reason that, even in this post-human world, inhabited solely by Kate and the natural history of her culture, Kate has a body and a memory. Embodied and situated, her recollection of the world that has ceased to exist questions the gender hierarchies that highlight men's experiences while disregarding women's lives. Her life as a woman. What's more: her life as a woman writer.

A VANISHING POINT

Markson begins the fragmentary path of *Vanishing Point* with two shoe-boxes full of bibliographical reference cards and a character named Author. The boxes contain what appear to be isolated notes that include phrases, whether written by the artists themselves or about them, about their creative processes, their works, and their times. Author occasionally allows his voice to be heard, if only to say that he's tired, that he doesn't remember if he's taken a nap or not, that his sneakers seem to lead him to the wrong places. With an emphatically unfamiliar language and a considerably fragile memory of himself, Markson produces an Author who is beyond the dominion of what-is-one's-own.

"A decorator tainted with insanity, *Harper's Weekly* once called Gauguin," writes Markson. "Goethe wrote *Werther* in four weeks. Schiller wrote *William Tell* in six," states Markson. "I like a view but I like to sit with my back to it. Said Gertrude Stein," says Markson.

Author suffers from something slightly unusual in the head. Author doesn't feel like him-self. Author trips on objects and stumbles into walls that were once or otherwise familiar to him.

Markson asks: "Was *The Work of Art in the Age of Mechanical Reproduction* the most frequently cited critical essay in the second half of the twentieth century?" Markson says: "*Terrorists*. Which was in fact the literary term chosen to categorize the earliest nineteenth-century female Gothic novelists." Markson asserts: "Tacitus, when young, defending other young writers against the eternal Old Guard: What is different is not necessarily worse."

On page 96: "Author is experimenting with keeping himself out of here as much as possible because? / Can he really say? Why does he still have no idea whatever where things are headed either? Where can the book possibly wind up without him?"

Author, meanwhile, continues bumping into unexpected walls. Author is tired and suspects he should see a neurosurgeon. Author loses more and more control, any kind of control, over his discourse.

"Nominative. Genitive. Dative. Accusative. Ablative."

Textual citations appear with increasing frequency and without references. There is more and more information about where other authors died. The anti-textual citation. The out-of-text citation.

"The illusion that Deep Blue was somehow *thinking*."

About Virginia Woolf and about Author, sans transition:

> The one experience I shall never describe, Virginia Woolf called her intended suicide.

I have the feeling that I shall go mad. I hear voices and cannot concentrate on my work. I have fought against it, but cannot fight any longer.

The morning's recollection of the emptiness of the day before.

Its anticipation of the emptiness of the day to come.

"Ravenna, Dante died in," writes Markson. "Milan, Eugenio Montale died in."

"Giuseppe Ungaretti *anche*."

Author even manages a wink to *Wittgenstein's Mistress*: "Somebody is living on this beach."

"*Selah*, which marks the ends of verses in the Psalms, but the Hebrew meaning of which is unknown."

"And probably indicates no more than pause, or rest."

Selah.

A poet turns the pages and says: versicles.

A fiction writer turns the pages and says: long sentences.

Between the poet and the fiction writer: the silhouette of religion.

A novel without a story. A novel without a linear development. A cryptic novel. Self-referential. Schizophrenic. Wiseacre. Dying. A novel. A pause. Are they really verses? A rest. *Selah.*

A novel?

David Markson died in late May. He had written, it's true, his last novel. He was 82.

Brief Missives from Pompeii

The Production of Present

TIMELINE

In the Twitter world, "TL" can only mean one thing: timeline. Indeed, on Twitter, all writing is a timeline in continuous motion. Or the other way around: on Twitter, time is made of writing, incessantly appearing and disappearing. A present-day firefly. There is no time without writing: this is the first conclusion. Simultaneously, there is no writing that isn't time itself, passing. In this way, only the effort of collective writing (unerringly enunciated, constantly occurring) can make possible what is possible: that time exists. And that time, in existing, flashes by.

Of course, the TL is the set of rectangles filled with up to 280-character phrases that occupies the screen and seems to advance, only to disappear again. I think I've already mentioned the word "firefly." From top to bottom: vertical writing. From its existence within the screen of the present to its semi-existence in the records of what has already been: synaptic writing. Few things so sharply remind us that time's very business is to pass. Few things confirm what is no less intriguing by being so obvious: *so we're going to disappear, too?*

The tweet resembles many things that have existed in the past and which certainly still exist now: the aphorism, the haiku, the *poemínimo* (or "minimal poems," a term coined by Mexican poet Efraín Huerta), the *invención varia* (or "variable invention," a term coined by Mexican writer Juan José Arreola), the vignette, the loose phrase, the versicle, the sentence, the line. The difference lies in the medium. A tweet is a form of brief writing, yes, but it's also *onscreen* writing. What's more: a tweet is writing in the construct of *real time*. As Walter Benjamin (transcrivener par excellence) had already said in the fourteenth section of his *Theses on the Philosophy of*

History (with, aptly, an epigraph from Kaul Kraus; the goal is the origin): counter to the empty, homogenous time of the dominant ideology, we find *now-time*. Which is a full time that, in the moment of danger that is any and every quotation, makes the continuum of history jump. "Fashion has an eye for what is up-to-date, wherever it moves in the jungle of what was," he writes, expounding on the ways in which fashion "cites" the garments of the past.[1] So does the tweet: writing in brief, like so many other kinds of writing, but with and in and through today's technology. However, in pointing out the similarities, which is a laudable activity with respect to such a recent phenomenon, we shouldn't overlook the specificities.

An aphorism and a tweet can appear identical if read out of context. While both are texts of exceptional brevity, they embody different means of seeing and representing the world through writing. Once again, the major difference is the interface. Whether on paper or onscreen, an aphorism is typically a closed structure that presents itself as self-sufficient. A tweet, on the other hand, can only exist within the continuous flow of the TL. Always in connection with others, and always in the descending vertical movement that condemns it to a form of storage much like disappearance, tweeting is a form of collective writing that, in being based on a system of continuous juxtapositions, challenges certain basic elements of traditional narrative. Such elements range from bifurcation, which is assumed to be essential between the author and narrator of a text, to the existence of or need for a narrative arc in the account, as well as to the once-sacred idea of writing as a solitary exercise. Perhaps that's why tweetwriters have made generous use of so-called threads—a form of linear connection in a format that otherwise favors contrast and juxtaposition. In any case, these are just some elements (perhaps the most obvious ones) that betray the many ways in which the increasing use of digital technology has affected and is affecting both the process and the cultural significance of a practice that, when viewed within specific contexts, is never identical to itself.

Two examples. First, the work of Graciela Romero, who asserts in a tweet that *ya fue* (it's over and done with) is today's business. Second, the electronic writing of renowned Mexican writer Alberto Chimal, who has delightfully tackled transversal scrolling in his *Viajero del tiempo*. Time, then, is the-thing-that-comes-to-pass, and in both senses of "pass": what happens and what passes away. Time and its means of being, which is writing: measured time, physical time, time leaving a trail. Time with more *here* in it. Time that, because it's writing, is imagination.

Graciela Romero was @diamandina first: her name as a writer on Twitter. I remember the first tweet of hers I ever read: *Me haces falta de sobra. (Me haces falta* is a way to say "I miss you," but it literally means "I lack you"; *de sobra* indicates an excess of something; hence the paradoxical "I lack you too much.") I remember how the phrase made me laugh, then made me think, then made me laugh again, but this time with an awareness behind it—the tension between the two verbs *faltar* (to lack) and *sobrar* (to be in excess), and the phrase that in another context could be cliché. *Me haces falta.* What are you actually saying if you say "I lack you too much"? Among other things, you're saying that the phrase, which in Spanish sounds entirely natural, is in fact pure artifice. You're saying that the possibilities of wordplay are infinite and that, with the right keystrokes, these possibilities emerge in the wing-beats of the colloquial. You're saying that a playful, critical, attentive intelligence bobs about between the letters. You're saying, in other words, that there's *writing* in it. That's why I kept reading her. And became her "follower." What I mean, paraphrasing her, is that reading @diamandina is today's business.

Alberto Chimal, meanwhile, is already an established writer of books printed on paper (proof that the TL equally welcomes published and unpublished authors, as it should). Curiosity killed the cat, but curiosity is what keeps Alberto and his readers alive. Attuned to present-day technological fluctuations, Alberto not only made his Twitter account a channel of active, recurrent information; he also uses it to write. His morning and evening greetings—a ritual that now marks the passing of time in numerous timelines—are proof, as are those journeys occasionally embarked upon by a Traveler who avails himself both of learned quotations and of winks to popular culture.[2]

Such a declaration is both scandalous and true. As Argentine thinker Josefina Ludmer once convincingly argued, and as I mentioned in the early pages of this book, these writings may not be literature (and we shouldn't care if they're not); they produce present.[3] This concept, she went on, is intimately connected to her reading of an essay by Tamara Kamenszain in which the latter author argued, apropos of certain contemporary Argentine poetry, that "a testimonial is proof of the present and not a realistic record of what happened."[4] This is Ludmer's point of departure. And this is my point of departure here. It's useless to argue whether the writing that takes place on the electronic platform known as Twitter is literature or not. Also irrelevant (though therein lies one of its major points of interest) is whether it's fiction or not. What's important when reading the TL is that the language it's made of is proof of the present. As Kamenszain has said, they aren't a realistic record of what is happening, but they constitute evidence of its happening. Both evidence and practice. In other words, a production of that enunciation of contemporaneity that so concerned Gertrude Stein.

TRACTATUS LOGICO-TWITTERUS

1. Let's put it this way: a tweet doesn't produce meaning; it produces present.

    1.1. A tweet doesn't tell what happened; it confirms that something is happening.

        1.1.1. A tweet is what is happening.

    1.2. Except for words, nothing happens as we tweet.

        1.2.1. The tweet's present is already a mediated present.

        1.2.2. The tweet's present is already a readymade.

        1.2.3. Facing keyboard and screens, Twitter users participate in a fictitious present.

            1.2.3.1. Something is happening: fiction conceals it. Nothing is happening: the tweet reveals it.

            1.2.3.2. A Twitter user is the best character of Her Self.

        1.2.4. The tweet's present is produced by a seated body.

    1.3. Because the tweet's present is already a readymade, there is no such thing as a sincere tweet.

        1.3.1. Every tweet is already implausible.

        1.3.2. A confessional tweet is a contradiction in terms.

        1.3.3. No one actually performs tweet-tease.

        1.3.4. Alter-produced and alter-directed, a tweet moves from outside outward.

            1.3.4.1. A tweet is a scene.

    1.4. The tweet's present, like the Twitter user's present, is based on principles of juxtaposition and montage.

        1.4.1. The tweet's present occurs in the random articulation of the TL.

            1.4.1.1. Even if the other tweet is by the same Twitter user, a tweet needs an other to exist.

                1.4.1.1.1. Every tweet is an echo.

                1.4.1.1.2. Every tweet is contact.

                1.4.1.1.3. Every tweet is a limbo.

            1.4.1.2. A tweet becomes a tweet only on a TL.

        1.4.2. The tweet's present is on the screen.

1.5. The function of erasure accentuates the ephemeral consistency of the tweet's present.

    1.5.1. A tweet is the shortest present.

    1.5.2. A tweet is the present in its most precarious form.

        1.5.2.1. Enormous collective effort is necessary to produce us as the tweet's present.

    1.5.3. The tweet's nature is erasure.

1.6. Like spores, tweets are reproduced via retweets, spreading from TL to TL.

    1.6.1. From TL to TL, the tweet's sporadic reproduction is a process of framing and reframing.

    1.6.2. From TL to TL, the tweet's sporadic reproduction excludes its fusion with another.

    1.6.3. Sporadically also means occasionally. A tweet.

1.7. Twitter: a live writing session.

    1.7.1. Twitter is the jazz of writing.

    1.7.2. A tweet interpellated by another: live writing.

        1.7.2.1. Written toward: the tweet.

        1.7.2.2. Every tweet is a zigzag.

    1.7.3. A chain of swift semantic reactions: the tweet's nerve impulse.

    1.7.4. Tiny metonymic operations: the dialogic tweet.

    1.7.5. Errant orthographies: the tweet's syntactic transformations.

1.8. The tweet's present: kaleidoscopic, protean, collective, sporadic.

1.9. Look: this tweet just disappeared.

BRIEF MISSIVES FROM POMPEII

There are various explanations for my recent addiction to Twitter. If I've accurately read the theoretical essays on this phenomenon of instantaneous communication established via written messages of no more than 280 characters, then these explanations are also complex. All roads now lead to Pompeii, not Rome. Our birthplace is no longer the eternal city whose ruins lie, layer upon layer, in a gesture of circular totality. Here and now, our birthplace is that other city petrified in a moment's glory: Pompeii. Cut. Slash. Interruption.

Once upon a time there was a *homo psychologicus*. He was a human being from industrial societies who built thick walls to separate the private from the public and thus to protect a deep, silent, stable, individual notion of the *I*. Because he had a secret, the *homo psychologicus* invented psychoanalysis, for example. In those days, having a rich "inner life" and a "personal history" were very important to him. Writing long, labyrinthine books (Roman books, in this sense), which nonetheless arrived at a well-established ending, was not only special for the writer who signed the text with his own name, thus unfastening the writer from the narrator and the character. It was also special for the reader, who, in another room of the private world, would silently receive the message informing her about her own inner recesses. One wrote, then, to be extraordinary, or because one was already extraordinary. One read for the same reasons. One among the finest representatives of this world—French, by the way; Mallarmé by name—would ultimately argue that life existed in order to be told in a book. Judging by the weight of the paper, books were fairly tedious objects at the time.

But the *homo psychologicus*, as we know, is over and done with. Today, in his place, forged not in the slow chore of Roman ruins but in the imperious instant of Pompeii, is the *homo technologicus*: a post-human being who inhabits the physical and virtual spaces of computer societies for whom the *I* isn't a secret or a depth, much less an interiority, but rather (quite the contrary) a form of visibility. Always connected to diverse digitalities, the *technologicus* writes in transparent rooms lined with screens; in fact, she is often accompanied by people. There, she writes down the life that only exists in order to appear, inscribed, in fragments circulating constantly throughout that exteriority (if I may use a vintage term) known as Web 2.0.

Both cases involve writing about life. But in the irascible competition between fiction and nonfiction (as such things are called in the ex-empire of the United States), nonfiction is winning by a landslide. A strange but suggestive combination between the cult of personality and an alter-directed notion of the *I* within a regime of total visibility has led billions of post-human beings to hurl themselves into the act of transmitting written messages about what's happening to them right at that very Pompeiic second. With no totalizing plot or teleological objective of any kind, these bits of writing cross cybernetic space with no other goal than to appear wherever they appear: that is, before the legitimizing eyes of their equal other. Reading is, after all, a means of verification. There are no secrets.

Because I'm a DM (digital migrant), I've come to Twitter a few years late. This delay, however, does nothing to diminish the intensity or pleasure of my new tweetaddiction. My excitable explorations of this twenty-first-century Mexican Pompeii have led me to numerous treasures: for one, the horizontal dissemination of information (I've discovered more cultural and political minutiae thanks to the readings and highlightings of my Twitter community, from Alberto Chimal and Ernesto Priego's links to Yuri Herrera and Irma Gallo's commentary, than from any other form of media); for another, the critical exercise of citizen journalism (the information produced and propagated about the Chile earthquake is all the evidence I need); and, above all, the forms of writing that respond, voluminously and constantly, to the question/abracadabra confronting every tweet. To which we could add: what's happening (to language)? Due to the malformations of my trade, I look for writing in everything I do. Against all odds, I've found this, too, in tweets. I have the sense, for example, that tweetwriters like @diamandina and @franklozanodr care about writing and about appearing onscreen, in that order. More than reporting on what's happening (although they do), these two writers from Guadalajara (which is the most I've learned about their whereabouts) write about what's happening to language. Their texts allow us to witness what's happening when Oulipo has taken the helm and all of society conforms to the maxim of the 280 blows. It would take me entire pages to analyze what they do in a way that does them justice, but for now I'll mention how comically and dazzlingly they disassemble popular language, often changing letters that turn a word into several more or repositioning words within a sentence, thus transforming it into something unfamiliar. For example, there's @diamandina's *Me haces falta de sobra* (discussed above), or *Que-herida* (a pun eliding *querida*, or "dear," and *qué herida*, "how hurt"), which has appeared at this very instant on my screen inside a horizontal box signed by @franklozanodr. These tweets are marked not only by a profound awareness of the everyday twists and turns of colloquial speech, but also by a playful transgression of syntax and spelling. Which is what tells me that there's *writing* in them. Which means I pay attention, I implicate myself. In a territory not fully covered by aphorism, but which doesn't go so far as the *poemínimo*, @diamandina writes: *Desde 1998 te estaba esperando en 2008* (I've been waiting for you in 2008 since 1998). Or *El acto malabárico de poner en movimiento tantos celos al mismo tiempo* (the juggling act of tossing many jealousies into the air at the same time). Or *Reaccionaria: preferiría no preferir no hacerlo* (Reactionary: I'd prefer not to prefer not to). Or *Mis planes tienen una agilidad sorprendente para dar vuelta en u* (My plans have a surprising knack for making U-turns). And by @franklozanodr: *Recuerdas ese jardín. No lo tuvimos* (Remember that garden? We never had it.) Or *Yo en realidad tengo una piedra en el corazón, y oídos sordos* (I actually have a stone in my heart, and deaf ears). Or *Y rueda la piedra, gira en su pértiga sonámbula hasta su conversión en polvo* (And the stone rolls, turns around its somnambulist pole until it's turned to dust). I've been quoting them for days at the slightest provocation, and that (Lord help me, I'm going to say something truly awful—which I often do, truth be told) is something I don't even do with Tolstoy.

POMPEIIAN EROTOGRAPHIES

Orthography, as we know, is a set of conventions for writing a language, including norms of spelling, hyphenation, capitalization, word breaks, emphasis, and punctuation. Another source adds (and I'm paraphrasing here) that orthography is based on the linguistic community's acceptance of a series of conventions in order to maintain the unity of the written language. What's clear to me, then, is that orthography is a tense, dynamic convention, since the "setting" of rules involves participation by perhaps dissimilar members of "the linguistic community." It's also clear that language tends toward dispersion and toward a who-knows-how-healthy form of spreading-about, given that entire organizations (such as the RAE, in the case of Spanish) have been founded in order to "maintain its unity."

I'm not sure how reliable my sources are (and I'll confess that they're Wikipedian in nature right now), but everything seems to indicate that meddling with orthography is no small matter. More than a simple distraction or an illiterate dalliance, challenging orthography means confronting the very forces that keep a language intact. A bad speller could easily be a perfectly ignorant person—but seen from another angle, viewed through the lenses of Twitter, he might also very well be a guerrilla of written language's centrifugal forces. And why would we want a language that, paraphrasing what canonical Mexican poet López Velarde said of his sparkling Homeland, is always faithful to itself?

To clarify: this isn't a plea in favor of spelling errors in general, whether they appear on paper or onscreen. What I want is to lay the groundwork for analyzing one of the methods most commonly employed by Mexican Pompeii's early twenty-first-century tweetwriters when they answer the question "What's happening (with language)?"

My theory is that, in using orthography as a field of action, these tweetwriters are altering the meaning of both specific words and entire phrases (whether of popular origin or book culture) in order to produce playful and critical perspectives on the everydayness they emerge from. In this way, from the offices where they work or their single-people's bedrooms, tweetwriters manage to produce the phrase (like a verse or aphorism or *po-emínimo*, when applicable) that continually shows how language is never natural or immovable or carved in stone. If it's language, it's playful. If it's language, transmitted through keyboards and different screens, then it's political. Maybe @pellini was right in declaring that *Ustedes son geniales, pero tienen un empleo mediocre y una vida triste* (You guys are brilliant, but you have mediocre jobs and sad lives). He's definitely right, though, when he says *Esa es la magia de tuiter* (That's the magic of Twitter). Archaeologists of barely hidden meanings and jugglers of well-made phrases, tweetwriters are people who have learned this old adage well, and for good: it's important to be able to laugh at yourself.

It's certainly interesting to meet writers in the labyrinths of New Pompeii who transition smoothly to the 280-phrase after typically using the paper platform. I'm thinking of Aurelio Asiain's translations, for example, or Isaí Moreno's thoughtful reflections, or the wordplay conjured on the other side of the pond by Jorge Harmodio in response to Jordi Soler's underlinings and annotations. On Twitter, you can find lipograms (Gael García Bernal published one a couple days ago, as a matter of fact), palindromes, exact translations, flash fiction. It's also interesting to discover other tweetwriters who may or may not publish on paper, but whose writing mode is predominantly electronic. They could pass for quips or witticisms, and when they are (as they might be), all of these 280-character (or less) phrases are ultimately something else: writing. It's clear to me that they contain grammatical awareness, active and defiant, anti-authoritarian and hardly trivial. Let's look at these entries by @hiperkarma: *De ahora en adelante, Usaré Mayúsculas Cuando Hable* (From this point forward, I Will Use Capital Letters When I Speak). In retweeting a phrase by @mutante, this is how @hiperkarma echoes orthographic transgressions: *No pienso poner ni una coma y dar así una libertad inusitada a la interpretación del texto escrito* (I won't add so much as a comma and thus grant an unusual freedom to the interpretation of the written text). She was the one who responded critically and fairly, from Monterrey, to the badly written ad published by the Gandhi bookstore chain: *Si tu límite de lectura son 140 caracteres. Te vamos a hacer leer. / Si tu puntuación es mala, les enseñaré a escribir* (If your reading limit is 140 characters. We'll make you read. / If your punctuation is bad, I'll teach you to write).

Their methods seem simple, but they have their tricks. These are the most frequent ones: first, the rearranging/substitution of letters within a word, and then the repositioning/replacement of one word for another

within a phrase. In both cases, the goal (intended or otherwise) is to produce a proliferation of meanings that denaturalize, and therefore question,
what will never again be the original "meaning." With a simple substitution
of the vowel *e* for the vowel *a*, the word *felicidad* (happiness), for example,
can become *falicidad*, a neo-noun that associates the *falo* (phallus) with the
initial word's positive definition. In *Me rehúso a que no me reúses* (I refuse
to tolerate the fact that you won't reuse me), @diamandina erases the silent
h in the second word that now, even without a hyphen between "re" and
"use," takes on an erotic dimension, if not an overtly sexual one. In *Instruc-
ciones para bailar matemáticamente: cuestión de seguir el algorritmo* (How
to dance mathematically: it's a matter of following the algorhythm), the
addition of a second "r" to the final word successfully and serendipitously
exchanges a dance beat for the methodology employed by the science of
numbers. The hashtag *#pornolibros* (@viajerovertical brought this one to
my attention) takes up the exercise—and takes it to the extreme—of switch-
ing certain letters in certain well-known book titles in order to produce a
double entendre. Joyce's *Culises* (which we might translate in English as
Ulasses) is one such example.

In a second method, the word remains intact, but its relocation within a
familiar phrase (a popular expression, for example, or the title of a song or
film) ultimately produces parodic or revelatory results. @diamandina once
said: *Engañifa. Albaricoque. No es por presumir, pero tengo felicidad de palabra* (Swindle. Apricot. I don't mean to brag, but I have a joy with words).
The *facilidad* of the colloquial expression (to have *facilidad de palabra* is
to have a way with words) has been exponentially elevated by *felicidad*—a
word that respects the rules of spelling, but whose location in this sentence
isn't "natural." Others, like @viajerovertical, draw from philosophy to raise
questions of literary theory, such as *¿La experiencia se conserva o se disuelve
en el texto?* (Is experience preserved or dissolved in the text?), or to conduct
personal reflections about memory and love, among other things: *Qué do-
lor el idilio en que uno solo es los dos amantes y el jardín y el pájaro* (What a
terrible utopia when you're the two lovers, the garden, and the bird all by
yourself). Tweetwriters also cull 140-character phrases by interacting with
English. @diamandina does it again, combining champagne bottles with
those of plastic packaging material: *A manera de brindis hay que caminar
sobre el* bubble wrap (Let's toast by stepping on bubble wrap).

What could be taken literally as a mistake, whether as an error of knowledge (not knowing the orthographical rules) or of mechanics (the typical typo), becomes the universe of tweetwriting. And it does so through
inventiveness and continual contact with the work of words, borne out in

brief phrases with intense evocative and parodic power. Which is why I've used the term "erotography" to categorize these experiments with alternative spellings that so characterize today's tweetwriters: the touch, the body-to-body contact with everyday words. The pleasure. Ah, yes: the pleasure of finally reading something fresh again. A final note: erotography has nothing to do, as far as I can tell, with the generally random spelling of Twitter or twiter or *tuiter* or *tuitah*.

A TWEET IS A BOUQUET.

10:05 am 18 Apr via web

FIRST DEFINITION OF THE PLACE:

> Language's emergency room: Twitter.
>
> 10:06 pm 31 Mar via web

THE CHARACTERS ENTER:

> Squanderers, crestfallens, extravagants, early birds, prodigals, runaways, foul-moutheds: Twitter users.
>
> 5:11 am 3 Apr via web

> Big Drama Queens of the keyboard: Twitter users.
>
> 4:31 am 3 Apr via web

> Forensic pathologists of the sentence: Twitter users.
>
> 10:06 pm 31 Mar via web

> Cannibals of the ABCs: Twitter users.
>
> 10:05 pm 31 Mar via web

THE AUTHOR'S POINT OF VIEW:

> Ever since I came to Twitter, I've mistrusted paragraphs longer than three lines.
>
> 12:21 pm 9 Apr via web

> Good habits: I used to be a long-distance runner, but now I discipline myself to reach 280.
>
> 12:20 pm 9 Apr via web

IT ALL STARTED WITH THE ERRATICS:

In the face of the correct sentence, the erratic phrase.
6:52 am 15 Apr via web

I like phrases that come out of nowhere and break the stillness of a paragraph. Oar against lake. Stone against riverbed.
10:53 am 15 Apr via web

The erratic phrase leads writing to where it was never headed.
Extra-vagrant.
10:31 am 15 Apr via web

But the goal is to err. To flow. To surpass. To bend.
6:57 am 15 Apr via web

If you're lucky, the tweet is that erratic phrase.
10:44 am 15 Apr via web

The phrase that comes out of nowhere always begs the question: who's
speaking? And where? So reading is dialogue.
10:55 am 15 Apr via web

If it belongs to you, an erratic phrase is produced as someone else's.
An echo.
7:05 am 15 Apr via web

In the erratic phrase, the I, if real at all, is a mere reflection.
7:06 am 15 Apr via web

THE MAGNETIC FIELD, OR NOTES TOWARD A THEORY OF ATTRACTION:

Maybe the task is to produce a magnetic field powerful enough to attract
the fleeting gaze of phrases coming out of nowhere.
11:14 am 15 Apr via web

A text/magnetic field traversed, more than written, by erratic phrases.
11:30 am 15 Apr via web

Text as magnetic field: a montage of attractions: a field of co-existence.
8:16 pm 28 Mar via web

THE TL-NOVEL:

The tweetnovel is a TL written by characters.
About 16 hours ago via web

As in any TL, how a tweet lets itself be affected/deformed by another is important to the tweetnovel.
About 16 hours ago via web

A true tweet always contains the other tweet that cuts across it.
9:15 pm 23 Apr via TweetDeck

A true tweet doesn't contain a message; it contains a secret.
9:10 pm 23 Apr via TweetDeck

More than expressing something, a tweet alludes to something else. That something else is precisely what the tweet doesn't know: its own blind spot.
9:12 pm 23 Apr via TweetDeck

A tweet is an agreement (not necessarily made between gentlemen).
9:11 pm 23 Apr via TweetDeck

The structure doesn't precede the TL-novel. The (juxtaposed) structure and not the (linear) anecdote is the discovery of the TL-novel.
About 15 hours ago via web

A tweet doesn't allow for the development of an idea (progress); it contrasts several (allegory). Benjamin would love it.
10:07 am 18 Apr via web

The TL-novel, then, reveals the plural production of a structure. The TL-novel doesn't tell.
About 15 hours ago via web

@alisma_deleon A TL is dialogic/coralic/echoic: texts from different origins, principle of juxtaposition, "I" unfolded. I think.
About 15 hours ago via web in reply to @alisma_deleon

@javier_raya Take a good look at your TL. There must be a couple narrative sequences written by "characters" ready to be extracted.
About 15 hours ago via web in reply to @javier_raya

@psicomaga @javier_raya @criveragarza // [Works of the divinities of chaos] >> there's a certain method to the juxtaposition and therefore to the chaos.
About 15 hours ago via web in reply to @psicomaga

I suspect that the person who only sees disorder in her TL still hasn't found the method in its most secret associations. That heartbeat.
12:46 pm 28 Apr via web

STYLE EXERCISES:

Your own noveltweet: read the novel, underline the tweets, cut them out, paste them on another page. Throw out the rest. Organize presentation.
About 16 hours ago via web

Textual purge: read a novel, underline the tweets, erase the rest. Voilà.
About 16 hours ago via web

Sometimes a story is a tweet in the context of another set of many words.
About 16 hours ago via web

You could look at it this way: an article is three or four tweets surrounded by text.
About 16 hours ago via web

WE'RE INTERRUPTING THE INTERRUPTION TO SAY:

The tweet melts in your mouth.
9:15 pm 23 Apr via TweetDeck

FOREIGN RELATIONS:

With an equal distribution of assets, by mutual agreement, and as the con-
sequence of irreconcilable differences: FB/Twitter divorce.
8:58 am 23 Apr via TweetDeck

FB and Twitter get divorced. In the distribution of assets, one kept propa-
ganda and the other kept writing. They'll get along fine, I think.
8:26 am 23 Apr via TweetDeck

SECOND DEFINITION OF PLACE:

Tweet is cluster.
10:05 18 Apr via web

Twitter is the Text's Surrounding Area.
11:11 pm 28 Mar via web

THE ORIGIN:

You started writing because of something else. That something-else is what
you should return to. Always.
8:00 am 23 Apr via TweetDeck

Writing's something-else, which is its origin, always speaks very softly.
8:21 am 23 Apr via TweetDeck

PRIVATE LIFE

Summer looks like winter out there (and the morning storm brings thunder
and lightning to prove it). Those who seem far away are close by and vice-
versa. Sometimes everything looks like a contradiction. We could say the
same of so-called private life. I wake up thinking about this, about private
life, about the secret that's supposed to inhabit the very heart of its definition. Certain high walls around the core of it. There, in the private realm
of space that bites its own tail, like a boa. A fastening clasp. A link. At the
other extreme, of course, is the exhibitionism of public life. Revelation. The
prudish and the discreet, it's said, keep quiet and preserve convention. Only
shameless extroverts wash their dirty laundry outside. Private life, as is also
believed, happens behind closed doors. If there's such a thing as "behind,"

and if the doors really close. There's something unnervingly smooth about the dichotomy that situates the secret and the private vis-à-vis revelation and the public; it makes them such symmetrical opposites that I can't help feeling suspicious. Paul Virilio had already complained (and in this, my goodness, he resembles Simon & Garfunkel) about those who don authoritarian airs in sentencing silence to silence[5]—flaunting, of course, the fact that silence is actually full of voices. So what?, I ask myself, echoing that complaint. Weren't doors made for the sole purpose of overhearing something on the other side of them?

The Universal Declaration of Human Rights protects it: "No one shall be subjected to arbitrary interference with his privacy, family, home or correspondence, nor to attacks upon his honor and reputation. Everyone has the right to the protection of the law against such interference or attacks." Georges Duby has dedicated at least five volumes of searing analysis to the subject, focusing on Europe from the Roman Empire until (according to the final title) the present day.[6] The history of everyday life, with special emphasis on the private sphere, has also yielded historical collections in Mexico (I'm thinking particularly of the volumes coordinated by Pilar Gonzalbo Aizpuru, which span from the Mesoamerican era to the twentieth century[7]). Even so, and perhaps only as a result of the storm that has since abated, I woke with the hunch, which is terrible and rather scandalous in itself, that Private Life (just like that, in capital letters, though spoken very softly) ended in 1844. That was the year Edgar Allan Poe wrote the story "The Purloined Letter," in which the Prefect of Paris asks for the detective Auguste Dupin's help in finding a stolen piece of correspondence. Dupin discovers that the supposedly stolen letter hadn't been taken anywhere, but was actually right there all along, in plain view of the outside eye. The letter is left out in the open, where no one thinks to look for it. That—as Poe seems to be telling us in his intricate, enjoyable story—might be what social networks, especially Twitter, are here to tell us. The more exposed (whether a letter or a private life), the less accessible.

In Poe's story, the authorities know who stole the letter (a sharp-eyed minister), and, in general, the place where the object can be found (the minister's house). However, after a painstaking, even exhaustive search, the police can't find it. Dupin, aware that the thief is not only a minister but also a poet and mathematician, reaches the conclusion that the letter isn't hidden, or at least not in a conventional sense. Dupin traces it to a different place: not deep in the depths of some extraordinary hideaway, but on the surface. And that's exactly where he finds it. In plain sight. The letter, wrinkled and facing away, looks different, but it's the very same.

About a hundred years later, Jacques Lacan analyzed this story in his famous Wednesday seminars (in the same city, curiously, where Poe set his original tale), this time titled *La Lettre volée*. The psychoanalyst was concerned, among other things, with promoting the following principle: "that in language our message comes to us from the Other, and—to state the rest of the principle—in an inverted form." He also put forth this question: "[I]f man were reduced to being nothing but the echoing locus of our discourse, wouldn't the question then come back to us, 'What is the point of our addressing our discourse to him?'"[8] Perhaps. It's very possible that the psychoanalyst was actually interested in many other matters, but, as he himself often said, the truth can only reside in a half-saying. In any case, Lacan doesn't suggest leaving things in plain view in order to hide them better, but rather to call attention to the basic fact that nothing, "however deep in the bowels of the earth a hand may seek to ensconce it, will ever be hidden there, since another hand can always retrieve it. . ." The mystery is both simple and strange, just as Poe had described it.

Toward the end of the first part of the seminar, after being "confirmed in our detour by the very object which draws us on into it," Lacan declared that a letter always reaches its destination. Or, in other words, that language delivers its sentence to whomever knows how to hear it. Edgar Allan Poe and Jacques Lacan seem to have shared a fascination with what is hidden in plain view; I think this much is clear.

There's an interesting game in Twitter that its habitual users are skilled at playing. As we know, one can respond to a particular message by using the @ symbol to identify directly both the person emitting and the person receiving (and, if applicable, answering) the message. The appearance of the @ thus constitutes a clear indication of how a "private" exchange is transpiring, in broad daylight, in the town square that is the TL. The invention of the invisible @—a trick that some attribute to @asiain and others with years of Twitter experience associate with the very origin of digital times—nonetheless sustains a "private" dialogue before the undetected gaze of those who are doubtlessly watching. The message is issued; hidden from itself, after crossing the minefield of eyes, it delivers its sentence to the recipient capable of reading it. The fact that this process occurs—and, what's more, that it has to occur in front of everyone else in order to be truly hidden—makes me think hard about the very concept of privacy in these times, when intimacy is produced and directed from the outside outward. These mornings of extimacy.

NIGHT SHIFT

What kinds of documents might a late-twenty-first-century anthropologist consult in order to puzzle out, in as much detail as possible, the private lives of early twenty-first-century men and women? If it were 2092 and I were that anthropologist, interested in exploring the recesses of human emotional and sexual life, I would certainly search among the TL records of the Twitter accounts that, according to recent news reports, were archived in their entirety by the Library of Congress from 2006 to 2017 and have been "selectively" archived ever since.

People don't tell the truth on Twitter; this we know. But, on Twitter, people exaggerate or project within a cultural context that both feeds and channels the imagination that will ultimately construct a character. In one of my early texts on the writing phenomenon that is Twitter, I said the following:

> 1.3. Because the tweet's present is already a readymade, there is no such thing as a sincere tweet.
>
> 1.3.1. Every tweet is already implausible.
>
> 1.3.2. A confessional tweet is a contradiction in terms.
>
> 1.3.3. No one actually performs tweet-tease.
>
> 1.3.4. Alter-produced and alter-directed, a tweet goes from outside outward.
>
> 1.3.4.1. A tweet is a scene.

Let's take it one step at a time. In maintaining that a tweet (a 280-character message that a Twitter user writes inside a rectangle in the upper portion of a screen) is a readymade, I sought to emphasize the mediated nature of its most essential definition. A readymade—an everyday found object that is thus revealed and displayed through an already codified form—is always available for use. For this reason and no other, I asserted above that the tweet was implausible (in the sense that, if the "plausible" is *1. adj. Having the appearance of truth,* then the "implausible" must be *1. adj. Having the appearance of falseness*). But I didn't stop there. I also said, and I uphold it, that there is no such thing as a confessional tweet. In other words, I said that, in being a readymade, a tweet might take on a confessional form in order to produce the effect of revelation and intimacy that many associate with catharsis. Which means, of course, that no one is in the position of performing tweet-tease. No one gets naked here—or if she does, then her nakedness is only a disguise. The tweet, which is exposed right as it comes into being, is produced outside (in language, onscreen, on the keyboard) and is directed, without a doubt, outside and outward: into the TL. A tweet is a teeny-tiny scene.

If at least 80 percent of the previous paragraph sounds sensible or at least documentable, then it's obvious that the anthropologist in 2092 won't find the truth of early twenty-first-century emotional and sexual lives in any TL. What the future anthropologist will find, though, is the collective construction of the limits of so-called intimate life. The anthropologist (likely female, by the way) would do well to question the truthfulness of the information at her disposal. But she would also do well to take it at face value in order to elucidate each and every one of the prior elements deployed in producing the terrain of intimacy itself. In the end, as Fernández Porta reminds us (my translation),

> intimacy is a concept that was constructed by the upper classes in the late nineteenth century in order to distinguish themselves from the working class. It was based on the possession of closed spaces (houses and rooms, but also impermeable social spaces) that assured a certain refinement in inner and relational life. Strictly speaking, this concept ceased to exist in the mid-twentieth century with the extension of means of spectacularization and advertising.[9]

The anthropologist would read, then, the early twentieth-century time-lines. If I could give her some advice, I'd tell her to concentrate especially on tweets posted at night. As the textual production of insomniacs, they range from about eleven p.m. to two or three in the morning. These are the most fragile hours: the sleepless will implore and the drunk will say something in the guise of the truth. Almost all tweets from the night shift apologize more or less explicitly for what some call, not without certain pride, their cheesiness. @altanoche, in Hermosillo, Mexico, makes declarations like this one: *Tengo ganas de meterme a la cama. Pero no a la mía* (I want to go to bed. But not mine). @reiben, a young writer from Tijuana, has even authored a series of pornotweets depicting a woman tied to a chair while others have violent sex in front of her. The fact that readers like @manchas or @DianitaGL or @javier_raya meddle in the TL's fragmentary narrative, volunteering when it's time to choose which character to play, remains compelling. Is this an example of the naturalization of violence against women that led to the femicide machine, or is this the reversal of violence enacted by willing male and female partners? The anthropologist will soon see for herself: ardent and cheerful, early twentieth-century Twitter users were willing to shelter and appropriate sequences and characters in sparking desire. @ciervovulnerado deserves a special mention. Nonchalant from the get-go, in playful command of popular blasphemy, this Twitter user from Xalapa has no qualms about naming body parts or what they do. Nor does she hesitate to describe her own family (her brother tweets, too), or to chronicle her encounters (real or imaginary) with different partners. @hiperkarma, a female Twitter user from Monterrey, brings a queer dimension into play. Even @MiguelCarbonell, who usually tweets about social topics, especially those affiliated with law, wastes no opportunities to quote Sabines or express his nostalgia or let out a long sigh in his midnight tweets.

Something smells fresh here, which is how we know it has nothing to do with Denmark. The anthropologist, even if she really were a he in the end, would be wise to read carefully and laugh heartily at the sleepless anti-confessions—or, better put, disconfessions—that forge this outside-outward intimacy in our present day. It's the end of the circle.

AGAINST LITERARY VALUE

The conviction that you are capable of discerning the so-called literary quality of a digital text, employing the norms and rituals that historically arose to analyze texts printed on paper, is like asking your wild, stormy crush to be your boyfriend when your secret goal is to make him the man of the house. Or vice-versa. Form and content forge a dynamic unity defined by a series of mutual interdependencies. This means that the medium or platform in which a text is written does matter, very much. I'm not saying anything new when I say that no text comes out of nowhere. No matter how brilliant its author may be, a text's creation involves the participation of the body and the set of technologies—from the most rudimentary brush to the multifaceted pencil to the contemporary computer—that enable the concrete existence of writing. These technologies and these bodies are certainly historical: they are the products of volatile hierarchical contexts in which writing has played many different roles. It isn't entirely surprising that an era of radical changes, like those we're experiencing now in pursuit of the digital revolution, would cause anxiety and suspicion among the spokespeople of the status quo. The voice of this neoconservative wave gets louder every time the thorny question of literary quality is raised. As if it were an essential matter and not a historical one, natural instead of contingent.

As John Guillory argues in *Cultural Capital: The Problem of Literary Canon Formation*, literature as such arose toward the end of the eighteenth century in order to give a name to bourgeois cultural capital. The term "literary" thus described a historically determined and cultural significant form of writing. Although throughout the nineteenth century and most of the twentieth the "literary" as a category would serve as a dominant organizing principle in the establishment of the canon, its hegemonic power declined in the late twentieth and early twenty-first centuries. There are many reasons for this deterioration, but Guillory names at least three, at least with respect to England: the institutionalization of vernacular English in eighteenth-century primary schools; the controversy in favor of the new modernist criticism instated in universities; and the emergence of a theory of the canon that complemented the literary curriculum in postgraduate schools. Literature, then, isn't a synonym for good or high-quality writing. Literature is the name that has been assigned to a certain form of writing published on paper, usually in the form of books, and which was constituted as a hegemonic element in the formation of canons throughout the modern period. If a form of writing isn't literary, it only means that it's the product of another historical era, and of both social and technological practices that are different from modernity's characteristic ones. It doesn't mean that its quality is greater or lesser, just that it responds to other conditions and expectations. As such, one must learn to read it.

Quality, defined as the set of properties that allow for something to be judged, isn't intrinsic to a text. Nothing, in fact, is intrinsic to a text. Nothing comes from a text without the reader invoking it. Better put: the only thing intrinsic to a text is its altered qualities. The text doesn't say and isn't said; the text gives itself, which means, in this case, that it gives itself over to being read. The text is produced where the *you* and the *I* emerge. The text exists when it's read, and it's there, in that critical, dynamic relationship, that its value exists. As Charles Bernstein argued with respect to the ever-controversial definition of what poetry is (or isn't) in a chapter of *The Attack of the Difficult Poems*, "[A] poem is any verbal construction that is designed as a poem. The designation of a verbal text as poetry cues a way of reading but does not address the work's quality."[10] The same could be said of literature. Only an essentialist view, and therefore an ahistorical one, would make "literary" synonymous with "quality." Only a conservative vision—that is, strongly tethered to the status quo and the hierarchies it entails—would seek the incessant repetition of a single means of producing textuality.

Why must every text be asked to present itself as if it had been written with the technology and behavioral standards of its nineteenth-century fellows? Because a small elite, fearing they will lose the holdings of power that fortify their aesthetics, continues to insist on it, bickering in the town square. For my part, I'm convinced that everyone has the right to keep writing her own version of the nineteenth-century if she wishes. What these neoconservatives can no longer do, though, is brandish a contingent, historical notion of literature as if it were a natural phenomenon, a feature intrinsic to all forms of writing. I'll remain an admirer of Dostoyevsky until the end of my days, and I'm sure that some of my work will continue to be produced on paper. But I'm equally excited about the possibilities for action at work in the task of writing today's technological transformations. The investigation of these possibilities, amid an active, clamorous community that has taken digital platforms by storm, is among the most interesting alternatives available right now. Because, among other reasons, there are no written rules; because we're making them up as we go. If, as Gertrude Stein once said, a writer's only obligation is to be a contemporary of her time, then exploring an era's different compositional forms is more a critical vocation than an opposition based on solely personal taste.

I'll cite what Kathy Acker said in "Writing, Identity, and Copyright in the Net Age" when I stress that "we need to regain some of the energy, as writers and as readers, that people have on the Internet when for the first time they e-mail, when they discover they can write anything, even to a stranger, even the most personal of matters. When they discover that strangers can communicate to each other."[11]

Writing against Violence

Make No Mistake: This Letter Is All Business

I'm thinking that I'm writing one of those letters people call "love" letters. But make no mistake: this letter is all business.

Letter from Juan Rulfo to Clara Aparicio, September 4, 1947

In an interview, Ricardo Piglia once expressed his interest in reconstructing the history of literature from a perspective that couldn't be farther from the thesis of artistic autonomy: by researching authors' different ways of earning a living. As I'd like to interpret it, his proposal, while unsurprising, was and remains a radical one. It's radical because, in asking how authors produce their lives, which is another way of asking about the conditions that allow or restrict the production of their texts, Piglia returns writing (or leads it, as the case may be) to the chameleonic, human, political realm of everyday practice. Defined this way, writing isn't the answer to a divine or inexplicable calling. It's not just a profession or a trade, but also, and above all, an embodied experience. Or, better put, an experiment that inevitably involves heart, brain, and hand; a matter more communal, and properly community-based, than merely individual. The question, which is innocent or obvious in appearance alone, directly attacks essentialist and romantic conceptions of the Author as an individual being, a being without adjectives. The question, which rightfully questions art's claim to autonomy, would have fascinated Tolstoy, Brecht, and Arlt (Piglia is right about this, too). I suspect that for those who define themselves or imagine themselves without context, without circumstances, and even without a body, there is no ruder or coarser or more violent question than "So what do you do for a living?" Which would naturally (if the natural even exists, of course) be followed by: what time do you get up in the morning? Do you have to leave your house to work? What kinds of people do you interact with in your everyday routine? Are these people different from you in terms of race, gender, and class? Do you go about your business in a hostile medium prone to self-criticism and often outright discouragement, or within a glass bell where praise and assurance are your daily bread? How much money do you make? Is it enough to feed you and your family? How many jobs do you have?

Indeed, there is a strange complicity between the Author and the History of Literature: that refusal to discuss the chronic materiality of existence. People talk, and at great length, especially in recent times and in the realm of fiction, about million-dollar advances or prizes with six-figure winnings. But they don't touch the subject of work: the work of writing. It's hardly unusual, especially in Latin America, to find writers opining on a vast array of topics in newspapers and TV programs. It's even increasingly common for journalists to ask and authors to respond, generously, to questions about their creative processes: what they're reading, the paragraphs they underline, how they keep their notes, whether they write by hand or type on a keyboard, a detailed account of their personal hang-ups, what their work space is like (complete with nearly always poetic descriptions of the light). Work, though, is the F-word of writing. Inspiration is fine, but money isn't. As if the very subject would soil them, almost no self-respecting author will stoop to addressing something so earthly and mundane, so constant and cold, as the coins she earns with the sweat off her brow. Allusions to awards or fellowships or some form of more-or-less remunerated work are more closely aligned with conceptions of prestige than explications of how they support themselves. In keeping silent, we writers aid and abet a narrative that systematically excludes any association between writing and work, writing and everyday processes of symbolic and material production. I, for one, make my living by teaching. Because Mexico's literary scene is cliquish, organized around meager state resources that lead to constant skirmishing, I decided that, if I really wanted to write, I was going to need a job. I knew, or at least imagined, that in a highly centralized country, where matters of gender and race matter a great deal, a woman from the border with no family connections in the capital city had slim chances of success in such an outlandish life choice: being a writer. Reading the biographies of women writers also convinced me that I'd need to become fully independent if I was to escape suicide or the early onset of madness. An academic degree from a US university has proven instrumental to my securing a job that basically pays my bills, allowing me to fulfill family responsibilities as a mostly functional human being. I've worked since I was eighteen years old, I will work through retirement age, and I will have published some books in between. Book royalties and public readings help but by no means suffice in themselves as a way for me to fully support myself and my family. Teaching, although it generally limits my writing time to the summer, has nonetheless granted me the stability I need to write.

There is considerable evidence that earthly coins and concrete foodstuffs are not a merely random or peripheral aspect of creative lives. Let's look at an example. Let's start, if only to start somewhere, with the great ones. Let's start with Juan Rulfo, for instance, the author of two paradigmatic books in the literary history of Latin America and the Spanish-speaking world overall: the novel *Pedro Páramo* (1955) and the short-story collection *El llano en llamas* (1953). Between 1944 and 1950, Juan Rulfo wrote eighty-one letters to Clara Aparicio, his formal girlfriend, later his betrothed, later his wife. The letters are intimate documents replete with sentimental turns in which (according to Alberto Vidal, who wrote the prologue to the collected letters[1]) one can glimpse the complex communicative vessels that navigate from "the raw material of life" to chit-chat about "literary occurrences" (my translation). These letters—and these are most definitely love letters—also contain a long list of *business*, which is what Rulfo seems to have called matters of everyday life, especially those associated with marriage.

Among the allusions to "tu muchacho," "mujercita," "chiquitina," and "Juan el tuyo" with which the missives start or end, a notion of companionship, even camaraderie, transpires. Rulfo is in love, and his intentions are shrouded in romantic language, but his views on marriage are less exalted and more practical. He portrays himself as the gleeful lover, but increasingly, as the courtship evolves, he also considers the daily responsibilities of shared life as a couple. As for the list of "business" he wishes to address and resolve in his letters, this includes succinct references to his job as a tire salesman; the request, which may or may not be granted, for a salary increase; and several mentions of the rage he feels on witnessing injustices in his workplace. They also, and perhaps especially, express the series of mundane concerns that hinge on the money he has. Or, to put it more accurately, the money he doesn't have: the rent on his apartment, his (desperate?) purchase of ten lottery tickets that earned him nothing, a request for a mythical list of essential kitchen appliances, a detailed description of Clara's bridal gown, even the happy news that "Aunt Lola has given us a Presto cooking pot."

I don't know whether a meticulous reading of these letters could help establish definitive links between that "raw material of life" and those "literary occurrences," and this isn't the kind of reading that interests me here.

But I do think, as Piglia does, that an exploration of how Rulfo supported himself would help us newly understand the material (and therefore political) strategies that our great experimentalist used in constructing his image. His image, that is, as a figure reluctant to complicate his life with (become an accomplice to?) the literary sphere of which he was otherwise, as a writer, part. Of course, I don't think the relationship between the two phenomena is so direct or so simple, so over-determined, or so much a product of a simplistic causal link. But in being indirect and complex, as such things tend to be, I'm interested in exploring it with all the rigor of someone investigating a mystery. For if even Rulfo is willing to admit that the missives he wrote were not strictly love but *business* letters, then we can demand that history, literature, canon-making endeavors, and the "autonomy" of art be just as open, if not necessarily honest, about it.

WRITING WORKSHOPS

Writing workshops are still a matter of heated debate in Mexico. While the practice of the *tertulia* or the non-academic writing class is widespread, both aspiring and established writers in Mexico have historically mistrusted the relationship between academia, with its formal training and vertical discipline, and creative classes, which they generally regard as opportunities to discuss ongoing work under the leadership of a practitioner. Countries like Colombia have been far more open to the emergence of writing classes in the university setting, developing entire MFA programs as early as in the 1990s. Argentina and Bolivia, among others, have followed suit. While the Autonomous University of Mexico City (UACM) launched an undergraduate major in creative writing not long ago, and while both private and public universities offer creative writing workshops as optional classes, an MFA as such, as a terminal academic degree, has yet to emerge. But has it?

It's an old question, and it will be asked as long as men and women talk with manuscripts tucked under their arms: is it possible to teach someone to write? US-American post-war culture responded with an enthusiastic and unequivocal yes, states Louis Menand in a 2009 *New Yorker* article. In "Show or Tell: Should Creative Writing Be Taught?," the Harvard professor and assiduous contributor both to the *New Yorker* and to the *New York Times Book Review* traverses the long, if modern, history of university creative writing programs in the US, both at the undergraduate and graduate level. And he reaches an optimistic verdict based on his personal experience: even though he never published a poem, his participation in one of these classes made him a participant "in this small and fragile enterprise, contemporary poetry," and he has felt its influence in all other decisions he's made throughout his life, as a reader and as a citizen. "I wouldn't trade it for anything,"[2] he says of his experience in one of those intensely personal, sometimes draining, and sometimes actually creative workshops now taught at many US-American universities. Junot Díaz, in his now famous essay "MFA vs. POC,"[3] tells quite a radically different story. This piece places emphasis on the racial and class imbalances—both in demographic and ideological terms—characterizing MFA culture in the early twenty-first-century US. Indeed, women and minorities of all kinds (including bilingual writers) have become increasingly vocal against the structural inadequacies, even complicities, of the MFA program as an institution in itself. Most don't call for its demise, arguing that spaces devoted to writing—and to the humanities in general—are diminishing dangerously in our neoliberal era. That said, there is a widespread and urgent call to redefine these programs according to the increasing gender and racial diversity of the contemporary US.

Menand takes the road most documented. Although writing-related classes have existed since 1897 (a class called Verse Making was taught at Iowa that year), the university concept of creative writing (generally known in Spanish as *creación literaria*) wasn't truly established until the 1920s. That was the inaugural year of the Bread Loaf Writer's Conference in Middlebury, where Robert Frost became the first writer-in-residence. In 1936, Iowa founded their now-famous writing workshops, granting a master's degree in fine arts to creative writers (which, as a terminal degree, is different from a Master of Science or Social Science degree) for the first time. After World War II, writers' programs only expanded. Johns Hopkins and Stanford gave the go-ahead to their own writing seminars in 1947. Cornell would do the same just a year later. The process multiplied in the 1960s, when more university professors were hired than ever before. By the start of the '80s, there were 69 creative writing programs in the US; the number has more recently risen to a shocking 822. Graduate programs (at the MA level, in this case) have grown at a comparable rate: the figure rose from 15 in 1975 to 153 by 2009.

As creative writing workshops have been strategically disseminated throughout the world, questions have emerged, especially in the case of Latin America, as to the true nature of their teachings. Thanks to Eric Bennet's *Workshops of the Empire: Stegner, Engel, and American Creative Writing during the Cold War* (2015) we know, for example, that the affirmation of a private over a community voice—so championed in creative writing classes throughout the US and abroad—had more to do with the cultural politics of the Cold War era than with aesthetic values per se. Better said: aesthetic battles closely affiliated with creative writing workshops were fought in a charged context, in which broader political issues pertaining to world dominance played fundamental roles. Indeed, as the US fought to gain ascendance as a world power, some astute intellectuals viewed literature and its teachings as a way to counteract left-wing ideologies they perceived as aligned, if not twinned, with communism.

While there are few rules, written or otherwise, on what a professor must teach in a writing class, Menand also pays attention to the relevant changes in emphasis registered throughout the twentieth century. There was "show vs. tell," which would become, more than a slogan, a true mantra of early twenty-first-century writing workshops; this trend was soon followed by the so-called "finding your voice" that so resounded in the 1960s and '70s. From then to now, it's clear that writing (its role and its place, its circle of influence, and its "technologies," its very instruction) has been transformed in accordance with broader social conversations. Few people who walk into a creative writing classroom set out to transmit "inspiration," but many believe it's possible to "practice" a trade. Will the concept of "show vs. tell"—the only apparently innocent, even self-evident rendering of the inner, private, personal voice—endure the trials of cross-cultural practice as writing workshops spread in settings, both within and outside the US, that place more value on community experiences and bonds? According to Namrata Podar, among other writers trained in transnational contexts and conversations, "show vs. tell" is more a "colonial relic" than an aesthetic value. Challenging the perceived objectivity of "show vs. tell," and exploring the political value of orality, Podar concludes that "orality here becomes a political stance, an ideological move reminding the reader over and again that what we consume as universal story craft, literary history, or aesthetic taste is anything but universal."[4]

The topic lends itself, as it should, to endless digs and interminable conversations. Unlike what has often been the case in countries such as Mexico, where most well-known writers have not (until now) attended MFA programs or even a writing workshop, an important battalion of contemporary US-American writers have graduated from university programs that may (or may not) have helped them develop their trade, but which evidently did not destroy their personal vocation or their talent. Menand reminds us that writers as heterogeneous as Raymond Carver, Joyce Carol Oates, and Ian McEwan emerged from university programs. Oates has a BA in creative writing from Syracuse, while Carver took classes at California State University, Chico, at Humboldt State College, and at Sacramento State College before becoming a Wallace Stegner Fellow at Stanford. McEwan studied with Malcolm Bradbury. More contemporary authors, like Rick Moody, Tama Janowitz, and Mona Simpson, attended creative writing classes almost at the same time in the Columbia graduate program; so did Michael Chabon, Alice Sebold, and Richard Ford at the University of California, Irvine. The growing presence of diverse writers, and of their culturally and politically shaped views on both craft and trade, have challenged the very basis of MFA programs and their goals. From the "we want to tell, not show," to the "we want to put an end to the privilege that allows the existence of MFAs in the first place," the battle for the creative writing class is on.

How this dilemma plays out in countries such as Mexico, or among Spanish-speaking writers working in the US, remains to be seen. As an aspiring writer in Mexico City, I hesitated to approach writing *tertulias* because they were mostly led by male writers with little, if any, teaching experience; besides, most didn't take women's writerly ambitions seriously. When I gathered enough courage to take a writing class, I was promptly expelled over a disagreement with the instructor over the relevance of Octavio Paz to Mexican culture. Are cafés and bohemian hangouts, then, actually more effective than the academic environment of an MFA program? The boys' club organized according to the mandate of masculinity, as Rita Segato would say? The living room salon for the wealthy and the white and the elite few? Is it really desirable for writing programs to exist in Mexican universities, or for MFA and PhD programs in creative writing in Spanish to multiply in the US—as they are doing as we speak?

Let's see.

RETHINKING CREATIVE WRITING WORKSHOPS

Maybe the question isn't actually "Is it possible to teach someone to write?" Perhaps the more relevant one would be "Is it possible or desirable to build sporadic communities in which the participants exchange and explore ways of reading and writing that interrogate reigning traditions?" The first question corresponds more or less to the metaphysical realm. The second question, though, addresses everyday, critical elements of both aesthetic and political practice. If we pose the first question as a kind of shortened version of the second, my answer is a resounding yes. Yes, it's possible. Yes, it's desirable.

Many of the creative writing workshops that have been operating in Mexico since the dawn of its modern era employ teaching methods that could be defined as vertical, authoritarian, and patriarchal. While exceptions to the rule do exist, most conventional literary circles worked according to what Rita Segato calls a pedagogy of cruelty:[5] a set of practices that teach its participants to transform what is alive, and its very vitality, into things, commodities. In such spaces, an authority figure—defined by experience, whether in the form of prestige or generational disparity—sets out to review and judge the "literary quality" of diverse manuscripts based on parameters deemed universal, if not transparent. In following these parameters, aspiring writers attend the workshop in order to subject themselves (I don't use the verb innocently) to external, allegedly objective judgment in order to "improve" their writing. "Improvement" here is loosely defined as a path of increasing perception, starting from the inferior stage of nonliterary writing to the superior stage of fully literary writing. To refine, perfect, purify. To hone. But don't these verbs, so often used to describe what happens in a creative writing workshop, give off a whiff of something sinister, even sadomasochistic? Something that evokes a broad range of authoritarian purges?

Perhaps we should start by ceasing to call them creative writing workshops and instead—in a more horizontal, more pluralistic, more twenty-first-century, less essentialist, less colonialist, less chauvinistic way—*community writing workshops*, replacing the individual voice so automatically ascribed to creativity with the enjambed presence of the community.

Perhaps we should consider the rash possibility that having written books, even good books, doesn't necessarily qualify their authors for participation in the delicate practice of critique and exchange that lies at the heart of workshop teaching. In this sense, perhaps it would be advisable to stop struggling against the professionalization of these practices and to start delving critically into imaginative, interactive teaching methods that enable a dynamic exploration of writing's different worlds. The lack of accountability that has so often passed for creative license in Mexico has led to flat-out abuse, curtailing the writing lives of innumerable women and other racially marginalized members of society. Maybe preparing future writers, and leaders of community writing workshops, in these alternative teaching methods could eventually help eliminate the abuses of power that have so frequently occurred in *tertulias* and literary gatherings under the guise of creative freedom. Perhaps, someday, it won't be unthinkable to call out those who promote competitiveness over solidarity, ruthlessness over thoroughness, authority over open deliberation, submissiveness over autonomy and outright rebellion.

Perhaps we should reflect on the fact that any writing workshop must also (necessarily, simultaneously) be a reading workshop. In this way, it must include discussion and meticulous critical debate over the diverse traditions that feed and have fed (sometimes in hardly harmonious ways) the history of the writings produced in specific places and at specific times. Perhaps it would be a good idea for community writing workshop attendees to consider that they're also and maybe especially attending them to read more widely, and more wildly. And to talk about a broad range of readings that question whatever parameters aspire to the status of universal transparency. Perhaps it would be a small but no less astounding victory if every participant left these workshops with the idea that no tradition is untouchable, much less unchangeable.

Perhaps it wouldn't be entirely crazy to remove the community writing workshop from the closed space of a classroom and take it instead to the sidewalk or the park or the plaza or the bus or the subway platform or any other space of social coexistence that illuminates the organic, necessary interaction between any form of writing and the community that contains it and gives it meaning. Perhaps it would be smart for a workshop participant not to believe that everything that happens within the verb "to write" happens in solitude or while sitting down or inside an ivory tower. Perhaps it wouldn't be wholly wrongheaded to remember and remind ourselves that, when we write, we are using a borrowed language. That is, a language that belongs to everyone and that we therefore reuse (with scare quotes or without them).

Perhaps it would be desirable to erase the verb *to subject*, which in Spanish also means "to submit to"—to erase even the echo of this word—from any expression that references participation in a workshop. The noun: judgment. The adjective: implacable. Perhaps there's no reason why verbs should sound like authority figures. Maybe they should emit resonances of the vital adventure that defines all kinds of writing: *to explore, to compare, to debate, to disrupt, to subvert, to invent, to propose, to go beyond.*

WORKSHOP AS A VERB

In *Letters to Alice: On First Reading Jane Austen*, the epistolary novel published by New Zealand writer Fay Weldon in 1984, a niece with writerly aspirations (the Alice of the title) is advised to think hard before submitting her manuscripts to other eyes. In the end (the book argues), the only word that really counted was the editor's—the figure who would decide to endorse a text, or not, for reasons that could be literary or otherwise. Everything else, says the narrator of the book and aunt of the main character, amounts to no more than either a well-intentioned idea-exchange or useless chit-chat among acquaintances.

It's a bit paradoxical to bring in Weldon's words right as I'm trying to make an argument in favor of the community of language-workers known as a creative writing workshop. It might be entirely outrageous to remind ourselves that, whatever we ultimately end up saying in these contorted, sometimes highly emotional, sometimes truly revelatory sessions, little or nothing will bear any weight against the last word: a publishing contract. But is it? Is the publishing contract and the editor's word the last word? Marguerite Duras believed that the book made the writer; there was no writer without a book. I am not about to argue that workshop members should dismiss the publication of their own work, but I'd like to say, however subtly, that the last word remains truly ours. It is up to us. Who, after all, has the right to call us writers? It took me years of practice and the publication of two books for me to spit out the phrase "I am a writer" in front of an immigration officer on the Tijuana-San Diego border. Nothing was the same after that. It can happen anywhere; all moments are propitious. What do we do when we read carefully, underlining sentences and scribbling notes in the margins, and then sit together around a table? Or when we walk around in groups, following prompts to activate our imaginations—to engage in a conversation, the conversation of our lives? In a world that values immediate gratification and profit at all costs, we gather together to pay close attention to each other's words and presence. We exchange informed remarks—consciously and in detail, rigorously and with compassion—on pieces of writing we are willing to show our faces for. Nothing more. But nothing less, either.

The true star of a literary workshop isn't the writing; it's the reading. Exposing the reader's role, her function as the true generator of texts, may be the most relevant and most productive element of a workshop. A student once asked me what I found most annoying about writing—or, better put, about writing-related stereotypes. I mulled this over for a while before I finally uttered the word: "inspiration." I have no problem admitting that certain moments lend themselves very nicely to bouts of writing. It's not an alien experience; it has happened to me. Even then, though, even in the midst of these glorious spells, I am still under the impression that, as a writer, I continue to make decisions about the materials I'm in contact with and moved by. The word "inspiration" prevents me (and I suspect it prevents others, too) from peering into the complex, multilayered, politically charged process we engage with in deciding which words come next, which ones should be removed, their rhythm, their spacing. A workshop offers time and space to enact these decisions, putting them out in the open for further consideration and discussion. Listening to the questions, qualms, and suggestions that others bring into play, after reading the work conscientiously, has allowed me to interrogate my instinctual reactions. In this sense, it has ultimately helped me *unlearn*. The operation of unlearning, which is revelatory at many levels, takes place out loud in the conversation that is the workshop; at the same time, it also takes place within ourselves, as we make space for deep listening as we work. This is what a workshop can achieve in its happiest moments.

It's not a matter of personal taste. It's not a discussion about what we like or dislike. I usually begin my workshops by reminding everyone that we are here to investigate how the engine works. The writing engine, I mean. Is it a use of intermittent punctuation that effectively reproduces the emotions at work in the plot? Is it the repetition of certain sounds, interwoven into a certain pattern, that produce a special rhythm when we read them? Is it a total absence of adjectives that, by stripping the nouns bare, brings the reader face-to-face with the tangibility of the world? Is it a reiterated *that*, reminding us that we're hearing something indirectly, in the low voice of a rumor or gossip? Often, the most difficult task is to plainly describe what we see in front of us. Such a description, while seemingly simple, engages complex epistemological and political operations we weigh into as we talk and listen.

The egos of writers and aspiring writers are legendary. In this sense, the most pertinent exercise for both may be the rewriting of texts offered up for review and critique. At the end of the day, is there any form of reading more radical and careful than rewriting itself? Limiting workshop comments to the writings being intervened-in, and omitting comments about the "original" texts used to make those interventions, reminds us that all writing is intervened writing. That all writing is, in fact, re-writing. It also reminds us that, whether we realize it or not, we're always writing in collaboration with others. Writing is not an isolated practice; it's a collective and collaborative endeavor. It is shared time. It is community in the making. Commenting on the intervention as if it were "the original," trying to discover the rules of both writing practices without being entirely sure what belongs to whom, also tends to remind us that our colleague—that guy, the one sitting beside me as my neighbor, my fellow—is above all a reader. A reader of books, yes, but also of beings, processes, souls.

It shouldn't come as a surprise that such workshops may generate alert, critical, uneasy, sometimes playful communities of people who long to experience more, not less, in language and in life, within the walls of the classroom and beyond them, in community work. Dive in. Chime in. Get lost. Interrupt. Pause. Pay attention. Break out. My sense is that then, and only then, are we truly writing. And in these circumstances, regardless of what Weldon's Alice was told, we have the last word.

READING LIKE A WRITER

The question "What did you think of the book (story) (poem)?" tends to be answered with a declaration comprising, mostly, the language of personal taste. *I like the book. I don't like the poem.* Depending on the parties involved, these basic replies may be followed (or not) with a similarly personal explanation. *I like the book because it reminds me of. I don't like the poem because it made me feel like. I like the story because I identified with. I don't like the novel because I don't think it's realistic that.* The problem with such declarations, which at first glance seem not only normal but even expected, is that they are ultimately a shortcut or a trap. There is a long intellectual process hidden (intentionally or otherwise) above or below each *I like it / I don't like it*—a process that can easily encompass, among many other elements, attitudes about language; notions of what is literary; speculations on the "appropriate" relationship between the literary and the social; ideas about what books should do with readers and the world; prejudices against writing by women or Black or Latinx writers and their literary excentric traditions. If we add the fact that it's often easy to replace *I like* with *This is good* or *This is high quality*, then we can better understand the danger of providing apparently simple answers to apparently innocent questions.

An answer/shortcut may be useful, it's true, if the matter at hand is a brief book recommendation or a friendly chat about the weather or the need to rid yourself of someone's company with a certain surgical swiftness. But if what's at stake is a critical analysis of a text or the attentive gaze of a reader who intends to write or is already writing, I very much fear that an *I like it / I don't like it* doesn't do much good. What's more: I'm afraid that an *I like it / I don't like it* amounts to nothing more than a way to keep from identifying the politics of the text—the set of historically determined and culturally relevant writing strategies at work in it. I'm afraid, then, that the *I like it / I don't like it* is a ruse directed primarily at the ego (the writer's and the reader's) in a way that avoids the truly relevant question: how was this text written? How does it work? Or, failing this, how doesn't it work?

Why is it common to ask "How was this made?" of a photograph or an installation, but not of a text? Because it's still commonly believed that a text is the result of divine or at least superhuman intervention, and that its only goal (particularly in the context of fiction) is to tell stories according to a realist narrative pact. What is it we're saying about writing, by contrast, when we ask "How was this written?"? We're saying that a text wasn't drawn from various inspirations or attempts to recreate *x* or *y* notion of reality, but rather that it was built out of the decisions we make—consciously and unconsciously—with respect to a language that does not belong to us. A language we have borrowed from a community of practitioners to whom we are now forever related, even indebted. Indeed, we are saying openly, unabashedly, that we are in debt. We owe. We're also saying that the multiple effects writing can provoke—whether strictly psychological or also aesthetic and even political—are intimately connected to the effectiveness, or lack thereof, of these decisions. We're saying that a text is a process of textual (production) and not a mechanism of (personal) expression. We're saying that, as in every human act, every writing-related decision is drawn from specific (that is to say, historical) traditions of writing that we would do well to learn more about, both as writers and as readers—so that we can confirm them or subvert them or do something halfway between the two. We're saying that the text, like reality itself, can always be something else, or is always on the verge of being something else. We're saying so many things!

Once critics become less interested in their personal preferences and more interested in the concrete material context, both internal and external, of each text, perhaps they'll regain the attention, the curiosity of those readers who are intrigued, still!, by the mysterious mechanisms of things. That heart. That beat.

TEXTUAL DATES

Not long ago, and without giving it much thought, I accepted an invitation to visit a high school in Mexico. As far as I could tell at the time, it was a normal invitation. Someone working in an institution is responsible for encouraging the practice of reading, and that someone immediately thinks to invite some author, whose presence will somehow contribute to the cause. The rest, as I understand it, goes more or less like this: the someone looks up an email address or phone number in an agenda, or contacts another someone who has told her she has the information at hand. In this case, this particular contact was a friend of mine from college, someone

I think highly of, which is why I accepted the invitation without paying much attention either to the conditions of the agreement or to the address of the school.

When I got up to speed, I found myself in Querétaro, facing a group of about fifty students whose teenage laps held copies of my short story collection *Ningún reloj cuenta esto*. This was the first hint that something strange was happening. Guided by the three or four teachers accompanying us in the room, the students, who were getting ready for Saint Patrick's Day festivities (this was, indeed, an Irish high school in the middle of Mexico), started asking questions, shyly at first and then with outright brazenness. "I want to know," said one student, "what the color blue means on page 43." "The end of the fourth story," said another, "really makes me mad." "I'm from Venezuela," another was compelled to say, "and I want you to know that what the first story says is totally true." "I wonder," another declared, "if any of your characters would ever dare to defend society's real values." I replied, with considerable frankness, that I didn't have the slightest idea what the color blue was doing on page 43 (and also, could you remind me what that story is about?), that they should explain their conception of "values," and that we could think, all of us together, about what an ending is really made of. And as I did so, I realized—with true astonishment, with measureless pleasure—that I was participating in an informed, attentive, certainly unexpected dialogue. This dialogue wasn't about the author and her world, about her likes and dislikes, about her genius, about how inexplicable it all is. It was, rather, a conversation about writing, about how a text is made and how it evolves. I'd gone there, I then understood, in order to meet with some young readers so we could talk about a fistful of words committed to paper. In Spanish, *cita* is a word able to express both a citation and a date. Words I had written, words I was willing to show my face for, were quoted here, before my very ears, and as the dialogue continued, I realized those words had become the site of an encounter. Love was in the air!

Moments later, when I realized that the whole effort of rallying teachers and bringing them the books and contacting the author of the book and buying the books and having them sent all the way from Mexico City (that's what we have to do, those of us who live elsewhere in this highly centralized country; we have to order them all the way from Mexico City) and then distributing them to the selected classrooms, was entirely the brainchild of a particular father (a recently converted reader, to be more precise), I felt a series of contradictory feelings I still can't describe. Out of the impossibility of describing it, I suppose, the project I'm about to discuss was born.

Citas Textuales (meaning, then, both textual citations and textual dates) is an initiative designed to pool the efforts of high school and college-level teachers of literature and other likeminded disciplines, book authors, cultural promoters, publishers, and bookstores in holding informed, dynamic gatherings between writers and readers. The idea is that for every invitation to participate in panels, talks, and all manner of dialogues (and even without them), the participants also organize a gathering with at least one group of students. All of this organization needs to happen far enough in advance for the teacher to assign the selected author's book (a couple months before the semester begins, or before the start of whatever unit is used to organize the school calendar) and for the publisher to distribute the books, applying the legal discounts available. The idea is that teachers, teachers committed to encouraging the practice of reading, will guide their students along the paths of the text. And that this rich interaction will spark the kinds of questions that can serve, once the author is physically present in the classroom, as the subject or pretext for a conversation. In short, the idea is to encourage reading by reading.

This is the type of initiative I tend to come up with only to confirm, and fast, that it's exhausting or insanely expensive or otherwise impossible. Different versions of Citas Textuales are carried out all the time, with order and flare, by institutions with more resources or more infrastructure. But in places where financial resources are scarce, or where the commitment to reading, or the humanities in general, is constantly under siege, Citas Textuales, whatever form they may take, don't come about easily. I wouldn't be recounting all of this here if the proverbial day hadn't come: the day I was invited by the press at the Universidad Veracruzana to participate in a panel as part of the annual book fair held in Xalapa. I wouldn't describe all of this if—doubting myself a little, but telling myself that courtesy doesn't do away with courage—I hadn't told Cecilia del Palacio, the director of the UV press, about this idea. And, moreover, that I also asked her institution support the project. I wouldn't say anything at all, you see, but she agreed. And then others did, too, with equal enthusiasm: cultural managers, literary program coordinators, and university professors all joined in. Writers have also risen to the occasion: Rosa Beltrán and Ana Clavel, two essential authors in contemporary Mexican literature, are now part of Citas Textuales. This little text, then, is here as an invitation for others to channel the project's open, playful spirit. I hope we'll all arrive on time (perfume is optional) to our next Cita Textual.

CHRONICLE OF A FIRST DATE

I'd taught two morning classes, one at 7:30 and another at 10:30. I'd also attended at least two meetings. In the middle of it all, I'd forgotten to eat lunch again. I reached the airport to take a 4:00 p.m. flight, which was delayed, as usual. I took advantage of the wait to start reading Ian McEwan's *On Chesil Beach*. One of those insipid industrial snacks and a cup of water kept my stomach entertained as the plane landed in Monterrey a little after 6 p.m. The city they call Sultan of the North. Ninety-seven degrees in the shade. The occasion, the first Cita Textual, was at 7:00 p.m. in the meeting room of the Antiguo Palacio Federal, the old federal palace.

That evening, I found myself in the typical condition of someone getting ready for a first date: excited, certainly, with the unresolved pleasure that sometimes accompanies risk-taking, but also obstinately fearful that, when all was said and done, I wouldn't like the prospect. Or, worse yet, that the conversation would be bland. Or the very worst: that whatever happened during the encounter would yield nothing more, once again, than boredom. My emotions, accumulated and contradictory, were numerous. And all of them, under a light that looked fully orange in its evening radiance, led me directly from the airport to the meeting place in a state of fatigue that often makes me a little delirious.

I wouldn't be writing this if the exchange that occurred at the first Cita Textual hadn't been dynamic, intimate, compelling. I wouldn't be writing now if I weren't willing to do it again.

The readers of my book *La cresta de Ilión* (recently translated into English as *The Iliac Crest*) were already there, seated around a set of tables arranged in a U-format. After the obligatory greetings, we began—like people who already know each other but haven't yet had the chance to chat—a profoundly natural conversation that ran over the hour-limit we'd set. There was some of everything. Non-rhetorical questions and sensible comments. From "How does this work?" to "So you're saying that you don't know what *x* means, either (in which *x* could be a color or a gesture or an unfamiliar language)?" Conspiratorial expressions all around. Focused more on the *how* or the *why* than on the *I like this / I don't like this*, the conversation advanced as if along a dirt road: with ups and downs, stumbles, sudden lurches. What I mean to say was: it was something real. Something human that arose around a book that had been read rigorously and in depth.

Both honest and polite, the Monterrey readers who attended that first gathering questioned, for example, how certain characters in the novel had been constructed: "Can a doctor talk like a writer? Is this really a man? Do women really act this way?" Among other things, these questions invited me to explicitly reflect on many notions of identity, about how it flows, about its blurry limits—notions that allowed me to compose a strange world of men who seem like women who seem like men. Or doctors who can talk, as Deleuze said, like dogs. From there, it wasn't long before we transitioned into remarks on the setting and an inevitable dialogue about the work of the Zacatecas-born writer Amparo Dávila (one or more of the novel's characters respond to this name). It wasn't long, either, before we were all reflecting on the function of the author. Which, more than disappearing, or dying (as a certain school of late twentieth-century thought had argued; I discuss this in the chapter on "Undead Authors"), opens up to accept the activity of the reader as an inevitable figure. The reader, after all, writes her own book as she reads.

If this is true, I told them in an attempt at winding down, then my job as a writer of books, as a writer of books that still respond to the name "novel" in the early twenty-first century, is to critically consider ("disrupt" is another way to say the same thing) each and every element that we *naturally* associate with novels. (This naturalness must be italicized.) In the first place, subverting the function of the author and the narrator and the characters and the sense of authenticity, among many other elements, is and will always be the novel's fundamental task. We all tell stories. The novelist (by contrast, or in addition) composes structures inside which, with the greater or lesser weight of a particular story, the aforementioned disruption takes place: a reader becomes the author of her own book. The only real character, the character who unfolds into all the different characters in a novel, is language. And in my experience, that—not the surprise or intrigue of a story—is what has led me to keep talking, sometimes for entire years, with a book. Celebrating, always in my own way, countless textual citations.

As I've said, I was tired. And I've said, it was the type of tiredness that generally makes me delirious. Now, a couple days after the experience, I think that if the depletion and the delirium had anything to do with this strange feeling of having been utterly *there*, wholly present in body and soul, then I'll take it as a lesson: I'll never show up to any date, textual or otherwise, first or last, without being that exhausted. In any case, the pulse of this most intimate conversation—which is often the conversation a book ends with—was felt thanks to the enthusiasm and efforts of Jaime Villarreal, Gabriela Torres, Víctor Barrera, Ximena Peredo, and Mario Cantú. I no longer remember the names of each and every reader who so kindly dedicated two hours of their Thursday to talk about a book in a meeting room in an old federal building, but this little chronicle, which is really a hug, is for them.

NONREQUIRED READINGS

These essays don't seek to applaud everything done (or not done) in San Francisco by the artist-couple comprising Dave Eggers and Vendela Vida, but it's difficult not to say anything at all about the book collection *The Best American Nonrequired Readings*. Edited by Eggers for some years now, Houghton Mifflin Harcourt publishes this collection in its highly prestigious, highly canonical *The Best American Series*, which includes volumes of the best short stories, the best travel writing, and work in other genres.

In opposition to the perspectives that privilege "the best" over "what I like most," this anthology of nonrequired readings isn't directed by experts in the field. What I mean to say is, there isn't some Authorized Voice (the use of the capital letters and the singular is intentional) that solemnly addresses posterity in a low voice, with the bad breath of someone who hasn't brushed his teeth in a long time, and then spits us a sermon with his fingers dramatically splayed across our foreheads. What there is, and obviously so, are the fresh, hedonistic readings of a group of middle and high school students who live and gather at least once a week in the Bay Area, specifically at the writing center called 826 Valencia. Behind all this, then, there is no expert beyond the reader, who is someone still moved by curiosity rather than hierarchy, by pleasure rather than submission. The reader, in short, for whom what is interesting matters more than what is prominent.

Everything has a place in this Borges-esque, non-classifying gaze: short stories, essays, comics, long-form journalism, any combination of the above. The only requirement, says editor Eggers in the prologue, is that the selections must be "engaging, somewhat direct in approach, have something to say about the world at the moment, and that they not be too long or about the relationship problems of wealthy people in Manhattan."[6] With this in mind, a twelve-student committee sets out to read, year after year, all the magazines, supplements, or publications-at-large that cross their path, neither writing off "better-known examples" nor limiting themselves to such texts. In this way, the 2005 volume, which is the one I have in front of me right now, includes texts originally published in the *New Yorker* ("Hell-Heaven," by the highly renowned Jhumpa Lahiri, who won the Pulitzer in 1999 for *Interpreter of Maladies*). But it also includes texts that first appeared in *McSweeney's* ("The Death of Mustango Salvaje," by Jessica Anthony, who had previously published only in a handful of magazines, but who was later anthologized in *Best New American Voices of 2006*), or in *Other Voices* ("Five Forgotten Instincts," by Dan Chaon, a Cleveland-based writer whom I will certainly be following from now on. Has anyone read *You Remind Me of Me*, published by Ballantine Books in 2004?). Incidentally, a story by

Daniel Alarcón, a Peruvian-born, Oakland-based writer who was awarded a Guggenheim Fellowship in 2008, is included here. This kind of eccentric, anti-hierarchical reading exercise ultimately yields an unprecedented mosaic of the writing produced in our northern neighbor. There are "indispensable" names that don't appear in the index for this reason alone, and other names still awaiting wider reader recognition.

These aren't the Father's readings, but rather the readings of numerous children (and grandchildren of all genders). Radial readings more than vertical ones. Centrifugal readings more than centripetal ones. This dedicated group of young men and women (and there are many of the second in this guild) offers us both an enjoyable and a rigorous approach to the texts being written in the US during a given year. This is how we come to encounter a highly politicized text by Tish Durkin, the journalist who lived in Baghdad from April 2003 to September 2004. Here, a thirty-six-year-old US-American soldier exclaims, from his privileged observation spot inside an army tank, "The wolf is obviously me. . . . The man in the eyeball is Evil." Or in a story by Lauren Weedman, based on a trivial anecdote, who manages to produce the kind of vulnerability and paranoia propelling a woman who not only reads her lover's diary but also keeps one of her own—to record what she gleans by snooping. Openly social or painfully intimate, these texts portray a country in constant struggle with itself.

Readers who read for pleasure, who hunt for the unsanctified, who don't worry about whether what they're reading is or isn't part of the canon or if the author they're getting to know has sold x or y number of books or is listed in the top five of x or y generation, will surely spend many fruitful hours exploring its pages. And might something interesting happen in Mexico, I wonder, if at least one of the many anthologies produced there every year were directed by a group of high school readers/students?

#CUENTWITOS

On May 20, as the final short fiction event of the series I curated for the 2010 Feria de León (an annual book fair held in the Mexican state of Guanajuato), I included a panel of *cuentuiteros* (short-story-tweeters). The term refers, of course, to people who write 140-character texts known as tweets (a tweet was still capped at 140 characters at that point). The original idea was to gather four or five Twitter users together in real time. After a brief presentation on each one's relationship to Twitter, there would be a live writing session. In this way, the idea wasn't to spend much time expounding on the subject, but rather to get down to business and spend an hour building a collective TL.

Both @isaimoreno and @Orfa, emerging writers with a couple of books under their belts, reacted with enthusiasm. @diamandina, one of the most sophisticated Twitter users on any TL (and whose words, besides a couple of stories, haven't yet experienced the stability of paper), also gamely joined the event. @PaolaTinoco served as moderator, but her true Twittery nature meant that she couldn't help but participate in the session. For my part, I resolved to rise to the occasion: I kept tweeting, too. All of our efforts were recorded on the two screens flanking the rectangular table. There, the TL hastily descended, our tweets appearing and disappearing in situ.

Perhaps it's the collective stamp of all Twitteresque activity, or an intrepid zeal for throwing parties at the slightest provocation, but we all decided it would be perfectly natural to invite the Twitter community to join us from cyberspace. To this end, we created the hashtag #cuentwitos (little tweet-stories). In this way, anyone who wished to chime in with a text under 140 characters could do so, wherever she happened to be. Some, we quickly realized, were tweeting from inside the very same room where the live session was held. But others (like Alberto Chimal, an established writer, almost legendary workshop teacher, and well-known Twitter user) did so from Mexico City, while others sent in their texts from beyond Mexican borders. Toward the end of the session—when, in Isaí Moreno's words, the process had run away from us completely—we were even receiving stories in Arabic. The #cuentwitos initiative had been a resounding success. And as if we lacked for evidence, we soon noticed that our hashtag, created in the provincial city of León, had become a national trending topic. For hours, as evidenced by its position between #jefediego (a Mexican politician affiliated with the PAN party) and #santosvstoluca (rival Mexican soccer teams), it was neck and neck with other social interest issues. That's when I stopped in my tracks. Since when have writing and professional soccer ever actually competed with each other? In what other field has writing ever shared popularity credits with gossip news?

I return here to the renowned South American theorist Josefina Ludmer, who says that post-autonomous writings are those which flee the ruses and confines of the literary and focus instead on producing the present. From César Aira to Bruno Morales, from Fabián Casas to María Sonia Cristoff, Ludmer has taken up the task of locating authors for whom everything economic is cultural and vice-versa. In addition, these writings are based on the fact (or, better put, confirm the fact) that reality is already fiction in itself, and that fiction is our everyday reality. If all of this is true, and I'm very tempted to believe that it is, the phenomenon that occurred in response to the hashtag #cuentwitos is more serious than we thought.

According to Twitter's own statistics, for quite a few hours on that day, May 20, 0.02 percent of tweet-production all over the world was dedicated to the production of writing. This figure may seem insignificant at first glance. But it isn't, if we consider that an average of fifty million tweets were being produced every day. All signs seem to show that, contrary to the scandalous rumors heralding the end of books and writing, this new generation of Digital Natives (DNs) is as or more interested in writing than their Nondigital counterparts. Certainly, the statistics clarify that what the DNs are interested in, especially Twitter users, are forms of writing that escape the straitjacket of literary autonomy. As argued by Paula Sibilia, another acclaimed Argentine theorist, participants in public and collective writings, both in electronic logs and in microblogs, privilege outwardly directed forms of the *I*, thus paving the way for writings that combine auto-fiction and nonfiction.[7] Whatever nickname sticks, whether post-autonomous or nonfiction, these writings invoke forms of reading that circumvent the sieve of what has heretofore been known and valued as "the literary."

The outpouring of responses to the hashtag #cuentwitos—which, as I've already said, ran away from us entirely—can be read as an intriguing sign of the challenges and characteristics that define writing today. Those interested in producing readers and fomenting contemporary forms of popular culture can't overlook the fact that, amid the decline of "literary" cultural capital, the practice of collective and technological writings is demanding attention and support. Moreover, the practice is thriving. Cultural institutions responsible for these processes would do well to turn their gaze toward twenty-first-century screens and thus engage with the sensibilities, practices, and visions that grant meaning to writing in the here and now.

On Alert

Writing in Spanish in the United States Today

One of the first acts of Donald Trump's presidency was to erase the Spanish text from the official White House website. It was not, as some explained at the time, a transitory measure to allow the administration to improve the information contained on the site, but a true declaration of principles. Erasure is the name of the game: pretending that more than fifty million Spanish-speakers do not live and work in the United States, the country with the second-most Spanish-speakers in the world (only after Mexico). Those who still hoped that the nationalist bravado that characterized Trump's campaign would be transformed, once he was president, into more moderate methods, understood then that the true winter had barely begun. Trump's attacks against immigrants, especially against poor and dark-skinned immigrants from Latin America and, among them, primarily those from Mexico, are the stamp of an agenda that promises to return white and homogenous greatness to the United States. Such nostalgia for a world that never existed in this nation of migrants has led hundreds of thousands to take part in insane chants that have called for the construction of great border walls, the proliferation of guns in our daily lives, and the punishment of diversity and difference. Perhaps it wasn't a mere coincidence, then, that we inaugurated the PhD in Creative Writing in Spanish at the University of Houston in the fall semester of 2017, just months after Trump took power. Creative writing programs in the United States have long been present and their history is well documented. They began at the start of the twentieth century and were consolidated in the sixties with the proliferation of what Eric Bennett calls "workshops of empire" when, within the context of the Cold War, the teaching of creative writing played an important role in the dissemination of North American values around the globe.[1] While the emergence of creative writing programs in Spanish is more recent, it is important to keep in mind the fundamental presence of the Master of Fine Arts (MFA) Program in Bilingual Creative Writing at the University of Texas at El Paso, directed until quite recently by Mexican writer Luis Arturo Ramos, as well as the emergence of programs housed at the University of Iowa (with the Spanish poet Ana Merino in charge) and at New York University (with writers such as Lila Zemborain, Sergio Chejec, and Diamela Eltit among the faculty). It is not an exaggeration to claim that launching a program in creative writing in Spanish at the doctoral level precisely in these times is an act of linguistic activism, fair and square. Corporate takeovers and neoliberal governments around the world have played major roles in defunding public education. Public universities, especially those designated as Hispanic Serving Institutions, remain the last bastion in the struggle for equal educational access. It is not a coincidence that this initiative has cohered on one of the most diverse campuses in the nation, located, moreover, in one of the most cosmopolitan cities in the United States. The PhD in Creative Writing in Spanish not only brings writing to the heart of North American academia but also its traditions of resistance, its unredeemed plurality, its multiple accents, its continuous vociferation. It arrives, I mean, not so much to adapt itself to the established rules, but to contribute its vision and its pedagogies, its objectives, and its modes of quotidian practices. Fred Moten and Stefano Harney have already spoken about the presence of the *undercommons* in the university— those maroon communities that, far from adapting to university debt, to university authority, to the verticality of the university, employ their time and their multiple sets of knowledge to open doors and windows.[2] This is how the gust of our present blows in through the windows. This is how our contemporaneity finds its place in our rooms. It is a long story, however. And it is affected by current demographic changes in the United States of late, as well as by the increase in institutions of higher learning where Spanish, while proudly remaining a language of labor, is also used as a language of critical inquiry and creation. The growing migration of Latin American writers to the United States at the turn of the twenty-first century has played an important role in this process as well. Here, I am less interested in the identity politics involved in these questions—do those who write in Spanish in the United States become "American," "Mexican-American," "Latin" writers?—and more in the politics of writing, which are politics surrounding the materiality of language, the conditions under which Spanish-language writings are produced and distributed in the United States.[3] I'm interested, then, in its potential.

It is clear that when *McOndo* and *Se habla español: Voces latinas en Estados Unidos* were published in 1996 and 2000, respectively, these controversial anthologies reflected the rising presence of the United States in the imaginary of Latin American writers.[4] But, as Diana Palaversich notes in her discussion of these books, "out of the thirty-six voices included in [*McOndo*], only fourteen are Latino voices, the other twenty-two belong to authors that live in Latin America, the vast majority of which have never lived in the northern country."[5] Indeed, much in the manner of Boom writers, whom at least McOndistas perceived as the canonical enemy they vowed to uproot and replace, some of these authors developed a fragile or intermittent relationship with the United States, giving talks here and there or teaching entire semesters at various universities but seldom establishing themselves in the United States. Those were the privileged Latin American professors who would teach class but as visiting professors rarely had to attend committee meetings or carry out the enormous—though sometimes invisible—work that keeps the university running. The panorama could not look more different only sixteen years later. Pushed by the economic crisis in Spain (a highly regarded migratory route for many Latin American writers throughout the twentieth century) and lured by the economic opportunities offered by departments of Hispanic studies (which do not require authors to speak English) in the United States, many writers from Latin America managed to find a place to live and a place to write in this country, and they continued their writing careers, often in Spanish and in close conversation with Latin American traditions. Gustavo Sáinz and Jorge Aguilar Mora are among those who crossed the border to live and work in US universities for stretches of time back in the 1970s, constituting an early generation of "American" writers born in Mexico while living and producing in the United States.[6] But teaching positions in departments of literature or Spanish would not have been enough to steadily attract the attention of writers from Latin America for long periods of time. These writers—most of them children of the middle class—not only needed a place to live and work, but also a context, an atmosphere conducive to writing, and writing in Spanish at that, in conditions they had to perceive as safe and advantageous compared to what they left behind. Two intertwined processes emerged in the early twenty-first century: on the one hand, the already mentioned emergence of MFA programs in creative writing in Spanish and, on the other hand, and quite simultaneously, the increasing awareness in the literary field that writing and academia were not necessarily opposing arenas, but most surely complementary ones. Years of professionalization promoted by the State (as in the case of Mexico, where grants and publication support has fueled much of the writing pouring out of the country in recent years) or by the market (as in Spain, where large publishing houses and literary agencies took root in the middle of the twentieth century) were instrumental in weakening the romantic belief that writers—true writers—lived outside of academia, and society altogether. How many ways do we have of saying that *the ivory tower of the tormented genius* has come to an end?

A new generation of migrating writers from Latin America—which includes but is not limited to Edmundo Paz Soldán, Yuri Herrera, Valeria Luiselli, Lina Meruane, Pedro Ángel Palou, Álvaro Enrigue, Rodrigo Hasbún, Claudia Salzar, Carlos Yushimito, Carmen Boullosa—had published important books before establishing themselves in California, New Orleans, or New York, but the majority of their recent work has been envisaged and developed while living and working in the United States. While some critics have easily labeled, and often dismissed, the writing experience of these migrating Latin American writers in the United States as evidence of the globalization's overwhelming scope, I am interested in framing this experience within what Spivak called planetarity: a concept that, instead of emphasizing the circulation of commodities and capital, underlines the experiences of bodies when they come into contact—tense, volatile, dynamic—with a globe in which nature and culture are inextricably linked.[7] Indeed, much can be gained by replacing the "global agent" of a seemingly smooth capitalist world with a "planetary subject" able to embrace a sense of alterity as "continuously derived from us." For, as Spivak argued, "alterity is not our dialectic negation, it contains us as much as it flings us away."[8] The crossing of planetary borders between Latin America and the United States involves a complex geopolitical operation between coloniality and its limits. As many immigrants to the United States coming from peripheral areas of the world that are rich in natural resources and heavy on labor exploitation know, speaking/writing in Spanish—a language perceived by many in the United States as belonging to labor and not necessarily to literary artistry or creation—is not so simple. Migrating Latin American authors face difficult dilemmas with what Silvia Rivera Cusicanqui has called a ch'ixi epistemology: "an awareness of the border or a border consciousness . . . a contact zone that allows us to live inside and outside of the capitalist machine, using and simultaneously demolishing the instrumental reason born from its very entrails."[9] In her analysis of contemporary Aymara culture within the larger context of capitalist exploitation in Bolivia and Latin America at large, Cusicanqui has placed special emphasis on the various ways in which "semiotic movers" generate "methods of translation and integration of present and future entities." She shows, above all, a special interest in the production of "ch'ixi languages, polluted and tainted, an aymarized Spanish that allows a critical dialogue with state development and initiatives for the rural world."[10] Just as Guaman Poma de Ayala wrote to the king of Spain in Spanish, these migrating Latin American writers write both in Spanish and English with the "vigilant colonial ego" in check, while allowing their writing to embrace a plethora of "social, vital, and even cosmic elements able to articulate what words cannot in a society of colonial silences."[11]

Marjorie Perloff has called the practice of incorporating foreign words or syntax into texts that are otherwise written in conventional English exophonic writing.[12] Her examples go as far back as T. S. Elliot and Ezra Pound and extend to include recent works by Caroline Bergvall, the Norwegian-French writer and artist, or Yoko Tawada, the Japanese-born novelist who also writes in German. Eschewing the political and colonial contexts in which these exchanges take place and limiting her analysis to the formal implications of these practices, Perloff undercuts the political dimension of those who write, to put it in Cusicanqui's terms, from "both inside and outside of the capitalist machine . . . using and simultaneously demolishing the instrumental reason" and its many languages. Mixe linguist Yásnaya Aguilar has persuasively argued that the only difference between indigenous and other languages in the Americas is that the former ones live and manage to thrive without the backing of a State—or even in spite of having one working against them. They are languages without a standing army. Spanish, the language imposed by the conquest and an experience of colonization that lasted at least three hundred years, is indeed a language with a State and an army within the territories we know as Latin America (with the clear exception of Brazil and a few other countries). Yet, once Spanish crosses one of the most powerful and dramatic borders of our globalized world on the backs and in the mouths of undocumented migrants, it too becomes a language without a State and without an army. A ch'ixi language. A ch'ixi consciousness embodied in polluted and tainted words, in grammatical constructions and peculiar syntax that, immediately, go on to occupy the lowest rung among the hierarchies of languages protected by the North American State. And we have certainly felt this situation worsen in the Trump era. Resulting from both migratory experiences and a contested context in which struggles over colonization takes prominence, ch'ixi languages cannot simply be described as a mere blend or fusion of tongues. It is the use of *Spanglish* that characterized some of Chicana literature, for example. But it is also more. Always aware of the many layers of the colonial experience, each ch'ixi enunciation would look for ways to both "use and demolish" the very context out of which it emerges.

In the essay "The '90s," poet Juliana Spahr noted the surge among contemporary bilingual or multilingual writers to move away from standard English—
less to address their own identity than to discuss the histories of English and
English-language colonialism both within the United States and around the
world.[13] Paying attention to works written in pidgins or creoles, and linking
this movement to "the disquieting linguistic disorientation of immigration,"
Spahr argued that such a move went hand in hand with a growing critical
stand against globalization and in favor of migrant and indigenous rights.
As Chicanxs writers have done and continue to do, authors interested in
tearing up English-language grammar did so both literally and metaphori-
cally. "But what I have come to see is that, by the end of the century," she
says, "while many writers continue to bring other languages into their English, they do this less to talk about their personal identity and more to talk
about English and its histories.[14]

There has never been a better time—even a more urgent time—to talk
about Spanish and its many histories, its many histories in/with the United
States, and its many histories with/within English. Written in Spanish in an
English-speaking context—either with or against, for or below—the works
of these migrating Latin American writers contain traces, material marks,
dents of sorts, of the myriad strategies of opposition, adaptation, in short,
negotiation in which willingly or unwillingly, consciously or unconsciously,
these writers participate. For while writers are, or should be, in control of
their tools, they are not expected to be fully aware, much less in control of,
the materials with which they work. Reading this kind of writing in all its
complexity might require us to move well beyond the identity matrix that
has dominated the literary field—and, more specifically, the Latin American literary field of study in the United States—to fully grapple with "what
exceeds from this subjective capture and from where it exceeds" in writings
written in Spanish that emerge from within the United States.[15] With a rising number of translations from Spanish into English (a current movement
notably led by female writers and female translators) and a good number of
Spanish-speaking authors writing both in English and in Spanish (which
include but are not limited to Daniel Alarcón, Santiago Vaquera-Vásquez,
Maura Javier Cárdenas and, more recently, Valeria Luiselli and Pola Oloixa-
rac, writing directly in English) it is possible that these planetary authors
who write in ch'ixi languages might teach us something about what it is
like to live both inside and outside the beast. They, in other words, might
teach us something about the exercise of writing as a critical practice and
as a state of alertness.

Let's Be Stubborn

José Emilio Pacheco, Elena Poniatowska, Fernando del Paso, Juan Villoro—these recipients of the José Emilio Pacheco Award are all essential writers in Mexican literature today. They are all admired for work that has taken endless risks around the boundaries of established genres, for blazing trails, for clearing the way: from short stories to essays, from poetry to chronicles, from theater to novels or interviews, collage, pastiche. And they are also authors who have always lent their ears to—who have always genuinely listened to—the voices of everyone making the language of *we*. Something important happens when a writer reflects with us on the material conditions that enable—or obstruct—writing itself; that is, life itself. When they do so, when they think with us and alongside us, when they engage in a conversation that belongs to us because it concerns us, these writers expand the life of what is *common*, the practice of what we share, in works both personal and plural. These writers have taught us that imagination doesn't live in an ivory tower, isolated from the worldly din, distant from the goings-on of our feet, hands, skins, and days. As the US-American poet Claudia Rankine has argued with respect to other authors, the ones I'm referring to today have taught me "to not assume that the presence of race deforms the creative act, renders the creative act sadly earthbound. We are ourselves earthbound. And race is one of the things that bound us there."[1] And here. Generous, concerned, attentive to the conditions of their time, these authors are not just openly admired and respected; they also, and perhaps more importantly, writers people seek out for accompaniment and guidance. They are beloved writers, and we, as readers, have greatly benefited from their hospitality, their embrace. The fact that my work—and by "my work" I mean "my texts"—has even been included among these authors' names reminds me that I'm barely getting started. Among the greatest virtues of this noble and ruthless trade is that every day, when you pick up your pen or sit down at your keyboard again, you surrender to the evidence: nothing about this is cumulative. You start from zero, if you really start at all. And you return all over again, if you're lucky, to that zero at the end of the day. Awards seem to shift from the past toward the present, confirming everything in their path. But the risk, the wager, far from confirming the linear trajectory of time, shakes it up and alters it. What will readers remember about these books and how? Will any of those sentences, any of those characters, find a place in our everyday conversations? Will they someday seep, as the French writer Antoine Volodine hoped they would, into our dreams? We can't yet know. And it's all right that we don't.

I've said on various occasions that a good portion of contemporary Latin American literature is being produced from inside the United States, often in Spanish, sometimes in English. The trend is hardly new. The trend, moreover, is not just a fad. José Emilio Pacheco, whose name was given to this prize, was part of an early generation of Spanish-speaking writers who made the United States, and especially US universities, a second home. Just like Gustavo Sáinz at Indiana University before him, or Ricardo Piglia at Princeton later on, José Emilio shaped students and readers during his constant visits to the University of Maryland. Many more of us arrived, too. Some, as I was, were carried along by a family tradition of northward migration—a tradition of long walks, as Gloria Anzaldúa would say—into the cities and universities of Texas and California. Others moved away from migratory routes that had once led so many Latin American writers to Spain, opting in increasing numbers for the vertical path to the United States. Still others were attracted by the slow but steady discovery of the resources available at various Spanish-language literature departments in the US. Some fled dire conditions. Others landed on their feet after countless struggles. The migration of Spanish-speaking writers from below the Rio Grande thus changed its course: from a movement that had been massively horizontal (between Latin America and Spain) in prior decades, it became increasingly vertical (between the Spanish-speaking world and the US). In any case, there are a lot of us. We live in the country with the second-largest Spanish-speaking population in the world; the first is still Mexico. We're part of the nearly 50 million native speakers or the 11.6 million bilingual speakers of Spanish. We're among the speakers of a language, carried on the backs of both undocumented and documented workers, that becomes what the linguist Yásnaya Aguilar calls a stateless language as soon as it crosses the border—linked, in its fate or its consistency and its resistance, to the struggle of indigenous languages in Mexico. An unspoken rule dictates that literary awards created for Mexicans overwhelmingly go to Spanish-speaking writers living in Mexico, precluding the participation of Mexicans living in the US or Mexicans who speak and write in indigenous languages (unless the terms of the award explicitly state otherwise). It is especially telling that the organization of readers behind this award—one based in Yucatán, the FILEY; another based in the US, UC-Mexicanistas—have decided to recognize my work as a binational woman writer who lives and votes in both Mexico and the US, speaking two languages, often at once. Because I am convinced that writing is work, and that the work of many people and communities structure the languages I use to forge sentences, I believe that this award rightfully belongs to my deportee maternal grandparents, who found a way to remake their lives in the cotton fields surrounding the Tamaulipas-Texas border in the late 1930s. And to my paternal grandparents, who migrated north in search of better living conditions, making the US-Mexico border their home. The work of migrant workers, in fields and cities alike, is not only an essential component of the Mexican economy; it is also essential for feeding many mouths across the US. Constant waves of migration have kept the Spanish language alive and well in homes and streets, paths and plazas. I would not have been able to keep writing and thinking and living in Spanish without the massive, comforting presence of migrants in the places where I live. An award like this one is thus a welcome pause, a fleeting respite, in a time of outright hostility and increasing criminalization of migrants both in the US and in Mexico. I've come here from the very same country that has just eliminated Spanish from the White House website, and I'm reminded—almost immediately, almost automatically—of the recent words of a powerful US-American poet, Julie Carr:

My country, said the boy to the girl, likes its children shot through

My country, said the girl to the boy, likes its women weighted or flayed

My country, said the boy, tears away. We've never really loved the human.

A mother's

just a wisp.[2]

In that country, where Spanish has been and proudly remains a language of labor, and where it is also a language of creative labor, there are lots of us writing today. And we write in hopes, among so many other hopes, of cutting through the hateful rhetoric that governs public discourse and of reaching past the paralysis and isolation and terror it causes. In these extreme, drastic, polarized times, which force us onto the streets and urge us to rethink what's "natural" about daily events, we need, more than ever, something on which writing has always depended: critical thinking. Thinking with others. Action and everyday practice with others.

I'd like to think that this is why we're here today. Because I refuse to believe that we've come together here, in the glorious city of Mérida, Yucatán, just to participate blindly or in complicity with the manipulation of a market or an industry that grows more abstract and more unchallengeable the larger it gets. We're not so innocent as all that; we're not so naïve. In the same way, I refuse to believe that we've been summoned by the soft, melancholy, self-glorifying whimper of an entity (Literature with a capital L) that hasn't left its ivory tower for decades. I want to believe quite the opposite, and that's why I've come, and that's why I've come together with you. I want to believe that what we're doing when we open a book or a text means participating in something much more intimate and much more urgent at the same time. We came to acknowledge each other in our specificities and our differences. And we came, too—maybe especially—to engage in a conversation that may have begun in a phrase on the lips of a character whose appearance only we know, and on whom now depends whatever we do with the rest of our lives. We've come for what happens after we read, but that was produced by reading: we've come to question each other. When we do so, when we look at each other with critical, discerning eyes, we are propelled to reinvent ourselves, to forge a new life, a practice of living in which our days once again clasp hands with wonder.

And does this mean anything when we're besieged by hordes of tragic days, right at the beginning of a time that promises only darkness and terror, whether in the form of massive deportations or gasoline price gouges, shortages, inflation, corruption, precariousness? I'm here to tell you that the answer is yes. That it means more today than it did before. More than it ever has.

We're told that everything is ruined, the country is ruined, the world is ruined, and we have enough evidence to believe what we hear. But we have to be careful about agreeing too readily with the allegations of defeat and despair. We need to lend our ears and pay attention. Because, when we're told that everything is ruined, what we're often actually being told is that *we* are ruined. We're told, as Fred Moten argues in his beautiful and combative book *The Undercommons*,[3] that we have to correct ourselves. That obedience—any kind of obedience, as long as it's docile, as long as it's absolute—will be rewarded with survival. But what books taught me before they taught me anything else was to doubt. To question. And that's why I say that I owe books my rebellion.

There isn't one single version of history, I was told by every work of fiction I've ever read, by every poem. Whatever seems natural and inevitable is, in fact, just one of many paths the world can take, I was told in its own way by every essay, every story. The possibilities are here, I was told by every book, and they're marked, underlined, ready to leap out into the world and produce reality. Experience. Material life. Something concrete. Because books don't always help us get to know ourselves, which is another way of confirming ourselves. They also help us *not* know ourselves, to spark something inside us that we'd only suspected was there—or something that completely takes us by surprise, overcoming us.

We've been told for a long time that writing is a solitary activity fated to be performed by a select few. And here's another thing I've come here to say: don't believe that for a minute. Writing is a labor carried out among many, a task through which we connect with others. It is, in fact, a being-with-others. There are no soloists; there's only accompaniment, borrowing once again from Fred Moten. Writing isn't solitude. Writing is in the reach of everyone who practices language. Writing is, in fact, our reach, our scope.

Writing compels us to pay attention. It forces us to see others without ceasing to see ourselves. When we do, when we invite ourselves to engage in this mirrored game, writing takes us by the hand and leads us far away from indolence: the eternally comfortable position among those interested in confirming the state of things, the incredibly common position among those who (even as they know, and as they see) decide to enlist in the armies of indifference. Indolence—the incapacity to feel pain or someone else's pain, which in Spanish is *dolerse*—is militant indifference. When we say that a book moves us, what we're actually saying is that a book has liberated us from indolence. Only when we manage to get beyond indolence can we question our surroundings about the causes of hardship or misfortune. This is why feeling pain goes beyond empathy. This is why feeling pain has nothing to do with victimizing the victim, making her into a passive sufferer or one lacking in agency. This is why feeling pain leads to the creation of communities of empathy. Feeling pain, grieving, is a critical stance.

If writing, as Ricardo Piglia would say,[4] enables us to question the origin of paradox (without paradox, he said very early on in his "Theses on the Short Story," there is no story), then it also, and for the same reason, enables us to question the causes of general misfortune. The reasons behind or below what doesn't fit. Of what, precisely because it doesn't fit, becomes of interest to literary inquiry. If writing makes room for this question, then it necessarily also makes room for the question of justice. Writing, then, enables the question of destruction. And once that destruction has occurred, it enables, in the very ruins it has sowed, the question of devastation. When everything seems normal or inescapable, when everything indicates that it was going to happen this way, writing leaps out and looks around and picks up the pen again and says, no. That wild, untamable word: NO. There's a crack here. It's difficult to explain—this points to something else, and that something else points to yet another one. The possibilities are vast, perhaps unheard of. But not unimaginable. This stubbornness in writing is what I've wanted for myself. And it's what I want to share with you today.

We're surrounded by a generalized capital punishment, Sergio Villalobos-Ruminott reminds us as he ruminates on the devastation wrought by contemporary capitalism on Latin America.[5] In Mexico, the so-called War on Drugs—which has been nothing more than a war against Mexico's own population, a war that has now killed one hundred thousand people and forcibly disappeared thirty thousand others—has not only produced a staggering amount of death. It has also fomented the plunder to which the living have been subjected. Evacuated, seemingly barren, deserted, the land and its hidden riches become, once again, the object of rapacious appropriation by the political and corporate elites, both national and international. This phenomenon has been documented by brave and extraordinary journalists: John Gibler, Daniela Rea, Marcela Turatti, Diego Osorno, and Federico Mastrogiovanni, among others. Confronted with this crushing accumulation of cruelty, with the ferocious, continuous, and lethal excavation into our bodies and our souls, we are left with the lesser forces—lesser but insistent, lesser but piercing, lesser but present in every fleck of dust wandering the cosmos—that enable this questioning, these questions. Writing, which has no answers, does have the gift of opening up spaces in our language and in our days and in our consciousness for the questions that really matter, the questions we've been carrying around for our whole lives, ever since we were thirteen or sixteen or whenever we started reading books or participating in the conversations that would mark us forever. Asking questions is a practice, a concrete action that, by invoking an answer, in demanding attention, transforms the very material of the interrogation itself.

I'm not an optimist; I'm stubborn. Maybe, as the writer Marina Azahua remarked to me in conversation not long ago, quoting one of her professors: we don't need hope, we need tenacity. We need to insist. We need to never take our finger from the pulse. We're told that it's time to take to the streets, but we've always been on the streets. This writing that doesn't hide its debt to others, this writing that *is* its debt to others, lives outside: sometimes huddled and frozen, sometimes gently sheltered by strangers. There is no contradiction between this constant, urgent taking-to-the-streets and this entering into the process of writing. We're talking about the right-side-up and the inside-out of the same process.

Let's not be optimistic. There's no reason to be. But let's always, always be stubborn.

Thank you.

Notes

ACKNOWLEDGMENTS

1. Claudia Rankine, *Citizen: An American Lyric* (Minneapolis: Graywolf Press, 2014).

INTRODUCTION

1. I will use the term *US-American* throughout the book to reflect the fact that *América*, in Spanish, refers to the Americas, or the totality of North, Central, and South America. Citizens of the United States, then, are not the only Americans out there; they, too, are members of the Americas as a whole.

2. Camilla Roy, "Introduction," in *Biting the Error: Writers Explore Narrative*, eds. Mary Burger, Robert Gluck, Camille Roy, and Gail Scott (Ontario: Coach House Books, 2004), 8.

3. Hélène Cixous, "The School of the Dead," in *Three Steps on the Ladder of Writing* (New York: Columbia University Press, 1993), 12.

4. Margaret Atwood, *Negotiating with the Dead: A Writer on Writing* (New York: Cambridge University Press, 2002).

5. Elias Khoury, *Gate of the Sun*, (New York: Archipelago Books, 2006).

6. Juan Rulfo, *Pedro Páramo*, (Mexico City: Fondo de Cultura Económica, 1964).

7. An analysis of these years is found in my book *Dolerse: Textos desde un país herido* (Oaxaca: Sur+ Ediciones, 2011); see also Jon Gibler, *Morir en México* (Oaxaca: Sur+ Ediciones, 2012); Diego Enrique Osorno, ed., *País de muertos: Crónicas contra la impunidad* (Mexico: Debate, 2011); Marcela Turatti and Daniela Rea, eds., *Entre las cenizas: Historias de vida en tiempos de muerte* (Oaxaca: Sur+ Ediciones, 2012).

8. Roberto Bolaño, *2066* (New York: Farrar, Straus & Giroux, 2008).

9. Alma Guillermoprieto, *72 migrantes* (Oaxaca: Almadía, 2011).

10. Achille Mbembe, "Necropolitics," *Public Culture* 15, no. 1 (Winter 2003): 11–40; see also Achille Mbembe, *On the Postcolony* (Berkeley: University of California Press, 2001).

11. Adriana Cavarero, *Horrorism: Naming Contemporary Violence* (New York: Columbia University Press, 2011); see also Cristina Rivera Garza and Javier Raya, "Corresponsales de guerra," *Milenio*, April 24, 2012.

12. Mbembe, "Necropolitics."

13. Rita Segato, *La guerra contra las mujeres* (Madrid: Traficantes de sueños, 2016), 57–89.

14. Giorgio Agamben, *State of Exception* (Chicago: University of Chicago Press, 2005).

15. See Raquel Gutiérrez, *Horizontes comunitario-populares: Producción de lo común más allá de las políticas estado-céntricas* (Madrid: Traficantes de Sueños, 2017).

16. Josefina Ludmer, "Literaturas postautónomas," *Ciberletras*, no. 17 (July 2007), www.lehman.cuny.edu/ciberletras/v17/ludmer.htm.

17. Kathy Acker, "The Killers," in Burger, Gluck, Roy, and Scott, *Biting the Error*, 18.

18. Carmen Giménez Smith, "Make America Mongrel Again," *Harriet Blog*, Poetry Foundation, April 19, 2018, www.poetryfoundation.org/harriet/2018/04/make-america-mongrel-again.

19. Robert Fitterman and Vanessa Place, *Notes on Conceptualisms*, (New York: Ugly Duckling Presse, 2009). (My translation into Spanish: *Notas sobre conceptualismos* (Mexico City: Conaculta, 2013); Kenneth Goldsmith, *Uncreative Writing: Managing Language in the Digital Age* (New York: Columbia University Press, 2011).

20. Eloy Fernández Porta, *Afterpop: La literatura de la implosión mediática* (Barcelona: Anagrama, 2009); *£*o$: La superproducción de los afectos* (Barcelona: Anagrama, 2010); and *Emociónese así: Anatomía de la alegría* (con publicación encubierta) (Barcelona: Anagrama, 2012).

21. Agustín Fernández Mallo, *Postpoesía: Hacia un nuevo paradigma* (Barcelona: Anagrama, 2009); and *El hacedor (de Borges), Remake* (Madrid: Alfaguara, 2011).

22. Fernández Mallo's short novel, however, circulates freely in the digital world. Consider es.scribd.com/doc/82634523/El-hacedor-Remake-Agustin-Fernandez-Mallo.

23. Vicente Luis Mora, *El lectoespectador* (Barcelona: Seix Barral, 2011).

24. Antoine Volodine, *Le Post-exotism en dix leçons, leçon onze* (Paris: Gallimard, 1998).

25. Damián Tabarovsky, *Literatura de izquierda* (2004; repr., Mexico City: Tumbona Ediciones, 2011).

26. Gertrude Stein, "How Writing is Written," in *How Writing is Written: Volume II of the Previously Uncollected Works of Gertrude Stein*, ed. Robert Bartlett Haas (Los Angeles: Black Sparrow Press, 1975), 151–60.

27. Luis Felipe Fabre, *Leyendo agujeros: Ensayos sobre desescritura, antiescritura y no escritura* (Mexico City: Conaculta, 2005).

28. Giovanni De Luna, *El cadáver del enemigo: Violencia y muerte en la guerra contemporánea* (Madrid: 451 Editores, 2007), 38.

29. De Luna, *El cadáver*, 40.

30. Néstor Perlongher, "Cadáveres," in *Alambres* (Buenos Aires: Último Reino, 1987). See Fabre, *Leyendo agujeros*, for an analysis of this poem.

31. Lev Manovich, *The Language of New Media* (Cambridge, MA: MIT Press, 2001).

32. The foundational work on this perspective is Antonio Negri and Michael Hard, *Empire* (Cambridge, MA: Harvard University Press, 2009). The concrete terms cited here are from Christian Marazzi, *Capital and Language: From the New Economy to the War Economy* (Los Angeles: Semiotext(e), 2008); and *Capital and Affects: The Politics of the Language Economy* (Cambridge, MA: MIT Press, 2011).

33. Franco "Bifo" Berardi, *After the Future* (Oakland, CA: AK Press, 2011).

34. Christian Marazzi, *The Violence of Financial Capitalism* (Los Angeles: Semiotext(e), 2010); André Gorz, *The Immaterial* (London: Seagull Books, 2010); Franco "Bifo" Berardi, *After the Future*, and *The Soul at Work: From Alienation to Autonomy* (Los Angeles: Semiotext(e), 2009).

35. Hariett Staff, "David Buuck on Performance Poetics," *Harriet Blog*, Poetry Foundation, February 7, 2013, www.poetryfoundation.org/harriet/2013/02/david-buuck-on-performance-poetics.

MY JOURNEY THROUGH TRANSKRIT

1. Gerardo Villanueva, *Transterra* (Guadalajara, Mexico: Litoral, 2008).

2. Gayatri Chakravorty Spivak, "Planetarity," in *Death of a Discipline* (New York: Columbia University Press, 2003).

3. Mike Davis, *Dead Cities: And Other Tales* (New York: New Press, 2003).

4. Juliana Spahr, "The '90s," *Boundary 2* 36, no. 3 (2009), 164.

5. Qtd. in Keijirō Suga, "Translation, Exophony, Omniphony," in *Yoko Tawada: Voices from Everywhere*, ed. Douglas Slaymaker (Lanham, MD: Lexington Books, 2007), 27–28.

6. Slavov Žižek, *The Parallax View* (Cambridge, MA: MIT Press, 2006).

7. Žižek, *The Parallax View*, 17.

8. Anne Michaels, *Fugitive Pieces* (New York: Vintage Books, 1996), 5.

9. Sarah Pollack, "The Peculiar Art of Cultural Formations: Roberto Bolaño and the Translation of Latin-American Literature in the United States," *TRANS-: Revue de litératture generale et comparée*, no. 5 (2008), doi.org/10.4000/trans.235.

10. Elizabeth Lowry in *Granta 103: The Rise of the British Jihad* (New York: Granta, 2008), 14–15.

11. Michaels, *Fugitive Pieces*.

12. *Real Academia Española (RAE)*, s.v. "deletrear," accessed July 9, 2020, dle.rae.es/deletrear (translated).

13. Marjorie Perloff, "Language in Migration: Multilingualism and Exophonic Writing in the New Poetics," in *Unoriginal Genius: Poetry by Other Means in the New Century* (Chicago: University of Chicago Press, 2002).

14. Quoted in Perloff, "Language in Migration," 136–37.

15. Elias Khoury, *The Gate of the Sun*, trans. Humphrey Davies (New York: Archipelago Books, 2006), 29.

16. Refers to the poem "A mi prima Águeda in Ramón López Velarde, *Sangre devota; Zozobra; El son del corazón* (Madrid: Ediciones Hiperión, 2001).

17. Marjorie Perloff, "The Oulipo Factor: The Procedural Poetics of Christian Bök and Caroline Bergvall," *Textual Practice* 18, no. 1, 23-45, DOI: 10.1080/0950236042000183250

DISAPPROPRIATION

1. Ramón López Velarde, *Poemas*, trans. M. W. Jacobs (Moorpark, CA: Floricanto Press, 2014).

2. Jean-Luc Nancy, *The Inoperative Community*, ed. Peter Connor, trans. Peter Connor, Lisa Garbus, Michael Holland, and Simona Sawhney (Minneapolis: University of Minnesota Press, 1991), 67.

3. Nancy, 66.

4. Nancy, 46.

5. Nancy, 19.

6. Nancy, 29.

7. Nancy, 29.

8. Nancy, 39.

9. Nancy, 40.

10. Nancy, 41.

11. Nancy, 35.

12. Nancy, 75.

13. Floriberto Díaz, "Comunidad y comunalidad," eds. Floriberto Díaz, Sofía Robles Hernández, and Rafael Cardoso Jiménez, *Escrito: Comunalidad, energya viva del pensamiento mixe - Ayuuktsënëä'yën - ayuujkwënmää'ny – ayuujkmëk'äjtën* (Mexico City: UNAM, 2007), 39.

14. Díaz, 59-60.

15. Díaz, 42.

16. Floriberto Díaz, "Principios comunitarios y derechos indios," in Díaz, Robles Hernández, and Cardoso Jiménez, *Escrito*, 59.

17. Floriberto Díaz, "Guía para la alfabetización mixe. Pasos que deberá seguir el Animador para la Cultura y Educación mixe" (ACEM), in Díaz, Robles Hernández, and Cardoso Jiménez, *Escrito*, 261.

18. Díaz, "Guía para," 263.

19. Díaz, "Guía para," 269.

20. Ulises Carrión, "The New Art of Making Books," *Kontexts* no. 6-7 (New York: Center for Book Arts, 1975).

21. Jacques Rancière, "Politique, identification, subjetivation," in *Aux bords du politique* (Paris: La Fabrique, 1998).

22. Carmen Giménez Smith, "Rosa Alcalá: An interview, a review," *Letras Latinas Blog*, November 3, 2011, letraslatinasblog.blogspot.com/2011/11/rosa-alcala-interview-review.html.

23. Cristina Rivera Garza, "Desapropiadamente," in the original Spanish-language edition of *Los muertos indóciles: Necroescrituras y Desapropiación* (Mexico City: Tusquets Editores, 2013).

24. Floriberto Díaz, *Escrito: Comunalidad, energía viva del pensamiento mixe*, eds. Sofía Robles Hernández and Rafael Cardoso Jiménez (Mexico City: UNAM, 2007).

25. Maurizio Lazzarato, "Struggle, Event, Media," in *The Green Room: Reconsidering the Documentary and Contemporary Art #1*, eds. Maria Lind and Hito Steyerl (Berlin: Sternberg Press, 2009), 216.

26. "Intercambio entre Boaventura de Sousa Santos y Gladys Tzul Tzul en LASA 2015," YouTube, June 16, 2015, www.youtube.com/watch?v=ohq5efaXQ-8.

27. See Christian Marazzi, *The Violence of Financial Capitalism* (Los Angeles: Semiotext(e), 2010).

28. Jacques Rancière, *Aisthesis: Scenes from the Aesthetic Regime of Art* (New York: Verso, 2013).

29. Rancière, *Aisthesis*, x.

30. James Agee, *Let Us Now Praise Famous Men: Three Tenant Families*, 1st Mariner Books edition (Boston: Houghton Mifflin, 2001).

31. Agee, *Let Us*, xii.

32. Agee, *Let Us*, 94.

33. Quoted in Rancière, *Aisthesis*, 94.

34. Rancière, *Aisthesis*, x.

35. John Roberts, *The Intangibilities of Form: Skilling and Deskilling in Art after the Readymade* (New York: Verso, 2007).

36. Roberts, *The Intangibilities*, 25.

37. Roberts, *The Intangibilities*, 34.

38. For a selection of texts discussing immaterial work, see Franco Berardi Bifo, *After the Future* (Chico, CA: AK Press, 2011); Christian Marazzi, *The Violence of Financial Capitalism* (Los Angeles: Semiotext(e), 2010); Andre Gorz, *The Immaterial* (London: Seagull Books, 2010).

39. Rancière, *Aisthesis*, 262.

40. Rancière, 262.

41. Rancière, 262.

42. Rancière, 250.

43. Onfray, *Teoría*, 233–40.

44. Onfray, *Teoría*, 222.

45. Saúl Hernández Vargas, "Comunalidad como tecnología traslúcida: Primeros apuntes a partir de una lectura de la *Sexta sección* de Alex Rivera (2003)" (paper presented at Congreso de UC-Mexicanistas, Mérida, Yucatán, March 2016).

46. Judith Butler, *Giving an Account of Oneself* (New York: Fordham University Press, 2005).

47. See the concept of the geology of violence in Sergio Villalobos Ruminott, *Heterografías de la violencia: Historia, nihilismo, destrucción* (Buenos Aires: Ediciones la Cebra, 2016).

48. Fred Moten and Stefano Hareny, *The Undercommons: Fugitive Planning and Black Study* (New York: Minor Compositions, 2013). This work was translated into Spanish as *Los abajocomunes*, trans. Cristina Rivera Garza and Juan Pablo Anaya (Mexico City: Campechana Mental and El Cráter Invertido, 2017).

49. Díaz, "Comunidad," 39. The translation included here is my own.

50. Díaz, "Comunidad," 42.

51. Raquel Gutiérrez, *Horizontes comunitario-populares: Producción de lo común más allá de las políticas estado-céntricas* (Madrid: Traficantes de sueños, 2017), 27.

52. Gutiérrez, *Horizontes*, 71

53. Jaime Luna's neologism *compartencia* is derived from the verb *compartir* (to share). Luna took the standard verb *compartir* and stretched it, we could say, by changing a single vowel, to become *comparter*. Then he conjugated it into *compartencia*: the verb becomes a noun. Hence my English-language adaptation of "shareng" from "sharing."

54. Jaime Martínez Luna, *El camino andado*, vol. 1 (Oaxaca: CMPIO/Coalición de Maestros y Promotores Indígenas de Oaxaca, CAMPO/Centro de Apoyo al Movimiento Popular Oaxaqueño, CEEESCI/Coordinación Estatal de Escuelas de Educación Secundaria Comunitaria Indígena, 2013).

55. See, among others, Francisco Estrada Medina's analysis, "Estética citacionista y copyleft: Antígona González de Sara Uribe," at *7000 robles* (blog), May 29, 2017, 7000robles.wordpress.com.

56. Arturo Fierros Hernández, *Historia de la salud pública en el Distrito Norte de la Baja California 1888-1923* (Tijuana: CENCA-CCT, 2014), 36; my translation.

57. Chris Kraus, *After Kathy Acker: A Literary Biography* (Los Angeles: Semiotext(e), 2017), 34.

58. Kraus, *After Kathy Acker*, 49.

59. These books by Kathy Acker were published as *Portrait of an Eye: Three Novels* (New York: Grove Press, 1997).

60. Kraus, *After Kathy Acker*, 81.

61. Vanessa Place and Robert Fitterman, *Notes on Conceptualisms* (New York: Ugly Duckling Presse, 2009). I translated this book into Spanish as *Notas sobre conceptualismos* (Mexico City: CONACULTA, 2013).

62. A quick summary of the concept of disappropriation can be found in "Disappropriation for Beginners," *Literal Magazine*, May 31, 2017.

63. Kraus, *After Kathy Acker*, 59. Some years later, now married to Peter Gordon, Acker also worked as a stripper in various San Diego bars frequented by workers and sailors.

64. Kraus, *After Kathy Acker*, 134.

65. Kathy Acker, "The Gift of Disease," Outward From Nothingness, August 15, 2013, outwardfromnothingness.com/the-gift-of-disease-i-el-don-de-la-enfermedad-i.

66. Kathy Acker, "The Gift of Disease."

67. Kraus, *After Kathy Acker*, 277.

68. Jean Genet, *The Collected Writings of Jean Genet*, trans. Edmund White

(Hopewell, NJ: Ecco Press, 1993), 311.

69. Genet, 310.

70. Genet, 310.

71. Genet, 314.

72. Genet, 314.

73. Genet, 314.

74. Genet, 314.

75. Genet, 319.

76. Genet, 314.

77. Genet, 328–29.

USES OF THE ARCHIVE

1. Jacques Derrida, *Archive Fever: A Freudian Impression*, trans. Eric Prenowitz (Chicago: University of Chicago Press, 1996), 3.

2. Derrida, 18.

3. Nathalie Piégay-Gros, *Le Futur anterieur de l'archive* (Quebec: Tangence éditeur, 2012), 20.

4. Text of *El exceso de pasado* was read at the Centre d'Études en Civilisations, Languages et Littératures Étrangères (CECILLE) at the Université de Lille, France, in June and published in the *Revista de Occidente*, no. 376 (September 2012).

5. Rodrigo Rey Rosa, *El material humano* (Barcelona: Anagrama, 2009).

6. Michael Davidson, *Ghostlier Demarcations: Modern Poetry and the Material World* (Berkeley: University of California Press, 1997), 139.

7. Muriel Rukeyser, "The Life of Poetry," in *A Muriel Rukeyser Reader*, ed. Jan Heller, (New York: W. W. Norton & Company, 1994), 122.

8. Alice Oswald, *Memorial* (London: Faber and Faber, 2011), 39.

9. Oswald, *Memorial*, 13.

10. Pierre Boulez and Cecile Favre-Gilly, *Boulez on Conducting: Conversations with Cécil Gilly*, trans. Richard Stokes (London: Faber & Faber, 2003), 98.

UNDEAD AUTHORS

1. Roland Barthes, "The Death of the Author," in *Image-Music-Text*, trans. and ed. Stephen Heath (London: Fontana Press, 1977); Michael Foucault, "What Is an Author?," *Language, Counter-Memory, Practice*, ed. Donald F. Bouchard (Ithaca, NY: Cornell University Press, 1977).

2. David Markson, *Wittgenstein's Mistress* (Champaign, IL: Dalkey Archive Press, 1988).

3. David Markson, *Reader's Block* (Champaign, IL: Dalkey Archive Press, 1996); *This Is Not a Novel* (Washington, DC: Counterpoint, 2001); *The Last Novel* (Washington, DC: Counterpoint, 2007).

4. David Foster Wallace, "Overlooked," *Salon*, April 12, 1999, www.salon.com/1999/04/12/wallace.

5. Charles Bernstein, *On Poetics* (Cambridge, MA: Harvard University Press, 1992).

6. David Markson, *Vanishing Point* (Berkeley, CA: Shoemaker & Hoard, 2004), 12–13.

7. All quotations in this section are translated from the Spanish-language edition: Peter Sloterdijk, *Venir al mundo, venir al lenguaje: Lecciones de Frankfurt* (Valencia: Pre-Textos, 2006).

8. The quotations in this section are translated from Michael Onfray, *Teoría del cuerpo enamorado: Por una erótica solar*, trans. Ximo Brotons (Valencia: Pre-Textos, 2002).

9. Judith Butler, *Giving an Account of Oneself* (New York: Fordham University Press, 2005).

10. Gertrude Stein, *The Autobiography of Alice B. Toklas* (1933; repr. New York: Vintage, 1990); Jamaica Kincaid, *The Autobiography of My Mother* (New York: Farrar, Strauss & Giroux, 1996); Anne Carson, *Autobiography of Red* (New York: Knopf, 1998).

11. Kathy Acker, "On Realism," in *Bodies of Work: Essays* (London: Serpent's Tail, 1997).

12. Ron Silliman, *The New Sentence* (New York: Roof Books, 1987).

13. Alessandro Baricco, *An Iliad* (New York: Knopf, 2006); Alice Oswald, *Memorial: An Excavation of the Iliad* (London: Faber & Faber, 2011).

14. Eric Santner, *On Creaturely Life: Rilke, Benjamin, Sebald* (Chicago: University of Chicago Press, 2006).

BRIEF MISSIVES FROM POMPEII

1. Walter Benjamin, "Theses on the Philosophy of History," in *Illuminations: Essays and Reflections* (Boston: Mariner Books, 2019), 196–210.

2. Graciela Romero and Alberto Chimal, "El viajero del tiempo y la chica del ya fue en mi TL: La Cámara Verde," *Periódico de Poesía*, no. 37 (March 2011), www.archivopdp.unam.mx/index.php/1687.

3. Ludmer, "Literaturas postautónomas."

4. Tamara Kamenszain, *La boca del testimonio: Lo que dice la poesía* (Buenos Aires: Norma, 2007).

5. Paul Virilio, "Silence on Trial," in *Art and Fear*, trans. by Julie Rose (London: Continuum, 2003), 67–97.

6. Georges Duby, *A History of Private Life*, five vols. (Cambridge: Harvard University Press, 1987).

7. Pilar Gonzalbo Aizpuru, *Historia de la vida cotidiana en México XVIII: Entre la tradición y el cambio* (Mexico City: Fondo de Cultura Económica, 2005). This is the third in a multivolume set of five books.

8. Jacques Lacan and Bruce Fink, *Écrits: The First Complete Edition in English* (New York: W. W. Norton, 2006), 3–4.

9. Eloy Fernández Porta, *La superproducción de los afectos* (Barcelona: Anagrama, 2010).

10. Charles Bernstein, *The Attack of the Difficult Poems: Essays and Inventions* (Chicago: University of Chicago Press, 2011), 43.

11. Kathy Acker, "Writing, Identity, and Copyright in the Net Age," in "Identities,"

special issue, *Journal of the Midwest Modern Language Association* 28, no. 1 (Spring 1995): 93–98.

WRITING AGAINST VIOLENCE

1. Juan Rulfo, *El aire de las colinas: Cartas a Clara* (Barcelona: Plaza y Janés, 2000).
2. Louis Menand, "Show or Tell: Should Creative Writing Be Taught?," *New Yorker*, June 8, 2009, www.newyorker.com/magazine/2009/06/08/show-or-tell.
3. Junot Díaz, "MFA vs. POC," *New Yorker*, April 30, 2014, www.newyorker.com/books/page-turner/mfa-vs-poc.
4. Namrata Podar, "Is 'Show Don't Tell' a Universal Truth or a Colonial Relic?," *Literary Hub*, September 2, 2016, lithub.com/is-show-dont-tell-a-universal-truth-or-a-colonial-relic.
5. Rita Segato, *La guerra contra las mujeres* (Madrid: Traficante de Sueños, 2016), 21.
6. *The Best American Nonrequired Reading 2005*, ed. Dave Eggers, Houghton Mifflin Company, Boston/New York, 2005, p. xi.
7. Paula Sibilia, *La intimidad como espectáculo* (Mexico City: Fondo de Cultura Económica, 2019).

ON ALERT

This section was translated by Sarah Booker.

1. Eric Bennett, *Workshops of Empire: Stegner, Engle, and American Creative Writing During the Cold War* (Iowa City: University of Iowa Press, 2015). For those interested in the relationship between creative writing and international politics during the Cold War, see also Mark McGurl, *The Program Era: Postwar Fiction and the Rise of Creative Writing* (Cambridge, MA: Harvard University Press, 2011); Francis Stonor, *The Cultural Cold War: The CIA and the World of Arts and Letters* (New York: New Press, 2013).
2. Fred Moten and Stefano Harney, *The Undercommons: Fugitive Planning and Black Study* (New York: Minor Compositions, 2013).
3. In other words, I'm less interested in what Alberto Moreiras calls the "Latin Americanism of the self" and more in what Juliana Spahr calls the compromised history of English with other languages. Helpful for thinking about this is Alberto Moreiras, "La fatalidad de (mi) subalternismo," in *Marranismo e inscripción: O el abandono de la conciencia desdichada* (Pozuelo de Alarcón, Spain: Escolar y Mayo Editores, 2016), 77–102; and "El segundo giro de la deconstrucción," also in *Marranismo e inscripción*, 117–35.
4. Alberto Fuguet and Sergio Gómez, eds., *McOndo* (Barcelona: Mondadori, 1996). Edmundo Paz Soldán and Alberto Fuguet, eds., *Se habla español: Voces latinas en Estados Unidos* (Madrid: Alfaguara, 2000).
5. Diana Palaversich wrote a magnificent book, *De Macondo a McOndo: Senderos de la postmodernidad latinoamericana*, Plaza y Valdés, Mexico City, 2005; but here I'm using her article "McOndo y otros mitos," available at www.literaturas.com, June 2033.
6. I use the adjective "American" in reference to the following description of the

writer Salvador Plascencia, author of the novel *The People of Paper*, McSweeney's, San Francisco, 2005; Harvest-Harcourt, San Diego, 2006, in Wikipedia: "American writer, born December 21, 1976 in Guadalajara, Mexico."

7. Gayatri Chakravorty Spivak, "Planetarity," *Death of a Discipline* (New York: Columbia University Press, 2005), 73.

8. Spivak, 73.

9. Silvia Rivera Cusicanqui, *Sociología de la imagen: Miradas chi'ixi desde la historia andina* (Buenos Aires: Tinta Limón, 2015), 207.

10. Cusicanqui, 207.

11. Cusicanqui, 213.

12. Perloff, "Language in Migration."

13. Spahr, "The '90s," 164.

14. Spahr, "The '90s," 164.

15. Alberto Moreiras, "Conversación en torno a la noción de infrapolítica," *Marranismo e inscripción, o el abandono de la conciencia desdichada* (Madrid: Escolar y Mayo Editores, 2016), 201.

LET'S BE STUBBORN

Adapted from the speech I delivered on receiving the 2017 Excelencia en las Letras José Emilio Pacheco Award organized by UC-Mexicanistas and the FILEY (Yucatán International Book Fair).

1. Claudia Rankine, *The Racial Imaginary: Writers on Race in the Life of the Mind* (Albany, NY: Fence Books, 2015), 18.

2. Julie Car, *Rag* (Oakland, CA: Omnidawn, 2014).

3. Fred Moten and Stefano Harvey, *The Undercommons: Fugitive Planning & Black Study* (Brooklyn: Autonomedia, 2013).

4. Ricardo Piglia, *Formas Breves* (Mexico City: Penguin Random House/Debolsillo, 2014).

5. Sergio Villalobos-Ruminott, *Heterografías de la violencia: Historia, nihilism, destrucción* (Buenos Aires: La Cebra, 2016).

CPSIA information can be obtained
at www.ICGtesting.com
Printed in the USA
LVHW092114230920
666905LV00009B/185

9 780826 501226